THE BOOK OF
BURGER

THE BOOK OF
BURGER

RACHAEL RAY

PHOTOGRAPHS BY ROMULO YANES

ATRIA PAPERBACK

NEW YORK   LONDON   TORONTO   SYDNEY   NEW DELHI

ATRIA PAPERBACK
A Division of Simon & Schuster, Inc.
1230 Avenue of the Americas
New York, NY 10020

First Atria Paperback edition June 2012

ATRIA PAPERBACK and colophon are trademarks of Simon & Schuster, Inc.

For information about special discounts for bulk purchases, please contact Simon & Schuster Special Sales at 1-866-506-1949 or business@simonandschuster.com.

The Simon & Schuster Speakers Bureau can bring authors to your live event. For more information or to book an event, contact the Simon & Schuster Speakers Bureau at 1-866-248-3049 or visit our website at www.simonspeakers.com.

Designed by Elizabeth Van Itallie

Photo of Rachael Ray in apron by Gasper Tringale

Photos featured on p. 278 of Bobby Flay, Josh Capon, Marc Murphy, Michael Schwartz, Rachael Ray, John Cusimano, Masaharu Morimoto, and Spike Mendelsohn all by Seth Browarnik/World Red Eye Productions

Photo of Katie Lee by Dale Stine

Manufactured in the United States of America

10   9   8   7   6   5   4   3   2   1

Library of Congress Cataloging-in-Publication Data

Ray, Rachael.
The book of burger / by Rachael Ray.
    p.   cm.
Includes index.
    1. Hamburgers.   2. Cooking (Meat)   I. Title.
TX749.5.B43R39   2012
641.82'4—dc23   20120057222

ISBN 978-1-4516-5969-6
ISBN 978-1-4516-5970-2 (ebook)

Dedicated to messy eaters,
to people who know how
to take a wide-open bite out of life
and a bite out of a burger

CONTENTS

Thank You IX

Introduction: Meat 'n' Greet X

BURGERS 1

Beef and Veal Burgers 4

Pork Burgers 66

Chicken and Turkey Burgers 78

Lamb Burgers 109

Veggie Burgers 114

Seafood Burgers 119

SLIDERS 128

Beef, Pork (and 1 Lamb!) Sliders 131

Chicken and Turkey Sliders 162

Seafood Sliders 171

SANDWICHES AND DOGS 174

Beef, Pork, and Chicken Sandwiches 177

Seafood and Veggie Sandwiches 194

Hot Dogs and Sausages 199

SLOPPIES 214

Beef, Pork, and Lamb Sloppies 216

Chicken, Turkey, and Veggie Sloppies 230

SIDES AND SAUCES 240

All Kinds of Fries 243

Other Sides 261

Dippers, Fry Gravies, Sauces, and Ketchups 271

BURGER BASH

BURGER BASH 279
Spike Mendelsohn 280
Masaharu Morimoto 282
Katie Lee 283
Michael Symon 284
Michael Schwartz 288
Bobby Flay 291
Michael Schlow 292
Craig Koketsu 294
Chris Santos 296
Marc Murphy 298
Franklin Becker 302
Josh Capon 304

ESSAYS

Pat LaFrieda: A Homemade Burger Blend 24
Adam Perry Lang: The Perfect Bun 60
Josh Ozersky: My Love for Burgers 172
Michael Symon: Building the Perfect Burger 239

Index 305

The Book of Burger:
An Atria Smart Book
Rachael tells you all about her new
smart book.

You will find tags like the ones below throughout this book. You can use them to access enhanced digital content. To do so, simply download the free app at gettag.mobi. Then hold your phone's camera a few inches away from the tag and enjoy what comes next. You can also visit pages.simonandschuster.com/TheBookofBurgerTags to access this content.

If you access content through a mobile device, message and data rates may apply.

Rachael's burger tips!
(Page xi) Rachael shares some tips you will find in many of the recipes in this book.

Meet Josh Ozersky.
(Page 172) Rachael introduces you to Josh Ozersky.

Meet Pat LaFrieda.
(Page 25) Rachael introduces you to Pat LaFrieda.

Meet Michael Symon.
(Page 239) Rachael introduces you to Michael Symon.

Grinding your own beef with Pat LaFrieda.
(Page 25) Pat LaFrieda shares his techniques for making homemade burgers.

Experience Rachael Ray's Burger Bash.
(Page 279) Check out the South Beach and New York City Wine & Food Festival Burger Bashes.

Watch Rachael make her "Big Spicy Mac."
(Page 42) Rachael demos the burger featured on the front cover.

Tips from Rachael for hosting your own burger bash!
(Page 279) Rach shows you how to entertain guests with sliders, and various sides and sauces featured in this book.

Meet Adam Perry Lang.
(Page 61) Rachael introduces you to Adam Perry Lang.

View the latest bonus content.
(Page 323) Check back here for bonus recipes, new videos, and more!

THANK YOU

Thank you to the great chefs who contributed to our Burger Bash section. They help me prove that great food should be for everyone. When they put their expertise to work inside the bun, they prove that fine food can also be fun.

Thank you to Kappy, Andrew Kaplan. We met years ago at the SoBe Wine and Food Festival, and today he runs our children's initiative, which will receive a portion of my proceeds from this book. Together, we feed hungry kids, improve the nutrition standards in our public schools, and provide scholarships to any public school student who wishes to make a career in a food-related industry. Aside from his great direction of our Yum-o! organization, he also finds time to have my back (and those of many others, as well) on special projects. He oversees the reproduction of my food (when I cannot be at a shoot or on-site), and that's like leaving him as guardian to my baby (my dog, Isaboo). I owe you a burger, for sure. Kappy, you are a great chef and writer in your own right, and I look forward to others discovering what I already know: You're it and a bag of chips.

Thank you to my essay contributors who love burgers as much as I do: Adam Perry Lang, Mike Symon, Pat LaFrieda, and Josh Ozersky.

Thanks to my new family members at Atria, headed by Judith Curr, including Johanna Castillo and an A Team, for making The Book of Burger look so tasty and for streamlining, as much as possible, my wordy and sometimes rambling recipes and notes.

Thank you to photographer Romulo Yanes and his team for shooting drool-worthy portraits of my burgers and sandwiches.

Thanks to Michelle Boxer for organizing hundreds and hundreds of recipes for me from so many files and notebooks, a tough job for a woman who cooks very few meals and truly hates ground meat of any kind. Not a fan of the burger. Best I can say to you? Phew! It's over! Time to start organizing the next book. I'll try and go easy on the burgers.

INTRODUCTION: MEAT 'N' GREET

Burgers are iconic. They symbolize what amounts to a mantra: informality, hearty appetite, good times, and the inclusion of all (that's what the buns are for).

I have become obsessed with burgers, playing with the expectations and idea of what you can actually fit inside a bun. This *Book of Burger* is a collection of my favorites as well as some burgers created by great chefs who have taken home trophies at our annual South Beach Wine and Food Festival and NYC Wine and Food Festival Burger Bash over the years. The idea behind this large collection of a single type of food is to inspire you to flip a few burgers of mine, then create a real whopper of your own.

Each burger recipe is easy to follow and stacks up to burger greatness, no matter how simple or complicated, but some toppings are more time-consuming than others.

Burger making should have a set of rules, but for each burger cook, the rules may vary, because what makes a burger taste great is so subjective. I have very few rules, but I am true to them. Here they are:

Many burger lovers feel that burger season should be confined to outdoor grilling season. I prefer the all-weather, indoor method of a good old cast-iron skillet for my burgers. Griddles and cast-iron skillets create a delicious crust on the meat, resulting in deeply flavored burgers, while outdoor grilling can hide flavors in char and smoke. By all means, if you like to get your char on, take my burgers for a walk outside. BTW, if you love smoky meats, burgers are not the only occupants in this book. Check

out the best sandwich I have ever made: 7-Hour Smoked Brisket. It's a mindblower. It was created as a gift to my husband, and it's a gift that keeps giving back to everyone who braves it.

For more even cooking, when forming patties, make the center of the patty thinner than the edges, because patties plump when you cook them (as of yet they do not make Spanx for burger bulge).

Before you form patties, bring the meat to room temperature and pat off excess liquid using a paper towel. Form an even mound of meat in a bowl and score the meat with the side of your hand into equal portions. This will help you to avoid the "runt burger." This is when you form the last patty and discover it is half the size of the others. Then you have to carefully rip off bits of raw meat from the other patties to equal out what becomes the Frankenburger.

Season your burgers with kosher salt. Kosher salt makes an extra crispy crust on burgers.

Let the pan get hot, over medium-high heat, before cooking the patties.

Burgers are not made of beef alone. I can make a tasty burger from at least a dozen varieties of ground meats and seafood and vegetables. But regardless of the patty type, it's important to choose the right ingredients. When it comes to a beef burger, if you do not grind your own blend or have a butcher that offers one, you should go with ground chuck for a tasty patty. If you are limiting animal fats in your diet, go with ground sirloin or buffalo and cut back on cooking time by 1 to 2 minutes so the lean meat does not dry out. Ground turkey makes a tasty burger and I use it in several recipes in this book. I prefer a white and dark meat blend, heavy on the dark meat. For ground turkey and in blends, the fat content should not be less than the ground beef options you prefer, so read labels carefully. Ground turkey breast is up to 99 percent fat free, so you must compensate for that lean meat with moisture from vegetables or the addition of fats like olive oil.

Making your own mix is fun and very simple to do with a meat-grinding attachment on your stand mixer. My blend follows here. Experiment with your own mix when you have the time. Butchers make great collaborators and will often save you a little of this and a little of that to pick and choose from.

Know your rolls. Try a few brands and bakeries and get an arsenal to mix and match with different types of burgers. For Sloppy Joes, I like a soft roll; for burgers, brioche rolls are largely a favorite; but for certain recipes, I prefer a crusty kaiser or maybe a ciabatta roll. For patty melts, buy whole pullman loaves (whole loaves of white bread, unsliced) and cut your own half-inch-thick slices. By prebuttering the outside-facing pieces of patty melts with a light coat of butter, you'll get even more of a golden brown color.

Sliders are your friends. They are a fun and affordable option for many a gathering. Any recipe can be adapted to fit a smaller dinner-sized roll; count on 3 ounces per patty, 8 sliders per most base recipes in this book. Cook up two slider choices at a time and plan on keeping new, hot patties flipping for three rounds.

A fun way to serve these is BYOB: Bring Your Own Burger. Invite guests to bring fixings or flavored burger meat; it's potluck with buns.

Flip out! Enjoy *The Book of Burger*.

—Rachael

RR BURGER BLEND

MAKES 3 POUNDS GROUND MEAT:
8 BURGERS OR 16 SLIDER-SIZE BURGERS

1½ pounds **boneless beef chuck,** cut into 1-inch cubes

¾ pound **boneless beef sirloin,** cut into 1-inch cubes

¾ pound **beef brisket,** cut into 1-inch cubes

Place the meat grinder parts, such as the grind worm, knife, and coarse grinding plate, in the freezer to chill, approximately 30 minutes. Keep the cubed meat in the refrigerator until just before you plan to send it through the grinder. After the meat is ground, keep it covered and cold until ready to use. Bring to room temperature before forming patties.

Meat may be frozen in 1½-pound packages for up to 4 weeks. Pat dry before freezing and place in freezerproof bags, tightly sealed. Defrost in the refrigerator. Pat meat dry once defrosted. Bring to room temperature before forming patties.

Rachael's burger rules!

BURGERS

BEEF AND VEAL BURGERS

4 Big Beef Burgers with Crunchy Sour Cream Onion Rings

7 Audacious, Herbacious Beef Burgers

8 Beef 'n' Bean Burrito Burgers

9 Burgers with Bacon Bits and Blue

10 Burgers all'Amatriciana

11 Buttered-Toast Swiss Patty Burger

12 Chili Mac 'n' Cheese Burgers

14 Chipotle Burgers with Nacho Top

15 Coarse-Ground Chuck Burgers with Garlic–Black Pepper Parmesan Sauce and Roasted Tomatoes with Basil and Balsamic Drizzle

16 French Onion Dip Burgers

18 Drunken Burgers with Stilton

19 Goat Cheese Burgers with Beets

20 Grilled Cheese Burgers with Bacon and Tomato

21 Lasagna Burgers

22 Meat and Mashed Potatoes Burger

23 Meat Lover's Burger

26 Cuban Patty Melts with Yellow Mustard Slaw

27 Patty Melts with Eggs

28 Pimiento Mac 'n' Cheese Cheeseburgers

29 Sauerbraten Burgers

30 Bœuf Bourguignon Burgers

31 Bloody Mary Cheeseburgers

33 Stroganoff-Style Knife-and-Fork Burgers

35 The Adirondacker

36 Chili Burgers with Charred Pico de Gallo

37 Wellington Burgers

38 Welsh Rarebit Burgers

39 Goulash Burgers

40 Beer-Braised Bacon Bacon Cheeseburgers

41 Double-Decker Animal Style

42 Rach's "Big Spicy Mac"

44 Florentine Burgers

45 "Smoke and Fireworks" Bacon-Wrapped Chipotle Burgers

47 Sage-Scented Burgers with Fontina and Roasted Squash

48 Spaghetti and Meatball Burgers

50 Meatball Hero Burgers

52 The Ultimate Salami Burgers

54 Shepherd's Pie Knife-and-Fork Burgers

56 Uptown Burger au Poivre with Brandy Cream Sauce

57 Uptown Burgers with Porcini Steak Sauce

58 Blue-Rugula Burgers

63 French Onion Burgers

64 Italian Meat Loaf Long Boy Burgers

65 Saltimbocca Burgers

PORK BURGERS

66 5-Spice Burgers with Warm Mu Shu Slaw

68 Brat Burgers with Sauerkraut or Sweet Onions

69 Cajun Pork Burgers

70 Country Pork and Peppercorn Burgers

71 Banh Mi Burgers

73 Hot Sausage Burgers with Broccoli Rabe

74 "The Wurst" Reuben Burgers

76 Long Boy Sausage Burgers with Pickled Fennel and Pepperonata

CHICKEN AND TURKEY BURGERS

78 Adirondack Red Wing Burgers

79 Chicken Kiev Burgers with Russian Slaw

80 Italian BBQ Chicken Burgers

82 Spanikopita Burgers

83 Provençal Burgers with Pissaladière Topping

85 Indian-Spiced Patties with Yogurt Sauce

86 Marsala Burgers

87 Rachel Patty Melts

88 Buffalo Turkey Burgers with Blue Cheese Dressing

90 California Turkey Club Burgers

91 Cobb-Style Turkey Burger Club with Green Ranch Dressing

92 Cranberry Bog Turkey Burgers

94 Curried Turkey Burgers

95 Hawaii Burgers

96 Caribbean Burgers with Mango Salsa

98 Hungarian Turkey Burgers with Smoked Gouda

99 Jerk Burgers

101 Cubano Burgers

102 Chicken or Turkey Burgers with Caesar Pesto

103 Spinach-Artichoke Burgers

104 Onion-and-Mushroom-Smothered Turkey Burgers with Swiss

105 Open-Face Turkey Burgers with Potpie Gravy

106 Turkey Tikka Burgers with Indian Corn

LAMB BURGERS

109 Middle Eastern Lamb Burgers with Baba Ghanoush

110 Lamb Burgers with Walnut and Feta Cheese Sauce

111 The Gyro Burger

112 Shish Ka Burgers

113 Berber Burgers

VEGGIE BURGERS

114 Portobello Burgers with Spinach Pesto

116 Falafel Burgers

117 Mediterranean Veggie Burgers with Provolone and Italian Ketchup

SEAFOOD BURGERS

119 Everything Bagel Salmon Burgers

120 Salmon Burgers with Tartar Sauce

121 Open-Face Salmon Burgers with Honey Mustard

122 Garlic-Ginger Salmon Burgers with Wasabi Mayo

123 French Tuna Burgers

124 Sicilian-Style Tuna or Swordfish Burgers

126 Fresh Tuna French-Style Cheeseburgers

127 Shrimp Burgers

BIG BEEF BURGERS with CRUNCHY SOUR CREAM ONION RINGS

SERVES 4

Make the onion rings: Fill a countertop fryer with oil or pour a few inches of oil into a large Dutch oven. Heat the oil to 350°F. (The oil is ready for frying when a 1-inch cube of white bread cooks to golden brown in 40 seconds.) Combine 1½ cups buttermilk and ½ cup sour cream in a bowl and add the onion rings; soak for a few minutes. On a plate, toss the flour with the chives; season generously with salt and pepper. Dip the onion rings in the seasoned flour, then again in the buttermilk, and again in the flour. Fry 1 or 2 rings at a time in the hot oil, turning once, until deep golden, about 4 minutes. Transfer to a rack to cool.

(CONTINUED ON PAGE 6)

SOUR CREAM ONION RINGS:

Vegetable oil, for frying

1½ cups buttermilk

½ cup sour cream

1 yellow onion, cut into 1-inch-thick slices and separated into rings

1½ cups flour

¼ cup finely chopped chives or scallions, whites and greens

Kosher salt and coarsely ground pepper

BURGERS:

2 pounds coarse-ground beef chuck

¼ cup Worcestershire sauce

EVOO (extra-virgin olive oil), for drizzling

Make the burgers: Heat a large skillet or griddle over medium-high heat.

In a large bowl, combine the beef, Worcestershire sauce, lots of pepper and a little salt; mix thoroughly. Score the mixture into 4 equal portions and form them into patties slightly thinner at the center than at the edges for even cooking and to ensure a flat surface (burgers plump as they cook). Drizzle the patties with EVOO. Cook the burgers, flipping once, 10 minutes for medium (adjust the timing for rarer or more well-done burgers).

While the burgers cook, make the dressing: In a small bowl, combine the buttermilk, sour cream, ketchup, garlic, herbs, and lemon juice; season with salt, pepper, and hot sauce.

Place the burgers on the roll bottoms and top with the lettuce, onion rings, and ranch dressing. Set the roll tops in place.

RED RANCH DRESSING:

½ cup **buttermilk**

½ cup **sour cream**

¼ cup good-quality **ketchup**, such as Heinz Organic

1 large clove **garlic**, grated or pasted (see Tip, page 138)

3 to 4 tablespoons finely chopped mixed fresh herbs (such as **chives**, **parsley**, and **dill**)

1 tablespoon fresh **lemon** juice

Hot sauce

4 **brioche rolls** or other **burger rolls** of choice, split

Chopped crisp **lettuce**, such as **iceberg** or **romaine heart**

TIP: You may have to make a special request for coarse-ground beef at your butcher or supermarket meat counter.

AUDACIOUS, HERBACIOUS BEEF BURGERS

SERVES 4

In a large bowl, combine the beef, chives, dill, parsley, and Worcestershire sauce. Season with salt and pepper and mix thoroughly. Score the mixture into 4 equal portions and form them into patties slightly thinner at the center than at the edges for even cooking and to ensure a flat surface (burgers plump when they cook). Drizzle the patties with EVOO.

Heat a large nonstick skillet or grill pan over medium-high heat. Cook the burgers, flipping once, 10 minutes for medium (adjust the timing for rarer or more well-done burgers).

Meanwhile, in a small bowl, combine the sour cream and honey mustard; season with salt and pepper. Spread the honey mustard sauce on the roll tops. Place the burgers on the roll bottoms and top with a smear of Boursin, sliced cukes, radishes, lettuce, and onion. Set the roll tops in place.

1½ pounds **ground beef chuck**

¼ cup chopped **chives**

¼ cup finely chopped **fresh dill**

¼ cup finely chopped **flat-leaf parsley**

2 tablespoons **Worcestershire sauce**

Kosher salt and **pepper**

EVOO (extra-virgin olive oil), for drizzling

¼ cup **sour cream**

¼ cup **honey mustard**

4 crusty **whole-grain kaiser rolls**, split and lightly toasted

1 (5-ounce) package **soft herb cheese**, such as Boursin

¼ **seedless cucumber**, thinly sliced

4 **radishes**, thinly sliced

4 leaves **red- or green-leaf lettuce**

4 thin slices **red onion**

BEEF 'N' BEAN BURRITO BURGERS

SERVES 4

All the flavors of your favorite bean, rice, and beef burrito in burger form!

Make the burgers: In a large bowl, combine the beef, beans, rice, grill seasoning, chile powder, cumin, and coriander; mix thoroughly. Score the mixture into 4 equal portions and form them into patties slightly thinner at the center than at the edges for even cooking and to ensure a flat surface (burgers plump as they cook).

Heat the oil, 1 turn of the pan, in a large skillet over medium-high heat. Cook the burgers, flipping once, 10 minutes for medium (adjust the timing for rarer or more well-done burgers).

While the burgers are cooking, make the guacamole: In a medium bowl, mash together the avocado flesh, onion, jalapeño, garlic, lime zest, and lime juice. Stir in the sour cream and season with salt.

Place a lettuce leaf and tomato slice on each roll bottom and top with a burger and guacamole. Set the roll tops in place.

BURRITO BURGERS:

1 pound **ground beef chuck**

½ cup **cooked black beans** or **canned black beans**, rinsed and drained

½ cup cold cooked **white** or **brown rice**

1 tablespoon **grill seasoning**, such as McCormick Montreal Steak Seasoning

1 tablespoon **ancho chile powder**

1½ teaspoons **ground cumin**

1½ teaspoons **ground coriander**

1 tablespoon **vegetable oil**

GUACAMOLE:

1 **avocado**

½ small **red onion**, finely chopped

1 **jalapeño** or **serrano chile**, seeded and finely chopped

1 clove **garlic**, grated or finely chopped

Grated zest and juice of 1 **lime**

½ cup **sour cream**

Kosher salt

4 leaves **red-leaf lettuce**

1 **tomato**, sliced

4 **crusty rolls**, split

BURGERS with BACON BITS and BLUE

SERVES 4

Heat a cast-iron skillet over medium-high to high heat. Cook the bacon until crisp, 3 to 4 minutes. Remove the bacon bits and drain on a paper towel–lined plate. Remove the pan from the heat and reserve the drippings in the pan.

In a large bowl, combine the beef, bacon bits, Worcestershire sauce, garlic, grated onion (grate it right over the bowl so the juices fall into the meat), parsley, salt, and lots of pepper; mix thoroughly. Score the mixture into 4 equal portions and form them into patties slightly thinner at the center than at the edges for even cooking and to ensure a flat surface (burgers plump as they cook).

Melt the butter in a small skillet over medium heat. Add the mushrooms and brown, 7 to 8 minutes; add the sliced onion and cook 8 to 10 minutes. If the pan gets dry, add a drizzle of EVOO. Season the cooked mushrooms with salt and pepper.

While the mushrooms are cooking, drizzle the patties with EVOO. Return the skillet with the drippings to medium-high heat. When hot, add the burgers and cook 10 minutes, flipping once, for medium (adjust the timing for rarer or more well-done burgers). Top the burgers with Stilton for the last minute or two of cooking, tenting the skillet with aluminum foil, if you like, to help melt the cheese.

Pile the watercress on the roll bottoms and top with the burgers, onions and mushrooms, and balsamic drizzle (if using). Set the roll tops in place.

8 slices **bacon**, chopped

2 pounds **ground beef chuck**

¼ cup **Worcestershire sauce**

4 cloves **garlic**, minced or grated

¼ cup grated **onion**

¼ cup finely chopped **flat-leaf parsley**

Kosher salt and **pepper**

2 tablespoons **butter**

¾ pound **cremini mushrooms**, sliced

1 **onion**, thinly sliced

EVOO (extra-virgin olive oil), for drizzling

½ cup crumbled **Stilton** or other piquant **blue cheese**

4 loosely packed cups **watercress** leaves

4 **burger rolls**, split, lightly toasted, and buttered

Balsamic drizzle, store-bought or homemade (optional; see page 15)

TIP: Whether you're toasting the rolls or bread for your burgers under the broiler, in a toaster, or in a toaster oven, do it as close as possible to when the burgers are ready.

BURGERS ALL'AMATRICIANA

SERVES 4

Preheat the oven to 400°F.

Arrange the tomato slices in a single layer on a baking sheet and drizzle with EVOO; season with salt and pepper, the sugar, and thyme. Roast for 30 minutes.

Meanwhile, heat 1 tablespoon EVOO, 1 turn of the pan, in a large nonstick skillet. Cook the pancetta and onion over medium heat until browned, about 5 minutes. Transfer to a large bowl to cool; wipe out the skillet and set aside.

Add the beef, garlic, and parsley to the pancetta-onion mixture; season with salt and pepper and mix thoroughly. Score the mixture into 4 equal portions and form them into patties slightly thinner at the center than at the edges for even cooking and to ensure a flat surface (burgers plump as they cook).

Heat the remaining 1 tablespoon EVOO, 1 turn of the pan, in the reserved skillet over medium-high heat. Cook the burgers until deeply browned and crisp on the bottoms, about 5 minutes, then flip and cook for 3 minutes longer for medium-rare and about 5 minutes longer for medium (adjust the timing for rarer or more well-done burgers).

When the tomatoes come out of the oven, preheat the broiler. Arrange the split rolls cut side up on a baking sheet and toast.

In a small bowl, microwave the butter until melted, about 20 seconds. Brush the butter on the toasted rolls and top with the Parmigiano-Reggiano. Broil for 1 minute.

Place the burgers on the roll bottoms and top with lettuce and some of the tomatoes. Set the roll tops in place. Pass the remaining tomatoes separately or save them for topping other sandwiches.

8 **plum tomatoes**, cored and sliced lengthwise into thirds

2 tablespoons **EVOO** (extra-virgin olive oil), plus more for drizzling

Kosher salt and **pepper**

A sprinkle of **sugar**

1 tablespoon **fresh thyme** leaves, chopped

4 (⅛-inch-thick) slices **pancetta**, chopped

1 small **red onion**, finely chopped

1½ pounds **ground beef chuck**

2 large cloves **garlic**, finely chopped or grated

⅓ cup finely chopped **flat-leaf parsley** (a generous handful)

4 crusty **kaiser rolls**, split

2 tablespoons **butter**

½ cup grated **Parmigiano-Reggiano cheese**

4 leaves **romaine lettuce**, shredded

BUTTERED-TOAST SWISS PATTY BURGER

SERVES 4

Melt 1 tablespoon butter in a medium skillet over medium-low heat. Add the onion and thyme, season with salt and pepper, and cook until the onion is lightly browned, about 15 minutes.

While the onion is cooking, combine the beef and Worcestershire sauce in a large bowl; season with salt and pepper and mix thoroughly. Score the mixture into 4 equal portions and form them into patties slightly thinner at the center than at the edges for even cooking and to ensure a flat surface (burgers plump as they cook). Heat the EVOO, ½ turn of the pan, in a large nonstick skillet over medium-high heat until very hot. Cook the burgers, turning once, 10 minutes for medium (adjust the timing for rarer or more well-done burgers). Top the burgers with the cheese for the last minute of cooking, tenting the skillet with aluminum foil, if you like, to help melt the cheese.

While the burgers are cooking, toast the bread, then spread with the remaining 2 tablespoons softened butter. Stir the mustard and chicken stock into the onions. Stir in the parsley, then remove from the heat.

Place a burger on each of 4 buttered toasts and top with some of the onions. Set the remaining buttered toast on top.

3 tablespoons **butter**, 2 of them softened

1 large **onion**, chopped

2 pinches of **ground thyme**

Kosher salt and **pepper**

1½ pounds **ground beef chuck**

1 tablespoon **Worcestershire sauce**

1½ teaspoons **EVOO** (extra-virgin olive oil)

4 thin slices **Swiss cheese**, such as Emmentaler

8 slices **sandwich bread**

1 tablespoon **Dijon mustard**

A splash of **chicken stock** or water

1 tablespoon finely chopped **flat-leaf parsley**

CHILI MAC 'N' CHEESE BURGERS

SERVES 4

Obvious. Cheeseburgers are great, so why not mac 'n' cheese on a burger?

Heat a drizzle of oil in a small skillet over medium-high heat. Add ½ pound of the beef and break it into crumbles as it browns. Add the onion, garlic, chile powder, coriander, cumin, salt, and pepper, and cook to soften the onion, about 5 minutes. Add the tomato paste, stir a minute, then deglaze pan with beer or stock.

Bring a medium saucepan of water to a boil. Salt the water and cook the macaroni to al dente.

While the pasta is cooking, in a second small saucepan, melt the butter over medium heat. Whisk in the flour and cook for 1 minute. Whisk in the milk and bring up to a bubble. Simmer until the sauce has thickened, about 2 minutes. Stir in the shredded cheese until melted.

Drain the pasta and toss with the cheese sauce, then fold in the chili. Keep warm.

Heat a grill pan or griddle over medium-high heat.

In a large bowl, combine the remaining 1½ pounds beef and the Worcestershire sauce; season with salt and pepper and mix thoroughly. Score the mixture into 4 equal portions and form them into patties slightly thinner at the center than at the edges for even cooking and to ensure a flat surface (burgers plump as they cook). Drizzle the patties with EVOO. Cook the burgers, flipping once, 10 minutes for medium (adjust the timing for rarer or more well-done burgers).

Place the burgers on the roll bottoms and top with chili mac. Set the roll tops in place.

EVOO (extra-virgin olive oil) or **vegetable oil**, for drizzling

2 pounds **ground beef chuck**

½ cup finely chopped **onion**

2 large cloves **garlic**, finely chopped

1 rounded tablespoon **mild (ancho)** or **hot (chipotle) chile powder**

1 teaspoon **ground coriander**

1 teaspoon **ground cumin**

Kosher salt and **pepper**

2 tablespoons **tomato paste**

½ cup **beer** or **beef stock**

1 cup **elbow macaroni**

2 tablespoons **butter**

2 tablespoons **flour**

1¼ cups **milk**

1 cup shredded **sharp yellow cheddar cheese**

2 tablespoons **Worcestershire sauce**

4 **burger rolls**, split

CHIPOTLE BURGERS with NACHO TOP

SERVES 6

Heat a large cast-iron skillet or griddle over medium-high heat.

In a mixing bowl, combine the beef, bacon, chipotle puree, Worcestershire sauce, garlic, and grated onion (grate it right over the bowl so the juices fall into the meat); season with salt and pepper and mix thoroughly. Score the mixture into 6 equal portions and form them into patties slightly thinner at the center than at the edges for even cooking and to ensure a flat surface (burgers plump as they cook). Drizzle the patties with a little oil. Cook the burgers 5 minutes on each side for medium, a minute less per side for rare, a minute more per side for medium-well.

While the burgers are cooking, make the *queso* sauce: Melt the butter in a small saucepan over medium heat. Whisk in the flour and cook for 1 minute. Whisk in the milk and bring up to a bubble. Simmer until the sauce has thickened, about 2 minutes. Stir in all the cheeses.

Place the burgers on the roll bottoms and top with *queso* sauce, chips, and other toppings of choice. Set the roll tops in place.

TIP: When you bring home a whole can of chipotle chiles in adobo sauce, seed the peppers and then puree them with the sauce in a food processor to make a smooth paste. Remove what you need and store the rest in a small plastic freezer bag (push the puree to the bottom of the bag to make a roll) in the freezer. The next time you need some, cut off about 1 inch of the puree for each tablespoon and return the rest to the freezer.

BURGERS:

1¾ pounds **ground beef chuck**

¼ pound **smoky bacon**, finely chopped

2 rounded tablespoons pureed **chipotle in adobo sauce** (see Tip)

2 tablespoons **Worcestershire sauce**

2 cloves **garlic**, finely chopped or grated

3 to 4 tablespoons grated **onion**

Kosher salt and **pepper**

Vegetable oil or **olive oil** for drizzling

6 **burger rolls**, split

3-CHEESE *QUESO* SAUCE:

2 tablespoons **butter**

1 rounded tablespoon **flour**

1 cup **milk**

1½ cups grated **Manchego cheese** (about ⅓ pound)

1 cup shredded **Monterey Jack cheese** (about ¼ pound)

¼ to ⅓ cup grated **Parmigiano-Reggiano cheese**

TOPPINGS:

Crispy **tortilla chips**—blue, yellow, or multigrain

Minced **red onion**

Chopped **cilantro**

Chopped seeded **tomato**

Pickled jalapeño slices

COARSE-GROUND CHUCK BURGERS with

Garlic–Black Pepper Parmesan Sauce and Roasted Tomatoes with Basil and Balsamic Drizzle

SERVES 4

Preheat the oven to 325°F.

Set a cooling rack over a baking sheet. Arrange the tomatoes on the rack, then drizzle with a touch of EVOO. Season with salt and pepper. Roast the tomatoes 45 minutes.

When the tomatoes are about ready, heat a large skillet over medium-high heat.

Season the beef with salt and pepper. Score the mixture into 4 equal portions and form them into patties slightly thinner at the center than at the edges for even cooking and to ensure a flat surface (burgers plump as they cook). Add the 2 tablespoons EVOO, 2 turns of the pan, to the hot skillet. Cook the burgers, flipping once, 10 minutes for medium (adjust the timing for rarer or more well-done burgers).

While the burgers are cooking, place a small saucepan over medium heat with the butter. Add the garlic and cook for about 1 minute. Add the flour and cook for 1 minute more. Whisk in the milk and bring up to a bubble. Season with salt and 1 teaspoon coarsely ground black pepper. Simmer until the sauce has thickened, about 2 minutes. Stir in the grated cheese.

Prepare the balsamic drizzle in small saucepan if not using store-bought.

Place lettuce on the roll bottoms and top with the burgers. Pour Parmigiano-Reggiano sauce over the burgers, set the roasted tomatoes in the sauce, scatter basil over the burgers, and garnish with the balsamic drizzle. Set the roll tops in place.

3 **vine-ripened tomatoes**, cored and sliced ¼ inch thick

2 tablespoons **EVOO** (extra-virgin olive oil), plus more for drizzling

Kosher salt and **pepper** for seasoning, plus 1 teaspoon coarsely ground pepper for the sauce

1½ pounds **coarse-ground beef chuck** (see Tip, page 6)

3 tablespoons **butter**

2 cloves **garlic**, finely chopped or grated

2 tablespoons **flour**

¾ cup **milk**

⅓ cup grated **Parmigiano-Reggiano cheese** (a couple of small handfuls)

Balsamic drizzle (see Tip)

Leaf lettuce

4 **kaiser rolls**, split and toasted

½ cup **basil** leaves (8 to 10), thinly sliced

TIP: Balsamic drizzle is available in some supermarkets, or make your own: Combine ½ cup balsamic vinegar and 2 tablespoons brown sugar in a small saucepan and reduce over medium heat until thick and syrupy, a couple of minutes.

FRENCH ONION DIP BURGERS

SERVES 6

Make the onion dip: Heat the butter in a skillet over medium heat. Add the sliced onions and bay leaf; season with salt, pepper, and ground thyme. Cook, stirring occasionally, until deep caramel in color and very soft, about 35 minutes. Deglaze the pan with beef consommé and cook until the liquid is almost absorbed. Cool the onions and discard the bay leaf. Stir the onions and sour cream together in a small bowl and adjust the seasoning.

When the onion dip is ready, make the burgers: Heat a griddle or large cast-iron skillet over medium-high heat.

In a large bowl, combine the beef, Worcestershire sauce, grated onion (grate it right over the bowl so the juices fall into the meat), and parsley; season with salt and pepper and mix well. Score the mixture into 6 equal portions and form them into patties slightly thinner at the center than at the edges for even cooking and to ensure a flat surface (burgers plump as they cook). Drizzle the patties with EVOO. Cook the burgers, flipping once, 10 minutes for medium (adjust the timing for rarer or more well-done burgers).

Place the burgers on the roll bottoms and top with a few layers of onion dip, potato chips, and a couple of pickle slices. Set the roll tops in place.

ONION DIP:

3 tablespoons **butter**

4 medium **onions**, thinly sliced

1 **fresh bay leaf**

Kosher salt and **pepper**

½ teaspoon **ground thyme**

1 cup canned **beef consommé**

1½ cups **sour cream**

BURGERS:

2 pounds **ground beef chuck**

¼ cup **Worcestershire sauce**

3 to 4 tablespoons grated **onion**

A handful of **flat-leaf parsley**, finely chopped

EVOO (extra-virgin olive oil), for drizzling

6 **brioche rolls**, split

36 good-quality ridged or thick-cut **potato chips** (look for chips cooked in olive oil)

Sliced **sweet pickles**

TIP: The grated onion and its juice will flavor the meat itself plus keep the burgers moist as you cook them.

DRUNKEN BURGERS with STILTON

SERVES 4

If you like, serve the burgers with Pub Hash Browns with Horseradish Sauce (page 268) on the side, spooning some of the horseradish sauce and bacon bits from the potatoes over the burgers, and open some cold beers to wash it down.

1 cup **dry sherry** or **ruby port**

1½ pounds **ground beef chuck**

3 tablespoons **Worcestershire sauce**

¼ cup very finely chopped **flat leaf parsley**

4 cloves **garlic**, grated or pasted (see Tip, page 138)

Kosher salt and coarsely ground **pepper**

EVOO (extra-virgin olive oil), for drizzling

2 large **shallots**, halved and very thinly sliced lengthwise

¾ pound **Stilton cheese**, crumbled

Upland cress or **watercress leaves**

4 **brioche rolls**, split

Bread-and-butter pickle slices

Bring the sherry or port to a boil in a small saucepan. Reduce to a low simmer and cook until reduced to ¼ to ⅓ cup, 15 to 20 minutes.

Heat a cast-iron skillet or griddle over medium-high heat.

In a large bowl, combine the beef, Worcestershire sauce, parsley, and garlic; season with kosher salt (it makes a nice crust) and lots of pepper. Mix to just combine—do not overwork the meat and do not form patties; just shape the beef mixture into an even mound and score with your hand into 4 portions.

Drizzle a little EVOO into the heated skillet. Place the 4 portions of burger mix into the pan and squish them into thick burgers with a spatula. Top the burgers liberally with the sliced shallots and press them into the meat. Cook the burgers 4 minutes for a good crust, then flip and cook the shallots into the meat, 4 minutes more (adjust the cooking time for rarer or more well-done burgers). Top with Stilton for the last minute or two of cooking, tenting the pan with aluminum foil, if you like, to help melt the cheese. Douse the burgers with the reduced sherry.

Place a little upland cress on the roll bottoms and top with sherry-Stilton burgers and pickle slices. Set the roll tops in place.

GOAT CHEESE BURGERS with BEETS

SERVES 4

Combine the fresh beet slices and enough water to cover in a medium saucepan. Bring to a boil, then reduce to a simmer and cook until tender, 10 to 12 minutes; drain. (If using canned beets, just drain them.)

Heat a large cast-iron skillet over medium-high heat.

In a large bowl, combine the beef, ⅓ cup chopped parsley, the garlic, and Worcestershire sauce; season with salt and pepper and mix thoroughly. Score the mixture into 4 equal portions and form them into patties thinner at the center than at the edges for even cooking and to ensure a flat surface (burgers plump as they cook). Coat the patties with the EVOO. Cook the burgers, flipping once, 10 minutes for medium (adjust the timing for rarer or more well-done burgers).

While the burgers are cooking, crumble the goat cheese into a small bowl. Add the sour cream, dill, thyme, lemon zest, and remaining 1 tablespoon parsley.

Place the burgers on the roll bottoms and top with the beet slices, goat cheese mixture, onion, and lettuce. Set the roll tops in place.

1 large **beet**, peeled and sliced ¼ inch thick, or 1 (14.5-ounce) can sliced beets

1½ pounds **ground beef chuck**

⅓ cup plus 1 tablespoon finely chopped **flat-leaf parsley** (a generous handful)

2 large cloves **garlic**, grated or finely chopped

2 tablespoons **Worcestershire sauce**

Kosher salt and **pepper**

1 tablespoon **EVOO** (extra-virgin olive oil)

3 ounces **goat cheese**

½ cup **sour cream, crème fraîche,** or **Greek yogurt**

1 tablespoon finely chopped **fresh dill**

1 tablespoon finely chopped **fresh thyme**

1 teaspoon grated **lemon** zest

4 **crusty rolls**, split

4 thin slices **red onion**

4 leaves **red-leaf lettuce**

GRILLED CHEESE BURGERS with BACON and TOMATO

SERVES 4

Heat 1 tablespoon EVOO, about 1 turn of the pan, in a medium skillet over medium-high heat. Add the onion and cook until tender, 4 to 5 minutes. Transfer the onion to a large bowl to cool.

When the onion has cooled enough to touch, add the beef and Worcestershire sauce; season with salt and pepper and mix thoroughly. Score the meat into 4 equal portions and shape them into thin patties slightly thinner at the center than at the edges for even cooking and to ensure a flat surface (burgers plump as they cook). Add the remaining 2 tablespoons EVOO, 2 turns of the pan, in a large nonstick skillet over medium-high heat. Cook the burgers, flipping once, 10 minutes for medium (adjust the timing for rarer or more well-done burgers).

While the burgers are cooking, butter up one side of each slice of bread, then flip over and spread mustard on the other side of each slice.

When the burgers have finished cooking, make your stacks by laying down 4 slices of white bread butter side down and topping them with a slice of Swiss cheese, a burger, another slice of cheese, 2 slices of bacon, and 2 slices of tomato. Cap the stack with a slice of bread (butter side up). Wipe out the pan that the burgers were cooked in and return it to medium heat. Add the stacks to the pan and cook, flipping once, until the bread is toasted golden brown and the cheese has melted, 2 to 3 minutes per side.

3 tablespoons **EVOO** (extra-virgin olive oil)

1 small **onion**, very finely chopped

1½ pounds **ground beef chuck**

1 tablespoon **Worcestershire sauce**

Kosher salt and **pepper**

3 to 4 tablespoons **butter**, softened

8 slices **white pullman bread**

3 to 4 tablespoons **Dijon mustard**

8 slices deli-sliced **Swiss cheese**

8 slices **bacon**, cooked until crisp

8 slices **tomato**

LASAGNA BURGERS

SERVES 4

In a large bowl, season the meat with plenty of salt and pepper and mix thoroughly. Score the mixture into 4 equal portions and form them into patties slightly thinner at the center than at the edges for even cooking and to ensure a flat surface (burgers plump as they cook).

Heat 2 tablespoons EVOO, 2 turns of the pan, in a saucepan over medium heat. Add the onion and garlic and cook until softened, about 5 minutes. Stir in the tomatoes and oregano and season with salt and pepper. Reduce the heat and simmer for 5 minutes; stir in the basil.

Heat a large skillet over medium-high heat. Drizzle the patties with EVOO. Cook the burgers, flipping once, 10 minutes for medium (adjust the timing for rarer or more well-done). Top the burgers with provolone or mozzarella for the last minute or two of cooking, tenting the skillet with aluminum foil, if you like, to help melt the cheese.

While the burgers are cooking, melt the butter in a small saucepan over medium heat. Whisk in the flour and cook for 1 minute. Whisk in the milk; season with salt, pepper, and the nutmeg. Cook until thickened, about 5 minutes. Stir in the ricotta and Parmigiano-Reggiano.

Spoon some red sauce on the roll bottoms and top with the burgers. Spoon more red sauce on top and then some cheese sauce. Set the roll tops in place.

1½ pounds **ground mix of beef, pork, and veal**

Kosher salt and **pepper**

2 tablespoons **EVOO** (extra-virgin olive oil), plus more for drizzling

1 small **onion**, finely chopped

2 cloves **garlic**, chopped

1 (15-ounce) can **crushed tomatoes**

½ teaspoon **dried oregano**

A handful **basil** leaves, shredded or torn

4 slices deli-sliced **provolone** or **mozzarella cheese**

2 tablespoons **butter**

2 tablespoons **flour**

1 cup **milk**

A few grates of **nutmeg**

½ cup **ricotta cheese**

¼ cup grated **Parmigiano-Reggiano cheese**

4 **burger rolls** or **ciabatta rolls**, split

MEAT and MASHED POTATOES BURGER

SERVES 4

Make the mashers: Place the potatoes in a saucepan and cover by 1 inch with water. Place over high heat and bring up to a bubble. Add some salt and boil the potatoes until tender, about 12 minutes. Turn off heat. Drain the potatoes and return them to the pot; let them sit for a minute to dry out. Add the cream or half-and-half, the butter, and egg. Mash with a potato masher or fork. Add the chives and season with salt and pepper; continue to mash to a fairly smooth consistency.

While the potatoes are cooking, start on the burgers: In a large bowl, combine the beef, Worcestershire sauce, parsley, and the grated onion (grate it right over the bowl so the juices fall into the meat); season with salt and pepper and mix thoroughly. Score the mixture into 4 equal portions and form them into patties slightly thinner at the center than at the edges for even cooking and to ensure a flat surface (burgers plump as they cook). Heat the EVOO, 2 turns of the pan, in a large skillet over medium-high heat. Cook the burgers, flipping once, 10 minutes for medium (adjust the timing for rarer or more well-done burgers).

Slather the roll bottoms with mustard and top with the watercress, burgers, and a pile of mashers. The mashers will be the glue to hold the roll tops in place.

MASHED POTATOES:

2 large **baking potatoes**, peeled and cut into chunks

Kosher salt and **pepper**

3 to 4 tablespoons **heavy cream** or **half-and-half**

1 tablespoon **butter**

1 large **egg**

2 to 3 tablespoons finely chopped **chives**

BURGERS:

2 pounds **ground beef chuck**

3 to 4 tablespoons **Worcestershire sauce**

A handful of **flat-leaf parsley** leaves, finely chopped

3 tablespoons grated **onion**

2 tablespoons **EVOO** (extra-virgin olive oil)

4 **poppy seed** or **plain kaiser rolls**, split and toasted

Dijon mustard

1 bunch **watercress**, trimmed of thick stems

MEAT LOVER'S BURGER

SERVES 4

Because my husband, John, cannot go more than three hours at home without bacon or some kind of *salumi*—ham, salami, or prosciutto—I have lots of bits of meat on hand at all times. This burger is a clever use of them.

Preheat the oven to 350°F. Arrange the tomatoes on a cooling rack set over a baking sheet and season with the oregano, salt, and pepper. Drizzle with EVOO and roast about 40 minutes to tart them up.

Heat a drizzle of EVOO in a large cast-iron or non-stick skillet over medium-high heat. Cook the pancetta, speck, or bacon, stirring, until browned, 8 to 10 minutes. Transfer to a bowl to cool. Wipe out the pan and reserve.

In a large bowl, combine the beef, garlic, parsley, a little salt, and lots of pepper. Chop the salumi and ham or prosciutto ends and then grind to fine bits in a food processor. Add to the beef in the bowl and mix thoroughly. Score the mixture into 4 equal portions and form them into patties slightly thinner at the center than at the edges for even cooking and to ensure a flat surface (burgers plump as they cook). Drizzle the patties with EVOO.

Return the skillet to medium-high heat and when hot, add the burgers and cook, flipping once, 10 minutes for medium (adjust the timing for rarer or more well-done burgers). Top the burgers with cheese for the last minute or two of cooking, tenting the pan with aluminum foil, if you like, to help melt the cheese.

Place the burgers on the roll bottoms and top with oven-roasted tomatoes, basil, arugula, red onion, and a drizzle of EVOO. Set the roll tops in place.

2 **plum tomatoes**, cored and sliced ½ inch thick

A sprinkle of **dried oregano**

Kosher salt and **pepper**

EVOO (extra-virgin olive oil), for drizzling

¼ pound **pancetta**, **speck**, or **bacon**, finely diced

1 pound **ground beef chuck**

2 large cloves **garlic**, minced or grated

A handful of **flat-leaf parsley**, finely chopped

About 2 ounces spicy salumi, such as **salami** pieces, **soppressata** bits, or **hot ham** ends

¼ pound **ham**, **prosciutto**, or **prosciutto cotto** ends

4 thick slices deli-sliced **provolone cheese**

4 **crusty rolls**, split

A handful of **basil** leaves, torn

A handful of **arugula** leaves

Thinly sliced **red onions**

A HOMEMADE BURGER BLEND
PAT LaFRIEDA

CEO, Pat LaFrieda Meat Purveyors

Being a native of the Bensonhurst section of Brooklyn, I was fortunate enough to grow up around plenty of Italian-American bakeries. It is there that I learned the lessons of freshness by eating my way through loaves and loaves of warm, fresh semolina bread. As a butcher who knows a little something about meat, I equate fresh bread with freshly ground beef. Fresh bread is at its best the day it is baked. Every day after that, it loses just a little bit of quality, texture, and flavor. It's the same thing with ground beef, and that is reason enough for you to grind your own beef at home.

Some of the fondest memories of my childhood involve tasting raw freshly ground beef right out of the grinder in my dad's butcher shop. I'd climb a ladder next to the industrial grinder and watch as my dad fed the fresh domestic beef into the machine. I was able to sniff the sweet aromas of the freshly ground beef, which can best be described as a cross between the center, rare part of a roast beef and the sweetness of fall corn. Dad ground the beef right into the palm of his hand, then sprinkled a pinch of salt over the top and reached up to me on the ladder to share a few ounces of love. At the age of ten, I was eating what every fine restaurant served for "steak tartare," but I always felt that my dad's was better; it was so fresh that I could taste the real difference between Dad's version and store-bought ground beef. If I hadn't been there myself to experience it firsthand, I never would have known what I was missing. I am going to help you to re-create this quality ground beef at home, for it will give hamburgers a completely different meaning for you.

Grinding your own meat at home also enables you to control what cuts of meat you are eating. Each cut or each selection of cuts will affect the fat content, texture, color, aroma, and flavor profile. It will also ensure that you can confirm the origin of the meat. (Many restaurants sell hamburgers that contain ingredients that you don't want to eat: mechanically deboned beef, fillers, nitrates, nitrites, and, worst of all to my mind, imported beef. The worst part about those added ingredients is that the restaurants don't have to tell you that they are included in what they are serving. If any hamburger product ever lists "100% Beef" as an accolade, you should *run*, for all that means is that there is no other species of animal, such as pork, in the mix. It doesn't mean that it isn't filled with "other things.") My favorite cuts of meat to grind are chuck roll steaks, flat iron steaks, briskets, and boneless short ribs. All of these cuts are easily found in most butcher shops. I use these cuts in equal ratios. The flat iron is closest to a New York strip steak in flavor but at a fraction of the price. The boneless short ribs are deep in beef flavor yet are a braising meat, which means it gives great texture to the grind. The chuck roll is an extension of the rib eye and tastes like prime rib. The buttery fat of the brisket brings it all together with sweetness. Any of these alone or any combination of these cuts will deliver a great flavor.

Safety is very important while making ground beef. Since *E. coli*—the main culprit for most ground beef–related illnesses—is found on the exterior of the muscles, it is very important that the cuts of meat are handled properly. If *E. coli* is present on the exterior, it will soon work its way throughout the mix after grinding. One has to make sure that all surfaces that come into contact with food are sanitized—and that includes all the parts of the grinder. I use a sanitizer and finish with a diluted bleach solution.

Ground beef is very safe; however, always keep in mind that rare or raw ground meat should not be fed to children or the elderly, for their immune systems are not strong enough to fight some pathogens. A simple rule to follow, when preparing meat for them, is to cook ground beef to an internal temperature of 165°F for at least one minute. A little-known fact is that when beef companies get a positive test for *E. coli* on meat, they don't destroy the product. The USDA requires that they sell it to other food companies that specialize in cooked products, such as precooked meatballs. It is there that a USDA inspector will ensure that tainted meat is cooked to 165°F to kill off any chance of the pathogen hurting anyone.

Whether you have a food processor, a meat grinder attachment, or a hand grinder, the most common myth is that you must chill all the parts—grinder knives, "screw," feed tray, and grinder plate—before using them. This is false; it is the meat that should be chilled. Chilling the grinder parts could make them more brittle and prone to metal flakes and shavings falling into the meat. It is better to concentrate the time you would spend to chill the parts on making sure all your work surfaces, knives, and all the parts of whatever equipment you are using are sanitized.

Regardless of what apparatus is used, the meat should not be cubed, but cut into strips as wide as the hole of the feed neck and as long as possible. The reason for this is simple: once the meat is fed into the machine, the "screw" will grab the tip of the strip and pull in the rest of the piece. One would not have to force the meat into the feed tube because the apparatus would already have a great grip on the strip. Once you have your meat cut into strips, place them on a plate and put the plate into the freezer for a good 5 minutes. You're not looking to freeze the meat, but to chill it so that it begins to get firm. Chilling strengthens the integrity of the muscle cells and prevents the meat from emulsifying under all the pressure of the grinder.

Now it's time to grind: If using a meat grinder—whether an old-fashioned hand-cranked model, an electric grinder, or an attachment for a stand mixer—always grind the meat twice using two different-sized grinder plates. If you are using a food processor, make sure that the knife and die plate are flush with each other.

Regardless of what you decide on for the fineness or coarseness of your final grind, use a coarser grind plate first, then run the ground beef through the grinder fitted with a finer disc. Following this technique will ensure that the muscle cells keep their integrity and composure and the meat will not emulsify into a paste. The whole point of grinding your own beef is to be sure you don't end up with mush but with a well-textured mixture that will make beautiful burgers.

Meet Pat LaFrieda.

Grinding your own beef with Pat LaFrieda.

CUBAN PATTY MELTS with YELLOW MUSTARD SLAW

SERVES 4

Make the slaw: Whisk the mustard, relish, and honey together in a mixing bowl. Whisk in the vegetable oil and toss the dressing with the coleslaw mix to coat. Season with salt and pepper.

Make the burgers: In a large bowl, combine the beef, marjoram or oregano, cumin, cilantro, grated onion (grate it right over the bowl so the juices fall into the meat), and garlic; season with salt and pepper and mix thoroughly. Score the mixture into 4 equal portions and form them into patties slightly thinner at the center than at the edges for even cooking and to ensure a flat surface (burgers plump as they cook).

Heat the EVOO, 1 turn of the pan, in a large skillet over medium-high heat. Cook the burgers 5 minutes; flip and cook 2 minutes. Squeeze lime juice over the burgers, then top with cheese. Tent the pan with aluminum foil, if you like, to help melt the cheese for the last minute or two of cooking (a total of 10 minutes for medium; adjust cooking time for rarer or more well-done burgers).

Place the burgers on 4 slices of buttered toast and top with the remaining toast. Cut on the diagonal, making 2 triangles. Serve with slaw and plantain chips alongside.

YELLOW MUSTARD SLAW:

¼ cup **yellow mustard**

3 tablespoons **dill relish**

¼ cup **honey** or **agave nectar**

⅓ cup **vegetable oil**

1 pound **coleslaw mix**

Kosher salt and **pepper**

BURGERS:

1½ pounds **ground beef chuck**

1½ teaspoons ground **dried marjoram** or **oregano**

1½ teaspoons **ground cumin**

¼ cup loosely packed **cilantro** leaves, finely chopped

3 to 4 tablespoons grated **onion**

3 to 4 cloves **garlic**, finely chopped

1 tablespoon **EVOO** (extra-virgin olive oil)

1 **lime**, halved

4 slices deli-sliced **Swiss cheese**

8 slices good-quality **white bread**, toasted and buttered

Store-bought **plantain chips**

PATTY MELTS with EGGS

SERVES 4

Preheat the broiler.

Halve the poblanos and seed them. Place them skin-side up on a baking sheet and blacken them under the broiler with the oven door ajar to let steam escape. (Or leave the poblanos whole and char them over an open flame on a stovetop burner.) Place the charred peppers in a bowl, cover with plastic wrap, and let cool. Once cool enough to handle, peel, seed, and thinly slice the peppers.

Preheat the oven to 375°F. Arrange the bacon on a slotted broiler pan or on a cooling rack set over a baking sheet and bake until crisp, 15 to 17 minutes.

Meanwhile, heat 1½ tablespoons butter in a large skillet over medium heat. Add the onion and cook until lightly browned, about 10 minutes; season with salt and pepper. Transfer the onion to a bowl and reserve the skillet.

In a large bowl, combine the beef with Worcestershire sauce; season with salt and pepper and mix thoroughly. Score the mixture into 4 equal portions and form them into very thin patties to fit the shape of your bread. Return the skillet to medium-high heat and add a drizzle of oil to the hot skillet. Cook the burgers, flipping once, 6 to 8 minutes for medium (adjust the cooking time for rarer or more well-done burgers). Transfer to a plate or baking sheet.

Wipe the pan clean and return to medium heat. Add another drizzle of oil and then crack the eggs into the pan; cook, turning once, to over-easy or over-medium. Transfer the eggs to a plate.

Scantly butter all the bread on 1 side. Place 4 bread slices buttered side down and top each with a few slices of poblano, 2 cheese slices, a burger, some bacon, an egg, 2 more cheese slices, and some onions. Top with the remaining bread slices, buttered side up.

Wipe out the skillet and return it to medium heat. Grill the sandwiches on medium heat, turning once, until deep golden, about 5 minutes.

1 large or 2 medium **poblano chiles**

8 slices **bacon**

1½ tablespoons **butter**, plus more for spreading

1 **onion**, finely chopped

Kosher salt and **pepper**

1½ pounds **ground beef chuck**

2 tablespoons **Worcestershire sauce**

EVOO (extra-virgin olive oil) or **vegetable oil**, for drizzling

4 **extra-large eggs**

8 slices **white bread**

16 slices **Monterey Jack** or **mild cheddar cheese**

PIMIENTO MAC 'N' CHEESE CHEESEBURGERS

SERVES 6

Make the mac 'n' cheese: Bring a pot of water to a boil. Salt the water and undercook the macaroni by 1 minute.

Meanwhile, melt the butter in a small saucepan over medium heat. Add the garlic and chile, and stir 3 minutes. Add the pimientos and heat through. Add the paprika, then the flour, and stir 1 minute. Whisk in the milk and bring up to a bubble. Simmer until the sauce has thickened, about 2 minutes. Season with salt and pepper and stir in the cheese to melt.

Drain the macaroni and stir it into the sauce.

Make the burgers: In a large bowl, combine the beef, Worcestershire sauce, and grated onion (grate it right over the bowl so the juices fall into the meat); season with salt and pepper and mix thoroughly. Score the mixture into 6 equal portions and form them into patties slightly thinner at the center and thicker at the edges for even cooking and to ensure a flat surface (burgers plump as they cook). Drizzle the patties lightly with oil.

Heat a large cast-iron skillet or griddle over medium-high heat. Cook the burgers, flipping once, 10 minutes for medium (adjust the timing for rarer or more well-done burgers).

Place the burgers on the roll bottoms and top with mac 'n' cheese and fixin's of choice. Set the roll tops in place.

MAC 'N' CHEESE:

Salt

1¼ cups **elbow macaroni**, about ⅓ pound

4 tablespoons (½ stick) **butter**

2 **cloves garlic**, finely chopped

1 **fresh red chile**, such as Fresno, finely chopped

2 (4-ounce) jars chopped **pimientos**, well drained and finely chopped

2 teaspoons **sweet paprika**

2 rounded tablespoons **flour**

1½ cups **milk**

Pepper

2 cups grated **extra-sharp cheddar cheese**

BURGERS:

2 pounds **ground beef chuck**

2 tablespoons **Worcestershire sauce**

3 to 4 tablespoons grated **onion**

Kosher **salt** and **pepper**

EVOO (extra-virgin olive oil) or **vegetable oil**, for drizzling

6 large, soft **burger rolls** or **brioche rolls**

OPTIONAL FIXIN'S:

Chopped **pickles**

Peppadew peppers

Chopped **lettuce**

Sliced or diced **tomatoes**

SAUERBRATEN BURGERS

SERVES 4

Make the cabbage: Heat the oil in a large skillet over medium-high heat. Add the caraway seeds and stir 30 seconds. Add the cabbage and season with salt and pepper. Stir in the sugar and vinegar. Partially cover the skillet and cook, stirring frequently, until tender.

Make the gravy: Heat the butter in a medium skillet over medium heat. Whisk in the flour and cook 1 minute. Whisk in the cider and stock, then Worcestershire sauce and gingersnap crumbs. Whisk until thickened and reduce the heat to low to keep warm.

Make the burgers: In a large bowl, combine the beef, parsley, grated onion (grate it right over the bowl so the juices fall into the meat), relish, and mustard; season with salt and pepper and mix thoroughly. Score the mixture into 4 equal portions and form them into patties slightly thinner at the center than at the edges for even cooking and to ensure a flat surface (burgers plump as they cook).

Heat a drizzle of oil in a cast-iron or other large skillet over medium-high heat. Cook the burgers, flipping once, 10 minutes for medium (adjust the timing for rarer or more well-done burgers). Transfer the burgers to the gravy and turn to coat.

Place the burgers on bread or roll bottoms and top with cabbage. Set the second slice of bread or roll tops in place. Serve the chips alongside and pass any remaining gravy around.

RED CABBAGE:

2 tablespoons **vegetable oil** or **olive oil**

1 teaspoon **caraway seeds**

¾ pound **red cabbage**, very thinly sliced

Kosher salt and **pepper**

1 tablespoon **superfine sugar**

3 tablespoons **cider vinegar**

SAUERBRATEN GRAVY:

2 tablespoons **butter**

2 tablespoons **flour**

½ cup **apple cider**

1 cup **beef stock**

2 tablespoons **Worcestershire sauce**

6 **gingersnaps**, processed into crumbs

BURGERS:

1½ pounds **ground beef chuck**

¼ cup finely chopped **flat-leaf parsley**

3 tablespoons grated **onion**

2 tablespoons **sweet pickle relish**

2 tablespoons **spicy brown/German-style mustard**

Vegetable oil or **olive oil**, for drizzling

8 slices good-quality **pumpernickel bread** or 4 **sourdough rolls**, split and lightly toasted

Salt-and-vinegar potato chips

BOEUF BOURGUIGNON BURGERS

SERVES 4

Heat a griddle or large cast-iron skillet over medium-high heat.

In a large bowl, combine the beef, wine, thyme, and shallot; season with salt and pepper and mix thoroughly. Score the mixture into 4 equal portions and form them into large patties slightly thinner at the center than at the edges for even cooking and to ensure a flat surface (burgers plump as they cook). Drizzle the patties with EVOO. Cook the burgers 10 minutes, flipping once, for medium (adjust the timing for rarer or more well-done burgers).

Place the burgers on the roll bottoms; top with pâté and lettuce. Spread mustard on the roll tops and scatter the sliced cornichons over the mustard. Set the roll tops in place.

1½ pounds **ground beef chuck**

½ cup **red burgundy wine**

2 tablespoons **fresh thyme**, finely chopped

1 **shallot**, finely chopped or grated

Kosher salt and **pepper**

EVOO (extra-virgin olive oil), for drizzling

4 **brioche rolls**, split and toasted

½-inch slice (about ¼ pound) **mousse-style pâté** (available near specialty cheeses in large markets), cut in 4 equal pieces

4 leaves **red-leaf lettuce**

Grainy mustard or **Dijon mustard**

4 **cornichon pickles** or **baby gherkins**, thinly sliced lengthwise

BLOODY MARY CHEESEBURGERS

SERVES 4

Heat a large cast-iron skillet or griddle over medium-high heat.

Make the burgers: In a large bowl, combine the beef, Worcestershire sauce, horseradish, Tabasco, celery, ketchup or chili sauce, cracker crumbs or breadcrumbs, and egg yolk. Season with kosher salt (it makes a nice crust) and pepper and mix thoroughly. Score the meat into 4 equal portions and form them into patties slightly thinner at the center than at the edges for even cooking and to ensure a flat surface (burgers plump as they cook). Add the EVOO, 1 turn of the pan, to the hot skillet. Cook the burgers, flipping once, 10 minutes for medium (adjust the timing for rarer or more well-done burgers). Top the burgers with the cheese for the last 2 minutes of cooking, tenting the skillet with aluminum foil, if you like, to help melt the cheese.

While the burgers are cooking, make the sauce: Stir the ketchup, horseradish, Worcestershire sauce, lemon juice, Tabasco, and minced celery together in a small bowl. Season with pepper.

Place the burgers on the roll bottoms and top with the sauce. Set the roll tops in place.

BURGERS:

1½ pounds **ground beef chuck**

2 tablespoons **Worcestershire sauce**

2 rounded tablespoons **prepared horseradish**

1 tablespoon **Tabasco sauce**

A small handful of **celery** tops and leaves, finely chopped

¼ cup good-quality **ketchup**, such as Heinz Organic, or Heinz **chili sauce**

½ cup **Ritz cracker** crumbs or **fine dry breadcrumbs**

1 **egg** yolk, lightly beaten

Kosher salt and coarsely ground **pepper**

1 tablespoon **EVOO** (extra-virgin olive oil)

4 slices deli-sliced **sharp cheddar cheese**

SAUCE:

¾ cup good-quality **ketchup**

1 rounded tablespoon **prepared horseradish**

1 tablespoon **Worcestershire sauce**

1 tablespoon fresh **lemon** juice

2 teaspoons **Tabasco sauce**

2 tablespoons minced **celery** tops

Coarsely ground **pepper**

4 **brioche rolls**, split and toasted

STROGANOFF-STYLE KNIFE-AND-FORK BURGERS

SERVES 4

When I was a kid my mom would make us these as special-occasion burgers. She served them on warmed oval-shaped steakhouse dinner plates topped with mushrooms or smothered onions with wine and lots of Swiss. The burgers sat on buttered white toast points, and we ate them with big silver dinner forks and steak knives. This stroganoff burger is a natural knife-and-fork burger. Serve with watercress salad with Dijon vinaigrette and cornichons alongside.

If you don't feel like making onion rings, chop up a few additional cornichons and top the burgers with those in place of the onion rings.

Make the onion rings: Fill a countertop fryer with oil or pour a few inches of oil into a large Dutch oven. Heat the oil to 350°F. (The oil is ready when a 1-inch cube of white bread cooks to golden brown in 40 seconds.)

While the oil heats up, cut two 1-inch-thick slices of onion and separate the slices into large rings. Pour the buttermilk into a bowl. On a plate, stir together the flour, chives, and lots of salt and pepper. Soak the rings a few minutes in the buttermilk. Dredge the rings in the seasoned flour, then dip them again in the buttermilk, and again in the flour. Fry 1 or 2 rings at a time until deep golden, about 4 minutes. Drain on a cooling rack.

Make the burgers: Heat a large skillet over medium-high heat.

(CONTINUED ON NEXT PAGE)

ONION RING GARNISH:

Vegetable oil or canola oil, for frying

1 yellow onion

2 cups buttermilk

3 cups flour

½ cup finely chopped chives

Kosher salt and coarsely ground pepper

BURGERS AND SAUCE:

2 pounds coarse-ground beef chuck (see Tip, page 6)

¼ cup Worcestershire sauce

1 tablespoon EVOO (extra-virgin olive oil), plus more for drizzling

2 tablespoons butter

½ pound button mushrooms, very thinly sliced

1 large shallot, finely chopped

1 large clove garlic, finely chopped

A couple of sprigs fresh thyme, leaves finely chopped

1 rounded tablespoon flour

A generous splash of dry sherry or white wine

1 (10.75-ounce) can beef consommé

¼ cup sour cream

4 slices good-quality white bread, toasted and lightly buttered

¼ cup finely chopped flat-leaf parsley

In a large bowl, combine the beef and Worcestershire sauce; season with lots of pepper and a little salt and mix thoroughly. Score the mixture into 4 equal portions and form them into patties slightly thinner at the center than at the edges for even cooking and to ensure a flat surface (burgers plump as they cook). Drizzle the patties with EVOO. Cook the burgers, flipping once, 10 minutes for medium (adjust the timing for rarer or more well-done burgers). Remove to a platter and let rest.

Make the sauce: Add 1 tablespoon EVOO and the butter to the pan, reduce the heat a bit, and sauté the mushrooms a few minutes. Add the shallot, garlic, and thyme; season with salt and pepper; and cook a couple of minutes more. Sprinkle the flour around the pan, stir for a minute or two, then add the sherry to deglaze. Add the consommé and cook until thickened. Stir in the sour cream to combine and remove from the heat.

Set the buttered toast on dinner plates. Top with the burgers. Pour the warm stroganoff sauce over the burgers and garnish each with 1 large onion ring and the chopped parsley. Pass any remaining onion rings around.

THE ADIRONDACKER

SERVES 4

This smoky cheeseburger's a star that hasn't forgotten where it came from. I grew up in the Adirondacks, a 6-million-acre park of mountains and lakes that I still call home. This bacon cheeseburger is an ode to my favorite smokehouse, Oscar's in Warrensburg, New York. They make the best bacon I've ever tasted, and their cheeses are almost as good.

8 slices **smoky bacon**

2 pounds **ground beef chuck**

2 tablespoons **Worcestershire sauce**

2 tablespoons **prepared horseradish**

Kosher salt and **pepper**

8 ounces shredded or sliced **extra-sharp white cheddar cheese**

1 cup **sour cream**

¼ cup finely chopped **flat-leaf parsley** (a generous handful)

A generous handful of finely chopped **chives**

A generous handful of finely chopped fresh **dill**

4 crusty **kaiser rolls**, split

1 bunch **watercress**, trimmed of thick stems, or **arugula**, chopped

Cook the bacon in a very large skillet until crisp. Transfer to paper towels to drain. Remove the pan from the heat and discard all but 1 tablespoon bacon fat.

In a large bowl, combine the beef, Worcestershire sauce, and horseradish; season with salt and pepper and mix thoroughly. Score the mixture into 4 equal portions and form them into patties slightly thinner at the center than at the edges for even cooking and to ensure a flat surface (burgers plump as they cook).

Return the skillet to medium-high heat. When the bacon fat is hot, cook the burgers, flipping once, 10 minutes for medium (adjust the cooking time for rarer or more well-done burgers). Top the burgers with the cheese for the last 2 minutes of cooking, tenting the skillet with aluminum foil, if you like, to help melt the cheese.

While the burgers are cooking, combine the sour cream, parsley, chives, dill, and lots of pepper.

Place the burgers on the roll bottoms and top each with 2 slices bacon and some watercress. Slather the roll tops with the sour cream sauce and set the tops in place.

CHILI BURGERS with CHARRED PICO DE GALLO

SERVES 4

Make the pico de gallo: Preheat the broiler. Halve and seed the tomatoes and jalapeño and place them on a rimmed baking sheet along with the onion wedges. Broil, turning once, until charred, about 15 minutes. Let cool. Chop the charred tomato, chile, and onion. Combine the vegetables with the cilantro and lime juice; season with salt.

Make the burgers: In a large bowl, combine the beef, beer, garlic, chili powder, coriander, cumin, grill seasoning (or kosher salt and coarse pepper), and Worcestershire sauce; mix thoroughly. Score the mixture into 4 equal portions and form them into patties slightly thinner at the center than at the edges for even cooking and to ensure a flat surface (burgers plump as they cook).

Heat the EVOO, 2 turns of the pan, in a large nonstick skillet over medium-high heat. Cook the burgers, flipping once, 10 minutes, for medium (adjust the cooking time for rarer or more well-done burgers). Top each burger with 2 slices of cheese for the last minute or two of cooking, tenting the pan with aluminum foil, if you like, to help melt the cheese.

Place lettuce on the roll bottoms and top with a burger and pico de gallo. Set the roll tops in place.

PICO DE GALLO:

4 plum tomatoes

1 large jalapeño chile

½ red onion, cut into 3 to 4 wedges

3 to 4 tablespoons chopped cilantro

Juice of 1 lime

Kosher salt

BURGERS:

1½ pounds ground beef chuck

½ cup beer

2 cloves garlic, grated or finely chopped

2 tablespoons chili powder

1 tablespoon ground coriander

1 tablespoon ground cumin

1 tablespoon grill seasoning such as McCormick Montreal Steak Seasoning or kosher salt and coarsely ground pepper to taste

1 tablespoon Worcestershire sauce

2 tablespoons EVOO (extra-virgin olive oil)

8 slices deli-sliced pepper jack cheese

Shredded romaine lettuce, for serving

4 kaiser rolls, preferably cornmeal-crusted, split and toasted

WELLINGTON BURGERS

SERVES 4

The Wellington is the Rolls-Royce of burgers: Dijon-buttered rolls topped with sirloin patties, sherried mushrooms, cornichons, and mousse pâté.

In a large bowl, combine the beef, shallot, parsley, and Worcestershire sauce; season with salt and pepper and mix thoroughly. Score the mixture into 4 equal portions and form them into patties slightly thinner at the center than at the edges for even cooking and to ensure a flat surface (burgers plump as they cook).

Heat a drizzle of EVOO in a large nonstick skillet over medium-high heat. When the pan is very hot, cook the burgers 4 minutes on each side for medium-rare, 6 minutes on each side for medium-well.

Meanwhile, melt 2 tablespoons butter with a drizzle of EVOO in a medium skillet over medium heat. Add the mushrooms and cook until tender, about 6 minutes. Pour in the sherry and let it cook off, about 30 seconds. Season the mushrooms with salt and pepper and remove from the heat.

Stir together the mustard and remaining 1 tablespoon softened butter. Spread the Dijon butter liberally on the roll bottoms. Top with the watercress, a burger, a pile of mushrooms, and a few chopped cornichons. Spread the mousse pâté on the roll tops and set them in place.

1½ pounds **ground sirloin**

1 **shallot**, finely chopped

2 to 3 tablespoons finely chopped **flat-leaf parsley**

1 tablespoon **Worcestershire sauce**

Kosher salt and **pepper**

EVOO (extra-virgin olive oil), for drizzling

3 tablespoons **butter**, 1 of them softened

½ pound **cremini** or **white mushrooms**, sliced

¼ cup **dry sherry**

2 tablespoons **Dijon mustard**

4 **brioche rolls** or other **burger rolls** of choice

1 small bunch **watercress**, trimmed of thick stems and chopped

½ cup chopped **cornichons** or **baby gherkin pickles**

½ pound **truffled mousse pâté**, at room temp

WELSH RAREBIT BURGERS

SERVES 4

I prefer to serve these burgers open-face. The rarebit sauce is too pretty to hide.

Preheat the oven to 350°F. Arrange the bacon on a slotted broiler pan or a cooling rack set over a baking sheet and bake until very crisp, 15 to 18 minutes. When the bacon is done, switch the oven setting to broil.

In a large bowl, combine the beef, shallot, and parsley; season with kosher salt and lots of pepper and mix thoroughly. Score the mixture into 4 equal portions and form them into patties slightly thinner at the center than at the edges for even cooking and to ensure a flat surface (burgers plump as they cook).

Heat a drizzle of EVOO in a large cast-iron skillet or nonstick skillet over high heat until very hot. Cook the burgers, flipping once, 8 minutes for medium-rare or 10 minutes for medium.

While the burgers are cooking, make the sauce: Melt the butter in a saucepan over medium heat. Whisk in the flour and cook until light brown, about 3 minutes. Stir in the Worcestershire sauce, mustard, and hot sauce, then whisk in the Guinness and cook the sauce until slightly thickened, 1 to 2 minutes. Reduce the heat to low and stir in the cheese until smooth. If you'd like a firmer sauce, temper an egg yolk (see Tip) and fold in.

Arrange the bread slices on a baking sheet and lightly toast them under the broiler. Pour the sauce over the toasts (using only half the sauce if you plan to serve the burgers open-face); broil until the cheese sauce is browned and bubbly, about 2 minutes. Place a burger on each of 4 slices, cover each with a handful of watercress, crisscross with 2 bacon slices, and top with a slice of tomato seasoned with salt and pepper. Serve open-face with knife and fork with extra sauce on the side, or cover with the remaining toasts, cheesy side down. Serve with chips.

8 slices center-cut **bacon**

1½ pounds **ground beef chuck**

1 **shallot**, finely chopped or grated, or 3 tablespoons grated **onion**

¼ cup finely chopped **flat-leaf parsley**

Kosher salt and coarsely ground **pepper**

EVOO (extra-virgin olive oil), for drizzling

2 tablespoons **butter**

2 tablespoons **flour**

2 tablespoons **Worcestershire sauce**

1 tablespoon **dry mustard** or 1 tablespoon **prepared English mustard**

1 teaspoon **hot sauce**

1 cup **stout**, such as Guinness

1 pound shredded **sharp yellow cheddar cheese** (about 4 cups)

1 **egg** yolk, beaten (optional)

8 slices (½-inch-thick) hand-cut, good-quality **white** or **pumpernickel pullman bread** (4 slices if serving the burgers open-face)

1 small bunch **watercress**, leaves only, chopped

4 thick slices **beefsteak tomato**

Salt-and-vinegar potato chips

TIP: To temper an egg yolk, beat it together with about ½ cup of the warm sauce in a small bowl, then stir back into the sauce. Be careful not to boil the sauce after adding the egg.

GOULASH BURGERS

SERVES 4

Make the sauce: Puree the roasted red peppers, sour cream, and shallot in a food processor. Season with salt and pepper.

Make the burgers: In a large bowl, combine the ground meat of choice, the garlic, grated onion (grate it right over the bowl so the juices fall into the meat), dill, parsley, and paprika; season with salt and pepper and mix thoroughly. Score the mixture into 4 equal portions and form them into patties slightly thinner at the center than at the edges for even cooking and to ensure a flat surface (burgers plump as they cook).

Heat the EVOO, 1 turn of the pan, in a large nonstick skillet over medium-high heat. When the oil is hot, add the burgers and cook, flipping once, 10 minutes for medium (adjust the time for rarer or more well-done burgers) or 12 minutes (or until juices run clear) for chicken and pork burgers.

Place the burgers on the roll bottoms and top with the radish slices and lettuce. Slather the roasted pepper sauce on the roll tops and set in place.

SAUCE:

2 **bottled roasted red peppers**, patted dry and coarsely chopped

1 cup **sour cream**

1 small **shallot**, chopped

Kosher salt and **pepper**

BURGERS:

1½ pounds **ground beef chuck**, **chicken**, or **pork**

2 cloves **garlic**, finely chopped

3 to 4 tablespoons grated **onion**

2 tablespoons finely chopped **fresh dill**

2 tablespoons finely chopped **flat-leaf parsley**

2 tablespoons **sweet paprika**

1 tablespoon **EVOO** (extra-virgin olive oil)

4 **brioche** or other **eggy rolls**, split, toasted, and buttered

2 **radishes**, thinly sliced and lightly salted

8 leaves **green-leaf** or **butter lettuce**

BEER-BRAISED BACON BACON CHEESEBURGERS

SERVES 4

Oscar's Hickory House in Warrensburg, New York, is a family outing favorite. We love their cheddar, and they have our hands-down favorite bacon. They ship (www.oscarssmoked meats.com). Get addicted. (P.S. They make doggie jerky, too.)

---

10 slices **smoky bacon**, 2 chopped, 8 left whole

1 tablespoon **EVOO** (extra-virgin olive oil)

1½ pounds **ground beef chuck**

2 tablespoons **Worcestershire sauce**

¼ cup grated **onion**

Kosher salt and **pepper**

A few hearty glugs of **stout**, such as Guinness (about ½ cup)

½ cup **sour cream**

1 tablespoon **prepared horseradish**

3 tablespoons **grainy mustard**

4 leaves **red-leaf lettuce**

1 **red onion**, sliced

4 **kaiser rolls**, split

4 slices **aged white cheddar cheese**, such as Oscar's "counter cheese"

Preheat the oven to 325°F. Arrange the 8 whole slices bacon on a slotted broiler pan or on a cooling rack set over a baking sheet and bake until crisp, 15 to 20 minutes.

Place a large skillet over medium heat with 1 tablespoon EVOO, 1 turn of the pan. While the pan is still cold, add the 2 slices chopped bacon. Cook the bacon as the pan heats up until crisp and golden brown, 3 minutes. Transfer the bacon bits to paper towel to cool. Reserve the drippings in the pan.

In a large bowl, combine the beef, Worcestershire sauce, bacon bits, and grated onion; season with salt and pepper and mix well. Score the mixture into 4 equal portions and form them into patties slightly thinner at the center than at the edges for even cooking and to ensure a flat surface (burgers plump as they cook). Return the skillet with the bacon fat to medium heat. When the fat is hot, cook the burgers until seared and golden brown, 4 to 5 minutes per side for medium. In the last minute of cooking, add the stout to the pan and cook until almost completely reduced and slightly thickened.

While the burgers are cooking, stir together the sour cream, horseradish, and mustard in a small bowl.

Place a lettuce leaf and some red onion slices on the roll bottoms. Top with burgers, and then with a slice of cheese, 2 strips of bacon, and a dollop of horseradish sauce. Set the roll tops in place.

DOUBLE-DECKER ANIMAL STYLE

SERVES 4

In-N-Out Burger invented the Double-Double Animal Style—and we invented your at-home version. Warning: You need all the stomach room you can get. Open double wide!

Make the sauce: In a small bowl, whisk together the sour cream, vinegar, and sugar. Stir in the ketchup and relish; season with salt and pepper.

Caramelize the onions: Heat the EVOO, 2 turns of the pan, in a skillet over medium heat. Add the onions and season with salt and pepper. Cook to light brown, stirring occasionally, about 15 minutes. Add the consommé and cook 10 to 15 minutes more until very soft and tender.

Make the burgers: In a large bowl, combine the beef, garlic, Worcestershire sauce, and parsley; season with kosher salt (it makes a nice crust) and pepper and mix thoroughly. Score the mixture into 4 equal portions and form each into 2 thin patties; drizzle with EVOO to coat lightly then sprinkle with a little extra salt. Top each patty with 1 tablespoon mustard.

Heat a large griddle over medium-high heat. Cook the burgers mustard-side up 4 minutes, flip, and cook 2 to 3 minutes more. (Cook the burgers in 2 batches if necessary.) Top the burgers with Swiss cheese for the last minute or two of cooking, tenting the griddle with aluminum foil, if you like, to help melt the cheese.

Stack 2 burgers with onions between them on the roll bottoms and top with pickles, tomato, lettuce, and special sauce. Set the roll tops in place.

SPECIAL SAUCE:

½ cup **sour cream**

1 tablespoon **white wine vinegar**

1 teaspoon **superfine sugar**

¼ cup good-quality **ketchup**, such as Heinz Organic

2 rounded tablespoons **dill relish**

Kosher salt and **pepper**

CARAMELIZED ONIONS:

2 tablespoons **EVOO** (extra-virgin olive oil)

2 large **onions**, chopped

½ cup **beef consommé** or **beef stock**

BURGERS WITH DIJON:

2 pounds **ground beef chuck**

4 cloves **garlic**, minced

¼ cup **Worcestershire sauce**

A handful of **flat-leaf parsley**, finely chopped

EVOO (extra-virgin olive oil), for drizzling

½ cup **Dijon** or **grainy Dijon mustard**

8 slices **Swiss** or **Comté cheese**

4 **brioche** or other **burger rolls**, split

Bread-and-butter pickle slices

Sliced **tomato**

Chopped **lettuce**

RACH'S "BIG SPICY MAC"

SERVES 4

Make the sauce: In a bowl, stir together the ketchup, relish, chiles, and sour cream; season with salt and pepper.

Make the burgers: In a large bowl, combine the beef, chili powder, coriander, cumin, and Worcestershire sauce; season with salt and pepper and mix thoroughly. Score the mixture into 4 equal portions and form 2 thin patties out of each section, creating 8 patties total.

Heat a drizzle of EVOO in a large skillet or griddle over medium-high heat. Cook half the burgers until browned and cooked through, about 2 minutes on each side. When you flip the burgers, top each with a slice of cheese. Set the first batch aside on a plate and cook the remaining burgers.

When the burgers are ready, assemble them in a double-decker style: Lay down 4 bun bottoms and top them with some of the sauce, a lettuce leaf, a burger, a couple of pickle slices, and a sprinkle of onion. Repeat with another layer (using 2 bun bottoms and 2 bun tops) of the same order. Add some sauce to the top buns, too, before you cap off each burger.

SAUCE:

1 cup good-quality **ketchup**, such as Heinz Organic

2 tablespoons **dill relish**

1 (4-ounce) can **diced green chiles**, drained and finely chopped

1 cup **sour cream**

Kosher salt and **pepper**

BURGERS:

2½ pounds **ground beef chuck**

2 tablespoons **chili powder**

1 tablespoon **ground coriander**

1 tablespoon **ground cumin**

¼ cup **Worcestershire sauce**

EVOO (extra-virgin olive oil), for drizzling

8 slices deli-sliced **cheddar cheese**

6 **sesame seed buns**, split (2 of the bun tops will be flipped over and put into the middle of the burgers)

Leaves from 1 head **green-leaf lettuce**

Sandwich-sliced pickles

1 small **onion**, chopped

Watch Rachael make her "Big Spicy Mac."

FLORENTINE BURGERS

SERVES 4

Heat 2 tablespoons EVOO, 2 turns of the pan, in a medium skillet over medium-high heat. Add the onion and garlic to the pan and cook until tender, 5 to 6 minutes. Turn the onion and garlic out into a bowl. Add the spinach to the onion and toss to combine. Add the ground meats, season with salt and pepper, and mix thoroughly. Score the mixture into 4 equal portions and form them into patties slightly thinner at the center than at the edges for even cooking and to ensure a flat surface (burgers plump as they cook).

Heat the remaining 2 tablespoons EVOO, 2 turns of the pan, and the sprig of rosemary in a large skillet over medium-high heat. Add the burgers to the hot pan and cook, flipping once, 12 minutes, or until the juices run clear.

While the burgers are cooking, make the sauce: Melt the butter in a small saucepan over medium heat. Sprinkle the flour over the melted butter and cook, stirring frequently, for about 1 minute. Whisk in the milk and cook until thickened, 1 to 2 minutes. Stir in the ricotta and Parmigiano-Reggiano and season with salt, pepper, and nutmeg.

Place the burgers on the roll bottoms and spoon the sauce over them. Set the roll tops in place.

4 tablespoons **EVOO** (extra-virgin olive oil)

1 small **onion**, chopped

2 cloves **garlic**, finely chopped or grated

1 (10-ounce) box **frozen chopped spinach**, thawed and wrung dry in a kitchen towel

1½ pounds **ground mix of beef, pork, and veal**

Kosher salt and **pepper**

1 sprig **fresh rosemary**

2 tablespoons **butter**

1 tablespoon **flour**

½ cup **milk**

¾ cup **ricotta cheese**

¼ cup grated **Parmigiano-Reggiano cheese**

Freshly grated **nutmeg**

4 **ciabatta rolls**, split

"SMOKE and FIREWORKS" BACON-WRAPPED CHIPOTLE BURGERS

SERVES 6

I made this for a Fourth of July tribute show with my friend Adam Perry Lang. He loves smoked everything, so I made this burger as smoky as possible.

Preheat the oven to 350°F. Arrange the bacon on a slotted broiler pan or on a cooling rack set over a baking sheet. Bake 10 minutes to cook the bacon halfway; set aside until cool enough to handle.

While the bacon is cooking, make the sauce: Combine all BBQ sauce ingredients in a small saucepan. Bring to a bubble and reduce the heat to low; simmer 15 to 20 minutes to thicken.

Place the sliced onion in a bowl; separate rings. Squeeze in the lime juice and season with salt and pepper.

In a large bowl, combine the beef, chipotle puree, and Worcestershire sauce; season with salt and pepper and a drizzle of EVOO and mix thoroughly. Score the meat into 6 equal portions and form them into patties slightly thinner in the center than at the edges for even cooking and to ensure a flat surface. Drizzle the patties with EVOO.

Heat a large griddle or skillet over medium to medium-high heat.

Cross 2 slices of bacon on a work surface, place a patty on top of the X, and wrap the bacon up and around the burger. Repeat to wrap all 6 patties. Cook the burgers with the bacon seam side down first until the bacon is crisp; flip and cook until the bacon on the second side is crisp, 10 to 12 minutes total for medium burgers. Top the burgers with cheese for the last minute of cooking, tenting the griddle with aluminum foil to help melt the cheese.

Place a little lettuce on the roll bottoms and top with the burgers, BBQ sauce, and onions. Set the roll tops in place.

12 slices smoky bacon

MY ALMOST FAMOUS BBQ SAUCE:

1 cup good-quality ketchup, such as Heinz Organic

2 large cloves garlic, finely chopped

2 tablespoons dark brown sugar

2 tablespoons dark amber maple syrup

2 tablespoons Worcestershire sauce

1½ tablespoons cider vinegar

1 teaspoon smoked sweet paprika

Coarsely ground pepper

ONIONS:

1 small red onion, sliced

1 lime

Kosher salt and pepper

BURGERS:

1½ pounds ground beef chuck

2 tablespoons pureed chipotle in adobo sauce (see Tip, page 14)

2 tablespoons Worcestershire sauce

EVOO (extra-virgin olive oil), for drizzling

12 slices yellow cheddar cheese

Finely chopped crisp lettuce

6 burger rolls, split

TIP: Always make sure to buy dark amber Grade A maple syrup. Colored corn syrup or syrup you can see through has very little flavor.

SAGE-SCENTED BURGERS with FONTINA and ROASTED SQUASH

SERVES 4

Preheat the oven to 425°F.

Lightly coat the squash slices with EVOO. Season with the nutmeg, salt, and pepper and spread the rings out on a baking sheet. Roast until tender and browned at the edges, 18 to 22 minutes.

Meanwhile, heat the butter in a skillet over medium heat until it foams. Increase the heat a touch and add the sage leaves. Cook until crisp. Transfer to paper towels to drain. Chop the sage leaves and reserve the browned butter separately.

In a large bowl, combine the veal and beef with the chopped crispy sage, the garlic, and Parmigiano-Reggiano; season with salt and pepper and mix thoroughly. Score the mixture into 4 equal pieces and form them into patties slightly thinner at the center than at the edges for even cooking and to ensure a flat surface (burgers plump as they cook). Drizzle the patties with EVOO.

Heat a griddle or large cast-iron skillet over medium-high heat. Cook the burgers, flipping once and basting with the reserved sage butter, 10 minutes for medium (adjust the cooking time for rarer or more well done burgers). Top the burgers with Fontina during the last minute or two of cooking, tenting the pan with aluminum foil, if you like, to help melt the cheese.

Drizzle the cooked squash with honey. Place the burgers on the roll bottoms and top with the squash. Set the bun tops in place.

½ small **butternut squash** or 1 **acorn squash**, peeled and sliced into ¼-inch-thick rounds

EVOO (extra-virgin olive oil), for drizzling

A few grates of **nutmeg**

Kosher salt and **pepper**

4 tablespoons (½ stick) **butter**

12 **sage leaves**

1 pound **ground veal**

½ pound **ground beef chuck**

1 large clove **garlic**, grated or pasted (see Tip, page 138)

A handful of grated **Parmigiano-Reggiano cheese**

½ to ¾ pound **Fontina Val d'Aosta** or other **Fontina cheese** or **Taleggio cheese**, sliced

Good-quality **honey**

4 **sesame brioche rolls**, split and lightly toasted

SPAGHETTI and MEATBALL BURGERS

SERVES 4

This is one of my favorite meatballs turned into a burger . . . a Spaghetti and Meatball Burger! This burger has it all—spaghetti and meat combined, then layered with cheese and tomato sauce on a garlic bread roll!

Heat a medium pot of water to a boil; add salt. Break the pasta strands in half and cook to al dente. Drain, cool, and reserve the pasta.

While the pasta is cooking, make the sauce: Heat the EVOO, 1 turn of the pan, in a small saucepan over medium heat and melt the butter into it. Add the garlic and stir a couple of minutes, then add the onion, bay leaf, tomato puree, oregano, and basil. Season with salt and pepper and simmer at a low bubble 20 minutes. Remove the onion and bay leaf.

Preheat the broiler.

Make the burgers: In a small bowl, soak the bread in the milk for a few minutes. In a separate bowl, combine the beef, parsley, Parmigiano-Reggiano, egg, garlic, and cold pasta. Squeeze out the bread and crumble over the beef. Season with salt and pepper and mix thoroughly. Score the mixture into 4 equal portions and form them into patties—let the pasta stick out from the sides—that are slightly thinner at the center than at the edges for even cooking and to ensure a flat surface (burgers plump as they cook).

Heat a thin, even layer of olive oil in a large skillet over medium-high heat. Cook the burgers, turning occasionally, until cooked through and crispy, 12 to 15 minutes. Douse the burgers with the sauce and top them with provolone or mozzarella. Turn off the heat and tent the skillet with aluminum foil to help melt the cheese.

Salt

¼ pound **bucatini** or **spaghetti**

SAUCE:

1 tablespoon **EVOO** (extra-virgin olive oil)

2 tablespoons **butter**

2 cloves **garlic**, chopped

½ small **white onion**, peeled

1 **bay leaf**

2 cups **tomato puree**

½ teaspoon **dried oregano** or **marjoram**

A few leaves **basil**, torn

Kosher salt and **pepper**

MEATBALL BURGERS:

2 (1-inch) slices **white bread**, crusts trimmed

¾ cup **milk**

1½ pounds **ground beef chuck**

2 to 3 tablespoons finely chopped **flat-leaf parsley**

⅓ cup grated **Parmigiano-Reggiano cheese**, a heavy handful

1 large **egg**, beaten

2 cloves **garlic**, grated or pasted (see Tip, page 138)

Olive oil, for frying

8 slices deli-sliced **provolone** or **mozzarella cheese**

While the burgers are cooking, make the garlic bread rolls: Broil the rolls until lightly toasted. Microwave or heat the EVOO, butter, and crushed garlic until the butter is melted. Brush the toasted rolls with the garlic butter and top with herbs and Parmigiano-Reggiano; broil to set the cheese, about 1 minute.

Place the burgers on the roll bottoms, spooning sauce from the pan over them. Set the roll tops in place.

GARLIC BREAD ROLLS:

4 **crusty rolls**, such as **ciabatta** or plain **kaiser**, split

1 tablespoon **EVOO** (extra-virgin olive oil)

2 tablespoons **butter**

1 clove **garlic**, crushed

1 tablespoon **fresh thyme**, chopped

1 tablespoon finely chopped **flat-leaf parsley**

½ cup grated **Parmigiano-Reggiano cheese**

MEATBALL HERO BURGERS

SERVES 6

This burger is a delicious roasted meatball that gets run through a bath of tomato sauce and topped with fresh mozzarella cheese, all served up on a sesame seed roll. It will be the hero of your meal.

Preheat the oven to 325°F.

Make the sauce: Process the onion, EVOO, fennel seeds, red pepper flakes, sugar, garlic, tomatoes, oregano, basil, salt, and pepper in a food processor until smooth. Transfer to a saucepan and gently simmer over low heat 30 minutes to thicken and to let the flavors combine.

Soak the bread in enough milk to cover in a small bowl.

In a large bowl, combine the beef, pork, fennel seeds, sage, granulated onion, cloves, red paper flakes, garlic, parsley, eggs, grated cheeses, and EVOO. Squeeze the excess milk from the bread and crumble the soaked bread as you add it to the bowl. Discard the milk. Season the burger mix with salt and pepper and mix throroughly.

Score the mixture into 6 equal portions and form them into oval patties, slightly thinner at the center than at the edges for even cooking and to ensure a flat surface (burgers plump as you cook them). Lay the patties out on a baking sheet and bake until cooked through, 20 to 25 minutes.

Switch the oven setting to broil when you remove the burgers from the oven. Place the rack in the center of oven.

Place the rolls on a baking sheet and toast under

SAUCE:

1 small **yellow onion**, coarsely chopped

2 tablespoons **EVOO** (extra-virgin olive oil)

½ teaspoon **fennel seeds**

½ teaspoon **crushed red pepper flakes**

½ teaspoon **sugar**

2 cloves **garlic**, grated or chopped

1 (28- or 32-ounce) can **San Marzano tomatoes**

Leaves from 1 sprig **fresh oregano** or **marjoram**, finely chopped, or 1 scant teaspoon **dried**

A few leaves of **basil**, torn

Kosher salt and **pepper**

MEATBALL BURGERS:

4 slices good-quality **white bread** or **Italian bread**, crusts removed

1 to 1½ cups **milk**

1 pound **ground beef chuck** or homemade ground beef blend (see Introduction, page x, and essay on page 24)

¾ pound **ground pork**

1 teaspoon **fennel seeds**

1 teaspoon **ground sage**

1 teaspoon **granulated onion**

¼ teaspoon **ground cloves**

1 teaspoon **crushed red pepper flakes**

3 cloves **garlic**, grated or minced

the broiler. Remove the tops from the baking sheet, turn the burgers in the sauce, and set them on the roll bottoms. Top with your choice of cheese and melt until bubbly under broiler. Top with torn basil and any remaining sauce and set the roll tops in place.

¼ cup **flat-leaf parsley** leaves, finely chopped

2 **large eggs**, beaten

¼ cup grated **Parmigiano-Reggiano cheese**

¼ cup grated **pecorino Romano cheese**

2 tablespoons **EVOO** (extra-virgin olive oil)

6 **Italian rolls** with sesame seeds, split

1-pound ball **fresh mozzarella cheese**, sliced, or ½ pound deli-sliced **mild provolone cheese**

Torn **basil**, for garnish

TIP: If you do not have fresh herbs on hand, use one-third the amount called for as dried herbs, about 1 teaspoon of dried for every tablespoon of fresh. Substitute such herbs as oregano, thyme, and sage, but I feel there is no substitute for fresh basil.

THE ULTIMATE SALAMI BURGERS

SERVES 4

This Italian-style burger gets piled high with crisp salami, provolone cheese, and chopped giardiniera relish. For a little extra oomph, top with some Quick Marinara Dipper for the ultimate burger experience.

Make the marinara dipper, if using.

Preheat the oven to 350°F.

Arrange the salami slices on a cooling rack set over a baking sheet and bake 10 minutes to crisp them up a bit. Remove from the oven and cool.

While the salami is cooling, make the burgers: Place the beef and pork in a large bowl and douse with the wine. Add the grated onion (grate it directly over the bowl so the juices fall into the meat), garlic, pepper, pecorino, oregano, and chile pepper and mix well. Score the mixture into 4 equal portions and form them into patties slightly thinner at the center than at the edges for even cooking and to ensure a flat surface (burgers plump as you cook them). Season the patties with kosher salt and drizzle some EVOO over them.

Heat a griddle or cast-iron skillet over medium-high heat. Cook the burgers, flipping once, 10 minutes for medium (adjust cooking time for rarer or more well-done burgers). Top the burgers with provolone for the last minute or two of cooking, tenting the griddle with aluminum foil if you like, to help melt the cheese.

While the burgers are cooking, make the Italian dressing. In a large bowl, toss the lettuce, tomatoes, red onion, and basil with 3 tablespoons of the dressing.

Place some chopped giardiniera on the roll bottoms

Quick Marinara Dipper (optional; page 271)

8 slices **hard salami** or **Genoa salami** (have the deli slice it a little on the thick side, not too thin)

BURGERS:

1 pound **ground beef chuck**

½ pound **ground pork**

⅓ cup **dry red wine**

3 to 4 tablespoons grated **onion**

2 large cloves **garlic**, grated or finely chopped

1 tablespoon coarsely ground **pepper**

A handful of grated **pecorino cheese**

1 teaspoon **dried oregano** or **marjoram**

1 **Fresno chile pepper**, very finely chopped, or 2 teaspoons **crushed red pepper flakes** (see Tip)

Kosher salt

EVOO (extra-virgin olive oil), for drizzling

4 slices deli-sliced **provolone** cheese (again, not too thin)

4 large **ciabatta rolls**

1 cup finely chopped **giardiniera** (Italian hot pickled vegetables), store-bought or homemade (page 183)

MARINATED VEGETABLES:

Italian Dressing (recipe follows)

1 cup chopped **lettuce**

Sliced **tomatoes**

and top with the burgers, 2 slices crispy salami, and the marinated vegetables. Set the roll tops in place. Pass the marinara (if using) separately.

Thinly sliced **red onion**

10 **basil** leaves, torn

ITALIAN DRESSING
MAKES ABOUT 1 CUP

In a medium bowl, combine the garlic, shallot, sugar, lemon juice, vinegar, thyme, basil, and parsley. Whisk while streaming in the EVOO. Season with salt and pepper and whisk in the mustard.

1 large clove **garlic**, grated

1 **shallot** minced, or 3 tablespoons grated **red onion**

1 rounded teaspoon **superfine sugar**

Juice of ½ **lemon**

3 tablespoons **red wine vinegar**

2 teaspoons **fresh thyme leaves**, finely chopped

1 tablespoon finely chopped **fresh basil**

1 tablespoon finely chopped **flat-leaf parsley**

½ cup **EVOO** (extra-virgin olive oil)

Kosher salt and **pepper**

1 rounded tablespoon **Dijon mustard**

TIP: Fresno chiles have a fruity, fairly mild heat. Leave the seeds in, which is where the heat lives. You may substitute another red chile, but chances are it will be hotter, so make sure to take the time to strip the seeds and ribs. Just make sure you wash your hands after preparing or working with chiles.

SHEPHERD'S PIE KNIFE-AND-FORK BURGERS

SERVES 4

Mashed potatoes? Check! Meat? Check! It's everything you love about a classic shepherd's pie—on a burger! What's there not to love?

Make the mashers: Cook the potatoes in a pot of boiling salted water to cover until tender, about 12 minutes. Drain the potatoes, return them to the pan, and mash with the milk, sour cream, horseradish, egg yolk, butter, and chives. Season with salt and pepper.

While the potatoes are cooking, make the burgers: Heat the 2 tablespoons oil, 2 turns of the pan, in a large skillet over medium heat. Add the mushrooms, carrot, celery, shallot, and garlic. Season with salt and pepper and cook until tender. Cool completely.

In a large bowl, combine the beef, Worcestershire sauce, and the cooled vegetables; season with salt and pepper and mix thoroughly. Score the mixture into 4 equal portions and form them into patties slightly thinner at the center than at the edges for even cooking and to ensure a flat surface (burgers plump as they cook). Drizzle the patties with oil.

Set the rack in the center of the oven and preheat the broiler to high. Heat a large griddle or cast-iron skillet over medium-high heat. Cook the burgers 10 minutes, flipping once, for medium (adjust the cooking time for rarer or more well-done burgers).

While the burgers are cooking, make the gravy: Melt the butter in a small skillet over medium heat. Whisk in the flour and cook for a minute. Whisk in the consommé and heat to a bubble. Cook until thickened, 2 to 3 minutes.

MASHED POTATOES:

2 large or 3 medium **russet (baking) potatoes**, peeled and cubed

¼ to ⅓ cup **milk**

2 tablespoons **sour cream**

2 tablespoons **prepared horseradish**

1 **egg** yolk, beaten

2 tablespoons **butter**

2 tablespoons finely chopped **chives**

Kosher salt and **pepper**

BURGERS:

2 tablespoons **olive oil** or **vegetable oil**, plus more for drizzling

¼ pound (5 to 6) **button mushrooms**, stemmed and very finely chopped

1 **carrot**, very finely chopped

1 rib **celery**, very finely chopped

1 **shallot**, very finely chopped

2 to 3 cloves **garlic**, very finely chopped

1½ pound **coarse-ground beef chuck** (see Tip, page 6)

3 tablespoons **Worcestershire sauce**

Stir in the Worcestershire sauce and mustard; season with pepper.

Transfer the burgers to a broiler pan. Top with mounds of mashed potatoes and set under the broiler to brown, 3 to 4 minutes.

Place the potato-topped burgers on the buttered toast and pour the gravy over them. Garnish with parsley and serve.

GRAVY:

2 tablespoons **butter**

2 tablespoons **flour**

1 (10.75-ounce) can **beef consommé**

1 tablespoon **Worcestershire sauce**

1 tablespoon **Dijon mustard**

4 slices **white bread**, toasted and lightly buttered

Chopped **flat-leaf parsley**

TIP: Add a little attitude to your mashed potatoes by adding a couple of peeled and cubed parsnips of equal size to the pot along with the potatoes.

UPTOWN BURGER AU POIVRE with BRANDY CREAM SAUCE

SERVES 4

Season the beef generously with salt and pepper and mix thoroughly. Score the meat into 4 equal portions and form them into patties slightly thinner at the center that at the edges for even cooking and to ensure a flat surface (burgers plump as they cook). Heat the EVOO, 1 turn of the pan, in a large nonstick skillet or grill pan over medium-high heat. Cook the burgers, flipping once, 10 minutes for medium (adjust the cooking time for rarer or more well-done burgers).

While the burgers are cooking, make the sauce: Melt the butter in a skillet over medium heat. Add the shallot and stir 2 to 3 minutes. Season with salt and pepper. Sprinkle in the flour and cook 1 minute. Whisk in the brandy (see Tip), bring to a boil, and reduce by half. Whisk in the cream and boil until reduced by half. Taste and adjust the salt and pepper; season with nutmeg.

Place the burgers on the roll bottoms and douse with the sauce. Set the roll tops in place.

BURGERS:

1½ pounds **coarse-ground sirloin** or your own "house blend" (see Introduction, page 6, and essay on page 24)

Kosher salt and cracked **pepper**

1 tablespoon **EVOO** (extra-virgin olive oil)

BRANDY CREAM SAUCE:

3 tablespoons **butter**

1 large **shallot**, minced

1 tablespoon **flour**

¼ cup **brandy**

1 cup **heavy cream**

A few grates of **nutmeg**

4 **brioche rolls**, split

TIP: Stand back from the pan when adding the brandy. There is a chance it may ignite.

UPTOWN BURGERS with PORCINI STEAK SAUCE

SERVES 4

As an alternative, slice up medium-rare flat iron steaks and serve on ciabatta rolls, topped with this sauce.

Make the sauce: Simmer the porcini in the stock in a small saucepan until the porcini are softened and the stock is reduced, 15 to 20 minutes. Transfer to a blender or food processor and process until smooth.

Heat a small drizzle of EVOO in a small saucepan over medium heat. Add the shallot and garlic and cook to soften. Add porcini puree, ketchup, Worcestershire sauce, vinegar, brown sugar, and pepper. Simmer over low heat until thickened, 15 to 20 minutes. Keep the sauce warm while making the burgers.

Season the beef with salt and pepper. Score the meat into 4 equal portions and form them into patties slightly thinner at the center than at the edges for even cooking and to ensure a flat surface, (burgers plump as they cook). Drizzle the patties with EVOO. Heat a large non-stick skillet or grill pan over medium-high heat. Cook the burgers, flipping once, 10 minutes for medium (adjust the cooking time for rarer or more well-done burgers).

Place the burgers on the roll bottoms and douse with sauce. Set the roll tops in place.

PORCINI STEAK SAUCE

A handful of **dried porcini mushrooms**

1½ cups **beef stock**

EVOO (extra-virgin olive oil)

1 **shallot**, finely chopped

2 cloves **garlic**, finely chopped

1 cup good-quality **ketchup**, such as Heinz Organic

¼ cup **Worcestershire sauce**

2 tablespoons good-quality **balsamic vinegar**

2 tablespoons **dark brown sugar**

A large pinch coarsely ground **pepper**

BURGERS:

1½ pounds **coarse-ground sirloin** or your own "house blend" (see Introduction, page 6, and essay on page 24)

Kosher salt and **pepper**

EVOO (extra-virgin olive oil), for drizzling

4 **brioche rolls**, split

BLUE-RUGULA BURGERS

SERVES 4

Cambazola blue is a soft cheese easily found in grocery stores. John and I prefer creamy Gorgonzola Dolce, but that can be tricky to find in a supermarket. If your market does not offer a thick, aged balsamic, simply simmer some down, sweetened with a little light brown sugar: ¼ cup balsamic vinegar to 1 scant tablespoon light brown sugar; simmer until syrupy.

Make the onions: Heat the butter and EVOO in a large skillet over medium heat. Add the onions, season with salt and pepper, and add the thyme and bay leaf. Cook, stirring occasionally, until the onions are caramelized, about 30 minutes. Add the stock, brown sugar, and vinegar and stir until the sugar is dissolved. Keep warm over low heat; remove bay leaf before serving.

Make the burgers: In a large bowl, combine the beef, garlic, Worcestershire sauce, and parsley; season with salt and pepper and mix thoroughly. Score the mixture into 4 equal portions and form them into patties slightly thinner at the center than at the edges for even cooking and to ensure a flat surface (burgers plump as they cook). Drizzle the patties with EVOO.

Heat a large nonstick skillet over medium-high heat. Cook the burgers 10 minutes, flipping once, for medium (adjust the cooking time for rarer or more well-done burgers). Top the burgers with Cambozola for the last minute or two of cooking, tenting the skillet with aluminum foil, if you like, to help melt the cheese.

Place the burgers on the roll bottoms, mound with caramelized onions, and top with a few leaves of arugula. Set the roll tops in place.

ONIONS:

3 tablespoons **butter**

1 tablespoon **EVOO** (extra-virgin olive oil)

2 **onions**, thinly sliced

Kosher salt and **pepper**

½ teaspoon **ground thyme**

1 **bay leaf**

½ cup **beef stock**

1 tablespoon **light brown sugar**

1 tablespoon good-quality **balsamic vinegar**

BURGERS:

1½ pounds **ground beef chuck**

2 cloves **garlic**, grated or finely chopped

2 tablespoons **Worcestershire sauce**

A handful of **flat-leaf parsley**, finely chopped

EVOO (extra-virgin olive oil), for drizzling

½ pound **Cambozola blue cheese**, thinly sliced

4 **brioche rolls**, split and lightly toasted

Arugula leaves, coarsely chopped

THE PERFECT BUN
ADAM PERRY LANG

Chef, restaurateur, author of *Serious Barbecue*, *BBQ25*, and *Charred & Scruffed*

Rachael often playfully teases me about my passion for the science behind meat and all things meat-related. Burgers are one of our favorite subjects. I enjoy exploring the "behind the scenes" details, investigating the complexity hiding beneath (and in this case, also on top of) the beloved burger. One of those details—the bun—is often overlooked. Usually, it is noticed only when it is stale, tough, or becomes a soppy mess. Let's take a microscope to one of the less-considered components of creating an amazing burger experience: the bun.

The consistency of the roll, the mouthfeel, and "chew" all contribute to the ultimate cross section of taste in each bite of burger. When you bite through a burger in the perfect bun, the result should be like looking at a cartoon image of a California surfer's board that has been expertly bitten by a shark: you should get a clear, precise bite (with no shifting of ingredients).

When choosing the right bun for my burger, there are three three possible options: the potato roll (my personal first choice), the enriched white roll, and a light version of a brioche roll. The first two rolls or buns are pure nostalgia, an off-the-shelf perfect match to "supporting" a great hamburger. The last choice, the brioche, has recently become more commonly available. Luckily for us, both potato rolls and enriched white rolls are perfect burger foils. The best part is that these rolls are easy to find. The light brioche bun is an excellent option, and one I often use, but because of the variation and artisanal nature of brioche (some brioche rolls are too sweet because of excessive sugar, and some too crumbly because of softer cake flour used), there is often great inconsistency. Therefore, a brioche roll can be a less suitable bun choice.

It is only when we take a look at some other types of rolls that we realize the importance of the bun. Sourdough rolls, although popular and readily available, tend to compete with and take away from the taste of the burger; I find the sourdough flavor a distraction. In my hands, a great burger thrives on a neutral bun. I look at the bun like a supporting actor, the costar, in a movie; the role (no pun intended) it plays needs to be great, but not better than the star of the show, in this case the burger itself. Texture is very important, and when a bun choice is too hard or chewy, "backsliding" can occur. "Backsliding" is a term used to describe the shift of the burger and accompaniments, and the resulting slide out the back of the bun is one of the most heartbreaking moments for me. To compensate when stuck in a "backsliding" situation, I often find myself cutting the hamburger in two, just to manage all the toppings and the meat itself.

Once you have chosen your bun, to determine the thickness of the hamburger patty, follow this guideline: lightly press the roll between your thumb and index finger just until the springiness stops. That distance between your thumb and index finger is the thickness that your patty should be.

To enhance the bun, I "cold-toast" the rolls. "Cold-toasting" is a term I came up with to describe pre-preparing the rolls. This technique creates another texture and enhances the complete burger taste. Cold-toasting also helps defend against soppiness. To cold-toast, lightly and evenly butter the rolls and then griddle-toast the buns until golden and lightly crisp. Let them cool at room temperature. This method helps the rolls maintain a moisture-resistant—notice I did not say moistureproof—defense, especially helpful if you are serving salad with the burgers. The cold-toasting also affects and enhances flavor vis-à-vis the caramelization of the natural (and sometimes not so natural) sugar found in the buns. This flavor transformation adds another dimension to the experience; it brings new flavors you wouldn't normally taste with an untoasted roll, without adding anything distracting. Using butter to cold-toast the rolls is a key step in preparing your hamburger. The butter provides a protective layer against moisture once the burger (and salad, if you're using

it—more on that in a minute) is added to the bun. Cold-toasting is also something you can do ahead of time, leaving you more time to hang out with your friends.

Once the rolls are cold-toasted and the burger is ready, assembly is important. My preference is to keep salad on the side—cold, crisp, and fresh—and add it just before eating. When I add salad to my burgers, the rule is: least wet item closest to the bun. For example, lettuce leaf first, then onion, then tomato, then thin pickle slices.

To me, saucy condiments are the bun's worst enemy. Condiments are often best suited for dipping, especially if the burger is not going to be eaten straight away. Condiments are often used as a crutch, compensating for a lack of moisture in the burger, but they wreak havoc on the roll. There are exceptions to this, like sliders, which are meant to be eaten quickly and in just a few bites; therefore, you can really lay the sauces on, and the rolls can hold for a while.

For your burger to shine, the subtle costarring support of a well-chosen and well-prepared bun can make all the difference.

Meet Adam Perry Lang.

FRENCH ONION BURGERS

SERVES 4

Serve along with 10-Cut Oven Fries (page 248) and Fry Gravy (page 272).

Heat 1 tablespoon EVOO, 1 turn of the pan, and the butter in a large skillet over medium heat. Add the onions, garlic, bay leaf, and thyme; season with salt and pepper. Cook, stirring occasionally, until the onions are well browned, about 20 minutes. Add the sherry and deglaze the pan, scraping up any bits from the bottom, and cook a couple of minutes longer to cook off most of the alcohol and concentrate the flavor. Remove from the heat; remove bay leaf.

Preheat the broiler.

When the onions are almost done, heat a grill pan or large skillet over medium-high heat.

In a large bowl, combine the beef, Worcestershire sauce, and parsley; season with salt and pepper and mix thoroughly. Score the mixture into 4 equal portions and form them into patties slightly thinner at the center than at the edges for even cooking and to ensure a flat surface (burgers plump as they cook). Drizzle the patties with a little EVOO. Cook the burgers, flipping once, 10 minutes for medium (adjust the cooking time for rarer or more well-done burgers).

Meanwhile, place the bread on a baking sheet and broil about 6 inches from the heat until both sides are lightly golden. Set 4 pieces of bread aside, mound the Gruyère onto the remaining bread rounds (just like the large croutons that top French onion soup). Return to the oven to melt the cheese, 1 to 2 minutes.

Dress the lettuce with the lemon juice and remaining 3 tablespoons EVOO. Season with salt and pepper.

Place the burgers on the plain toasts and top with mounds of caramelized onions and some of the dressed lettuce. Take the cheesy bread and set in place on top of the lettuce, cheesy-side down, of course.

4 tablespoons **EVOO** (extra-virgin olive oil), plus more for drizzling

2 tablespoons **butter**

2 large **onions**, thinly sliced

3 cloves **garlic**, grated or finely chopped

1 **fresh** or **dried bay leaf**

1 teaspoon **ground thyme**

Kosher salt and **pepper**

½ cup good-quality **dry sherry**

2 pounds **lean ground sirloin**

3 tablespoons **Worcestershire sauce**

A generous handful of **flat-leaf parsley**, finely chopped

½ loaf **fat French bread** (wider than a baguette), cut on a bias into 8 (1-inch-thick) slices

½ pound **Gruyère cheese**, shredded

2 **romaine lettuce hearts**, shredded

Juice of 1 **lemon**

ITALIAN MEAT LOAF LONG BOY BURGERS

SERVES 4

Preheat the oven to 325°F.

Halve the plum tomatoes lengthwise or slice the vine-ripened tomatoes crosswise. Arrange them on a cooling rack set over a baking sheet so the heat can surround the tomatoes while they roast. Drizzle with EVOO and season with thyme, salt, and pepper. Roast 45 minutes.

Make the burgers: Place the torn bread in a bowl, cover with milk, and let soak. Place the beef and pork in a separate bowl and season with salt and pepper. Pulse the mortadella or prosciutto in a food processor until finely chopped. Add the minced meat to the bowl with the pork and beef along with the egg. Wring excess milk out of the bread and mash it into moist crumbs between your fingers as you add it to the meat bowl. Add the garlic, parsley, rosemary, grated onion (grate it right over the bowl so the juices fall into the meat), pecorino, and the nutmeg. Mix thoroughly. Score the mixture into 4 equal portions and form them into oval patties slightly thinner at the center than at the edges for even cooking and to ensure a flat surface (burgers plump as they cook). Drizzle the patties with EVOO.

Heat a griddle or large skillet over medium-high heat. Cook the burgers, flipping once, 12 minutes, or until the juices run clear. Top the burgers with sliced mozzarella for the last minute or two of cooking, tenting the griddle with aluminum foil, if you like, to help melt the cheese.

Place the burgers on the ciabatta bottoms and top with roasted tomatoes and balsamic drizzle (if using). Set the ciabatta tops in place.

6 **plum tomatoes** or 3 **vine-ripened tomatoes**, cored

EVOO (extra-virgin olive oil), for drizzling

2 tablespoons **fresh thyme** leaves, chopped

Kosher salt and **pepper**

BURGERS:

2 slices good-quality **white bread**, crusts removed and torn into pieces

Milk, for soaking the bread

¾ pound **ground sirloin**

½ pound **ground pork**

½ pound very thinly sliced **mortadella** or **prosciutto**, coarsely chopped

1 **large egg**, lightly beaten

2 large cloves **garlic**, grated or minced

A handful of **flat-leaf parsley**, finely chopped

A couple of sprigs **fresh rosemary**, finely chopped

3 to 4 tablespoons grated **onion**

A couple of small handfuls grated **pecorino cheese**

⅛ teaspoon freshly grated **nutmeg**

1 pound **fresh mozzarella** or **smoked mozzarella**, sliced

4 **ciabatta rolls** or 4 roll-size chunks of **ciabatta bread**, split and lightly toasted

Balsamic drizzle, store-bought or homemade (optional; see Tip, page 15)

SALTIMBOCCA BURGERS

SERVES 4

4 tablespoons **EVOO** (extra-virgin olive oil)

¼ pound sliced **Prosciutto di Parma**

4 tablespoons (½ stick) **butter**

12 leaves **fresh sage**, thinly sliced

1½ pounds **ground veal** or **chicken**

3 cloves **garlic**, finely chopped

Kosher salt and **pepper**

½ pound **Fontina cheese**, sliced or shredded

2 cups chopped **romaine lettuce** (from the heart)

Juice of ½ **lemon**

4 **ciabatta** or **other crusty rolls**, split and toasted

Heat 1 tablespoon EVOO, 1 turn of the pan, in a large skillet over medium-high heat. Add the prosciutto and cook until crisp. Remove the crispy ham to a plate and break into irregular pieces.

Heat the butter in a small saucepan over medium heat until it foams. Increase the heat a touch and add the sage leaves. Cook until crisp, about 1 minute per side, and transfer to paper towels to drain, then chop. Reserve the browned butter separately.

In a large bowl, combine the veal or chicken, garlic, and crisp sage; season with salt and pepper and mix thoroughly. Score the mixture into 4 equal portions and form them into patties slightly thinner at the center than at the edges for even cooking and to ensure a flat surface (burgers plump as they cook).

Heat 1 tablespoon EVOO, 1 turn of the pan, in a large nonstick skillet over medium-high heat. Cook the burgers, flipping once and basting with brown butter, 10 to 12 minutes, or until the juices run clear. Top the burgers with the cheese during the last minute or two of cooking, tenting the skillet with aluminum foil, if you like, to help melt the cheese.

While the burgers are cooking, dress the lettuce in a medium bowl with the remaining 2 tablespoons EVOO and the lemon juice. Season with salt and pepper.

Place the burgers on the warm roll bottoms and top with crispy prosciutto and dressed lettuce. Set the roll tops in place.

5-SPICE BURGERS with WARM MU SHU SLAW

SERVES 4

Make the burgers: In a large bowl, combine the pork or chicken, 5-spice powder, garlic, ginger, scallions, tamari, and a drizzle of oil; mix thoroughly. Score the mixture into 4 equal portions and form them into patties slightly thinner at the center than at the edges for even cooking and to ensure a flat surface (burgers plump as they cook). Drizzle the patties with oil.

Heat a large nonstick skillet or grill pan over medium-high heat. Cook the burgers, flipping once, 10 to 12 minutes, or until the juices run clear.

While the burgers are cooking, make the slaw: Heat the oil, 2 turns of the pan, in a nonstick skillet over high heat. Cook the shiitakes 2 minutes. Add the cabbage and stir-fry 3 minutes. Add the scallions and hoisin sauce, toss to combine, and remove from the heat.

Place the burgers on the roll bottoms and pile high with slaw. Set the roll tops in place.

BURGERS:

1½ pounds **ground pork** or **chicken**

1 teaspoon **Chinese 5-spice powder**

2 cloves **garlic**, grated or pasted (see Tip, page 138)

1-inch piece **fresh ginger**, peeled and grated or minced

2 **scallions**, whites and greens, finely chopped

3 tablespoons **tamari** or **soy sauce**

Vegetable oil, for drizzling

MU SHU SLAW:

2 tablespoons **vegetable oil**

12 **fresh shiitake mushrooms**, stems discarded, caps thinly sliced

⅓ to ½ pound **cabbage**, such as napa or Savoy, shredded

2 or 3 **scallions**, whites and greens, thinly sliced on an angle

3 tablespoons **hoisin sauce**

4 **cornmeal-dusted** or **sesame kaiser rolls**, split and lightly toasted

BRAT BURGERS
with SAUERKRAUT or
SWEET ONIONS

SERVES 4

Heat the sauerkraut in a small saucepan and keep warm over low heat. If serving onions rather than kraut, melt 2 tablespoons butter in a large skillet over medium heat. Add the onions, season with salt and pepper, and cook until sweet and softened, about 15 minutes.

In a large bowl, combine the veal, pork, grated onion (grate it right over the bowl so the juices fall into the meat), garlic, ginger, paprika, coriander, nutmeg, and parsley; season with salt and pepper and mix thoroughly. Score the meat into 4 equal portions and form them into patties slightly thinner at the center than at the edges for even cooking and to ensure a flat surface (burgers plump as they cook).

Heat the EVOO, 1 turn of the pan, in a large nonstick skillet over medium-high heat. Melt 1 tablespoon butter into the oil. Cook the burgers, flipping once, 10 to 12 minutes, or until the juices run clear. Top the burgers with cheese (if using) for the last minute or two of cooking, tenting the skillet with aluminum foil, if you like, to help melt the cheese.

Stir the mustard into the sauerkraut or onions. Place the burgers on 4 slices of buttered toast and top with kraut or onions. Set the top bread slices in place.

2 cups **sauerkraut**, rinsed and drained, or 2 large **onions**, thinly sliced, and 2 tablespoons **butter** for cooking

Kosher salt and **pepper**

¾ pound **ground veal**

¾ pound **ground pork**

3 to 4 tablespoons grated **onion**

2 cloves **garlic**, grated

½ teaspoon **ground ginger**

½ teaspoon **sweet paprika**

¼ teaspoon **ground coriander**

¼ teaspoon freshly grated **nutmeg**

¼ cup **flat-leaf parsley**, very finely chopped

Kosher salt and **pepper**

1 tablespoon **EVOO** (extra-virgin olive oil)

1 tablespoon **butter**

½ pound **sharp white cheddar cheese**, shredded or sliced (optional)

¼ cup **grainy mustard**

8 slices (½-inch-thick) **pumpernickel bread**, lightly toasted and buttered

CAJUN PORK BURGERS

SERVES 5

Andouille is a smoky sausage that was introduced to the rest of the United States by its "home state" of Louisiana. It is often associated with Cajun dishes, ya know, like gumbo and jambalaya. You may substitute another smoked sausage in its place.

Make the burgers: Heat 1 tablespoon oil, 1 turn of the pan, in a skillet over medium-high heat. Add the celery, bell pepper, chopped onion, and garlic; season with salt and pepper. Let sweat 5 to 6 minutes. Transfer to a large bowl and cool.

Cut the sausage into large chunks and place in a food processor. Grind sausage into crumbles and transfer to the bowl with the cooled vegetables. Add the pork, thyme, and hot sauce; season with salt and pepper and mix thoroughly. Score the mixture into 5 equal portions and form them into patties slightly thinner at the center than at the edges for even cooking and to ensure a flat surface (burgers plump as they cook). Heat the remaining 1 tablespoon oil, 1 turn of the pan, in a large skillet or griddle over medium-high heat. Cook the burgers, flipping once, 12 minutes, or until the juices run clear.

While the burgers are cooking, make the sauce: In a small bowl, stir together the chili sauce, mayo, and relish.

Place the burgers on the roll bottoms and top with the special sauce, lettuce, tomato, and sliced onion. Set the roll tops in place.

BURGERS:

2 tablespoons **vegetable oil**

1 rib **celery**, finely chopped

½ **green bell pepper**, seeded and finely chopped

1 small **white onion**, finely chopped

3 cloves **garlic**, minced

Kosher salt and **pepper**

¾ pound **andouille sausage**, casings removed

1 pound **ground pork**

Leaves from 4 sprigs **fresh thyme**, chopped (about 1 tablespoon) or 1 teaspoon **dried thyme**

1 teaspoon **cayenne pepper sauce**, such as Frank's RedHot

SPECIAL SAUCE:

3 tablespoons **prepared chili sauce**, such as Heinz

3 tablespoons **mayo, reduced-fat mayo,** or **soy mayo**

3 tablespoons **sweet red pepper relish** or **dill relish**

5 **crusty rolls**, split

Bibb lettuce leaves or **hearts of romaine**

Sliced **vine-ripened tomato**

Sliced **red onion**

COUNTRY PORK and PEPPERCORN BURGERS

SERVES 4

In a large bowl, combine the pork, pepper, garlic, and thyme; season with salt and mix thoroughly. Score the mixture into 4 equal portions and form them into patties slightly thinner at the center than at the edges for even cooking and to ensure a flat surface (burgers plump as they cook).

Heat the EVOO, 2 turns of the pan, in a large skillet or griddle over medium-high heat. Cook the burgers, flipping once, 10 to 12 minutes, or until the juices run clear.

Place the burgers on toast slices or roll bottoms and top with lettuce, sliced pickles, and sliced shallot. Stir together the cranberry sauce or chutney and mustard and slather on the roll tops or top slices of toast and set in place.

2 pounds **ground pork**

1½ tablespoons very coarsely ground **pepper**

4 cloves **garlic**, grated or minced

1½ teaspoons **ground thyme**

Kosher salt

2 tablespoons **EVOO** (extra-virgin olive oil)

8 thick slices **white bread** or 4 **brioche rolls**, split, lightly toasted, and buttered

8 leaves **red-** or **green-leaf lettuce**

8 **cornichons** or **gherkin pickles**, thinly sliced

1 large **shallot**, thinly sliced into rings

3 tablespoons prepared **whole-berry cranberry sauce** or **chutney**

¼ cup **grainy mustard**

TIP: Ask your butcher for coarse-ground pork—it'll make a difference in this recipe.

BANH MI BURGERS

SERVES 4

These Vietnamese-style burgers are a delicious new twist on the classic!

Make the vegetables: Bring the sugar, salt, and vinegar to a boil in a small saucepan. Stir to dissolve the sugar, reduce the heat, and let simmer a couple of minutes. Combine the carrot, cucumber, radishes, and chile in a heatproof bowl. Pour the vinegar mixture over the vegetables and let stand at room temperature for about 30 minutes or until ready to use. The veggies will hold in the refrigerator for a few weeks.

Make the burgers: In a large bowl, combine the pork, grated onion (grate it right over the bowl so the juices fall into the meat), garlic, ginger, and coriander; season with salt and pepper. Grind the ham finely in a food processor. Add the ground ham and hot sauce to the pork and mix thoroughly. Score the mixture into 4 equal portions and form them into patties slightly thinner at the center than at the edges for even cooking and to ensure a flat surface (burgers plump as they cook). Heat the oil in a large nonstick skillet over medium-high heat. Cook the burgers, flipping once, 10 to 12 minutes, or until the juices run clear.

Place the lettuce on the bread bottoms and top with the burgers. Drain the vinegar from the vegetables and scatter them over the burgers. Top the veggies with cilantro or basil and mint. Set the bread tops in place.

VEGETABLES:

¼ cup **sugar**

1 teaspoon **kosher salt**

1 cup **rice vinegar** or **white wine vinegar**

1 large **carrot**, peeled and cut into matchsticks

½ **seedless cucumber**, cut into matchsticks

4 **radishes**, cut into matchsticks

1 small **Fresno** or **jalapeño chile**, seeded and thinly sliced

BURGERS:

1 pound **ground pork**

3 tablespoons grated **onion**

2 cloves **garlic**, grated or finely chopped

1-inch piece **fresh ginger**, peeled and grated or minced, or 1 teaspoon **ground ginger**

1½ teaspoons **ground coriander**

Kosher salt and **pepper**

½ pound deli-sliced **ham**, coarsely chopped

2 tablespoons **sriracha hot sauce**

1 tablespoon **vegetable oil**

Bibb lettuce leaves

French bread, cut into 5-inch pieces and split

Cilantro or **basil** leaves, coarsely chopped or torn

A handful of **mint** leaves, torn or coarsely chopped

HOT SAUSAGE BURGERS with BROCCOLI RABE

SERVES 4

In a large bowl, combine the pork, red pepper flakes, paprika, fennel seeds, sage, onion, and 4 cloves of the garlic; season with salt and pepper and mix thoroughly. Score the mixture into 4 equal portions and form them into patties slightly thinner at the center than at the edges for even cooking and to ensure a flat surface (burgers plump as they cook). Drizzle the patties with EVOO.

Bring a couple of inches of water to a boil in a large skillet. Salt the water, add the broccoli rabe, and cook 5 minutes. Drain the broccoli rabe and transfer it to a cutting board. Chop it into 2-inch pieces and set aside.

Wipe out the skillet. Heat 2 tablespoons EVOO, 2 turns of the pan, in the skillet over medium heat. Add the remaining 2 cloves garlic and the chile pepper. Stir 2 minutes, then add the chopped broccoli rabe. Season with the nutmeg, salt, and pepper.

Heat a drizzle of EVOO in another large skillet over medium-high heat. Cook the burgers, flipping once, 10 to 12 minutes, or until the juices run clear. Top each burger with 2 slices provolone for the last minute or two of cooking, tenting the skillet with aluminum foil, if you like, to help melt the cheese.

Place the burgers on the roll bottoms and top with the broccoli rabe. Set the roll tops in place.

1½ pounds **ground pork**

2 teaspoons **crushed red pepper flakes**

2 teaspoons **sweet paprika**

1½ teaspoons **fennel seeds**

1 teaspoon **ground sage**

1 teaspoon **granulated onion**

6 cloves **garlic**, minced

Kosher salt and **pepper**

2 tablespoons **EVOO** (extra-virgin olive oil), plus more for drizzling

1 small bundle **broccoli rabe**, trimmed of tough ends

1 small **Fresno chile pepper**, seeded and finely chopped

A few grates of **nutmeg**

8 slices deli-sliced **sharp provolone cheese**

4 **ciabatta rolls** or other **crusty rolls**, split

"THE WURST" REUBEN BURGERS

SERVES 4

Make the onions: Heat the butter in a medium skillet over medium heat. When melted, add the onion and cook until softened and tender, about 20 minutes. When the onion is done, add a splash of water and stir in the mustard.

Place the sauerkraut in a small saucepan and keep warm over low heat.

Make the sauce: Stir the sour cream, ketchup, and relish together in a small bowl; season with salt and pepper.

Make the burgers: In a large bowl, combine the ground meats, celery seeds, marjoram, ginger, nutmeg, cardamom, parsley, and vinegar; season with salt and pepper and mix thoroughly. Score the mixture into 4 equal portions and form them into patties slightly thinner at the center than at the edges for even cooking and to ensure a flat surface (burgers plump as they cook). Heat the EVOO, 1 turn of the pan, in a large nonstick skillet over medium-high heat. Cook the burgers, flipping once, 10 to 12 minutes, or until the juices run clear. Top the burgers with the Swiss cheese for the last minute or two of cooking, tenting the skillet with aluminum foil, if you like, to help melt the cheese.

Pile the onions on the roll bottoms and top with the burgers. Top with sauerkraut and sour cream sauce. Set the roll tops in place.

ONIONS:

2 tablespoons **butter**

1 large **onion**, quartered lengthwise then thinly sliced

2 tablespoons **spicy mustard**

1 (1-pound) package **sauerkraut**, rinsed and drained

SOUR CREAM SAUCE:

¾ cup **sour cream**

¼ cup good-quality **ketchup**, such as Heinz Organic

¼ cup **dill relish**

Kosher salt and **pepper**

BURGERS:

1½ pounds **ground mix of beef, pork, and veal**

1 teaspoon **celery seeds**

1 teaspoon **dried marjoram**

1 teaspoon **ground ginger**

½ teaspoon freshly grated **nutmeg**

½ teaspoon **ground cardamom**

¼ cup finely chopped **flat-leaf parsley** (a handful)

2 tablespoons **cider vinegar** or **white wine vinegar**

1 tablespoon **EVOO** (extra-virgin olive oil)

4 slices deli-sliced **Emmentaler Swiss cheese**, folded to fit burgers

4 **seeded** or **plain burger rolls**, split

LONG BOY SAUSAGE BURGERS with PICKLED FENNEL and PEPPERONATA

SERVES 4

This oval-shaped burger packs a punch with the pickled fennel and pepper relish. The garlic bun ain't too shabby either.

Cut the stalks off the fennel and cut the bulb in half down the middle. Carefully cut out the core, place the halves cut side down on a cutting board, and slice them thinly. (Or shave the halves with a mandoline.) Place the sliced fennel in small plastic food storage container. Combine ½ cup vinegar and ¼ cup water with 1 teaspoon salt and 3 tablespoons sugar in a small saucepan. Bring to a boil and stir to dissolve the salt and sugar. Pour over the fennel. Place the lid on the container and chill at least 1 hour.

When you're ready to make the burgers, heat 2 tablespoons EVOO, 2 turns of the pan, in a medium skillet over medium to medium-high heat. Add the bell peppers, onion, and sliced garlic, and season with salt and pepper. Cook until tender, 7 to 8 minutes. Sprinkle with 1 teaspoon sugar and add 1 tablespoon vinegar. Stir the pepper relish a minute more, then turn off the heat.

Preheat the broiler.

In a large bowl, combine the ground meats, fennel seeds, granulated garlic and onion, sage, and paprika; season with salt and pepper and mix thoroughly. Score the mixture into 4 equal portions and form them into oval patties slightly thinner at the center than the edges for even cooking and to ensure a flat surface (burgers plump as they cook). Drizzle the patties with EVOO. Heat a grill pan or large nonstick skillet over medium-high

1 large bulb **fennel**

½ cup plus 1 tablespoon **white wine vinegar** or **white balsamic vinegar**

Kosher salt and **pepper**

3 tablespoons plus 1 teaspoon **sugar**

2 tablespoons **EVOO** (extra-virgin olive oil), plus more for drizzling

2 large **red bell peppers**, seeded and chopped

1 small **red onion**, chopped

3 large cloves **garlic**, 2 thinly sliced, 1 clove crushed

1¼ pounds **ground pork**

¾ pound **ground beef chuck**

1 tablespoon **fennel seeds**, crushed

1 tablespoon **granulated garlic**

1 tablespoon **granulated onion**

1 tablespoon **ground** or **rubbed sage**

1½ tablespoons **smoked sweet paprika**

2 tablespoons **butter**

4 **club rolls** (oval-shaped crusty rolls about 5 inches long) or other 5- to 6-inch **Italian rolls**, split

4 tablespoons grated **pecorino Romano** or **Parmigiano-Reggiano cheese**

A handful of **basil** leaves, shredded

heat. Cook the burgers, flipping once, 10 to 12 minutes, or until the juices run clear.

Meanwhile, melt the butter in a drizzle of EVOO in a small saucepan. Add the crushed garlic and cook for 2 to 3 minutes over low heat to infuse the flavor of garlic into the melted butter. Lightly toast the split rolls under the broiler. Remove the bottoms from the broiler pan. Brush the roll tops with garlic butter and sprinkle liberally with grated cheese; return to the oven to brown the cheese a minute.

Spread the pepper relish on the roll bottoms and top with the burgers. Drain the fennel and scatter over the burgers. Top each burger with some of the basil and set the garlic roll tops in place.

TIP: To crush fennel (and other) seeds easily, press down on them with the flat side of your knife using the heel of your hand and steady pressure. Or pulse in a spice grinder.

ADIRONDACK RED WING BURGERS

SERVES 4

Heat 1 tablespoon EVOO, 1 turn of the pan, in a small skillet over medium heat. Add the carrot, celery, onion, and garlic and cook until tender, about 5 minutes. Transfer to a large bowl and let cool.

When the veggies are cool, add the turkey or chicken and poultry seasoning to the vegetable mixture; season with salt and pepper and mix thoroughly. Score the mixture into 4 equal portions and form them into patties slightly thinner at the center than at the edges for even cooking and to ensure a flat surface (burgers plump as they cook).

Heat the remaining 1 tablespoon EVOO, 1 turn of the pan, in a large skillet over medium heat. Cook the burgers, flipping once, 10 to 12 minutes, or until the juices run clear; transfer to a plate. Add the butter to the skillet. When melted, stir in the hot sauce. Add the burgers to the sauce and turn to coat. Top with the blue cheese crumbles and a cheddar slice. Tent with foil, turn off the heat, and let stand until the cheese is melted, about 1 minute.

Top each muffin bottom with some shredded lettuce and top with a burger and some relish. Set the muffin tops in place.

2 tablespoons **EVOO** (extra-virgin olive oil)

1 small **carrot**, peeled and finely chopped, grated, or minced

1 rib **celery**, with leafy tops, finely chopped

¼ cup finely chopped **onion**

2 cloves **garlic**, finely chopped

1½ pounds **ground turkey** or **chicken**

1 teaspoon **poultry seasoning**

Kosher salt and **pepper**

2 tablespoons **butter**

¼ cup **hot sauce**

½ cup **blue cheese** crumbles

4 slices deli-sliced **cheddar cheese**

4 **sandwich-size English muffins**, toasted

¼ head **iceberg lettuce**, shredded

¼ cup **dill relish**

CHICKEN KIEV BURGERS with RUSSIAN SLAW

SERVES 4

Butter makes a Kiev, so use a good-quality, rich organic butter for these burgers for the best flavor.

Make the burgers: On a cutting board, combine the chopped parsley, chives, and thyme. Press 4 of the 1-tablespoon pieces of cold butter into the herbs, coating them completely.

In a large bowl, combine the chicken, grated shallot, Worcestershire sauce, and mustard; season with salt and pepper and mix thoroughly. Divide the mixture into 4 mounds. Nest an herb-coated piece of cold butter into the center of the meat, and gently form a patty around the butter. The patties should be no more than 1 inch thick and slightly thinner at the center than at the edges for even cooking and to ensure a flat surface (burgers plump as they cook).

Heat 1 tablespoon EVOO, 1 turn of the pan, in a large skillet over medium-high heat. Melt in the remaining 2 tablespoons butter. When hot, cook the burgers, flipping once, 10 to 12 minutes, or until the juices run clear.

While the burgers are cooking, make the slaw: In a medium bowl, combine the sour cream, lemon juice, relish, and ketchup; season with salt and pepper. Add the cabbage and parsley and toss to combine.

Place the burgers (the herb butter waiting at the center) on the roll bottoms and top with the slaw and red onion. Set the roll tops in place.

BURGERS:

2 tablespoons finely chopped **flat-leaf parsley**

2 tablespoons finely chopped **chives**

1 tablespoon **fresh thyme** leaves, finely chopped

6 tablespoon-size tabs of cold **butter**

2 pounds **ground chicken** (a mix of white and dark meat; see page x)

2 to 3 tablespoons grated **shallot**

2 tablespoons **Worcestershire sauce**

2 tablespoons **Dijon mustard**

Kosher salt and **pepper**

1 tablespoon **EVOO** (extra-virgin olive oil)

RUSSIAN SLAW:

½ cup **sour cream**

Juice of ½ **lemon**

2 tablespoons **dill relish**

2 tablespoons good-quality **ketchup**, such as Heinz Organic

2 cups shredded **cabbage**

2 tablespoons chopped **flat-leaf parsley**

4 **kaiser rolls**, split

½ small **red onion**, thinly sliced

TIP: Coleslaw mix, found in the produce aisle of the supermarket, can be substituted for the shredded cabbage.

ITALIAN BBQ CHICKEN BURGERS

SERVES 4

Make the sauce: Heat 2 tablespoons EVOO, 2 turns of the pan, in a saucepan over medium-high heat. Add the pancetta and cook 3 to 4 minutes. Add the onion and season with salt and lots of pepper. Cook, stirring occasionally, until the onion begins to brown, about 10 minutes. Stir in the vinegar, brown sugar, Worcestershire sauce, and tomato sauce. Simmer, stirring occasionally, until thickened.

Make the burgers: In a large bowl, combine the chicken, Parmigiano-Reggiano, garlic, rosemary, thyme, fennel seeds, red pepper flakes, and poultry seasoning; season with salt and pepper and mix thoroughly. Score the mixture into 4 equal portions and form them into patties slightly thinner at the center than at the edges for even cooking and to ensure a flat surface (burgers plump as they cook). Drizzle the patties with EVOO.

Heat a large nonstick skillet or grill pan over medium-high heat. Cook the burgers, flipping once, 10 to 12 minutes, or until the juices run clear.

Place the burgers on the roll bottoms and top with the sauce, red onions, giardiniera, and chopped greens. Set the roll tops in place.

SAUCE:

2 tablespoons **EVOO** (extra-virgin olive oil), plus more for drizzling

¼ pound **pancetta**, chopped

1 small **onion**, finely chopped

Kosher salt and **pepper**

¼ cup **balsamic vinegar**

3 tablespoons **light brown sugar**

2 tablespoons **Worcestershire sauce**

1 cup or 1 (8-ounce) can **tomato sauce**

BURGERS:

2 pounds **ground chicken**

⅔ cup grated **Parmigiano-Reggiano** or **pecorino Romano cheese** (a couple of generous handfuls)

4 cloves **garlic**, grated or finely chopped

2 tablespoons **fresh rosemary**, finely chopped

2 tablespoons **fresh thyme**, finely chopped

1½ tablespoons **fennel seeds**, toasted

1 teaspoon **crushed red pepper flakes**

1 teaspoon **poultry seasoning**

4 **crusty rolls**, split

Thinly sliced **red onions**

Chopped **giardiniera** (Italian hot pickled vegetables), store-bought or homemade (page 183)

1½ to 2 cups **greens** (such as arugula, endive, and radicchio), chopped

TIP: A simple way to tell if chicken or turkey burgers are fully cooked is to poke a skewer or small knife into the very center. If the juices that run out are clear, the burger is cooked. If they are slightly pink, the burger needs a little more cooking.

SPANIKOPITA BURGERS

SERVES 4

Heat a drizzle of EVOO and the butter in a large skillet over medium heat. Add the onion, garlic, and oregano and season with salt and pepper. Cook the onion until tender, 5 to 6 minutes. Transfer to a large bowl to cool.

Separate the spinach as you add it to the bowl with the cool onions and garlic. Add the feta and chicken or turkey; season with salt and pepper and mix thoroughly. Score the mixture into 4 equal portions and form them into patties slightly thinner at the center than at the edges for even cooking and to ensure a flat surface (burgers plump as they cook).

Heat 1 tablespoon EVOO, 1 turn of the pan, in a large nonstick skillet over medium-high heat. Cook the burgers, flipping once, 10 to 12 minutes, or until the juices run clear.

Place the burgers on the roll bottoms and top with tomato, red onion, cucumber, lettuce, and pepperoncini rings. Set the roll tops in place.

1 tablespoon **EVOO** (extra-virgin olive oil), plus more for drizzling

1 tablespoon **butter**

½ small **onion**, finely chopped

2 cloves **garlic**, finely chopped

1 teaspoon **dried oregano**, lightly crushed in the palm

Kosher salt and coarsely ground **pepper**

1 (10-ounce) box **frozen chopped spinach**, thawed and wrung dry in a kitchen towel

¾ cup **feta crumbles**

1½ pounds **ground chicken** or **turkey breast**

4 **crusty rolls**, split

TOPPINGS:

Sliced **tomato**

Sliced **red onion**

Sliced **seedless cucumber**

Chopped **romaine lettuce**

Sliced bottled **pepperoncini** (hot Greek peppers)

PROVENÇAL BURGERS with PISSALADIÈRE TOPPING

SERVES 4

Make the topping: Heat the EVOO and butter in a large skillet over medium heat. Add the anchovies and stir until they "melt." Add the onions and cook until soft and sweet, 25 to 30 minutes, stirring occasionally. Stir in the garlic, parsley, and olives. Stir 2 minutes. Season with salt, if necessary, and pepper.

While the onions are cooking, make the burgers: In a large bowl, combine the ground meat of choice with the herbes de Provence, fennel seeds, lemon zest, and garlic; season with salt and pepper and mix thoroughly. Score the meat into 4 equal portions and form them into large patties slightly thinner at the center than at the edges for even cooking and to ensure a flat surface (burgers plump as they cook). Heat the EVOO, 1 turn of the pan, in a large nonstick skillet over medium-high heat. Cook the burgers, flipping once, 10 to 12 minutes, or until the juices run clear. (If you're cooking veal burgers and would like them slightly pink at the center, cook them 2 to 3 minutes less.) Top the burgers with cheese for the last minute or two of cooking time, tenting the pan with aluminum foil, if you like, to help melt the cheese.

Place the burgers on the roll bottoms and top with the pissaladière topping. Set the roll tops in place.

PISSALADIÈRE TOPPING:

1 tablespoon **EVOO** (extra-virgin olive oil)

2 tablespoons **butter**

4 to 6 flat **anchovy fillets**

2 large **onions**, very thinly sliced

2 cloves **garlic**, pasted (see Tip, page 138) or grated

¼ cup finely chopped **flat-leaf parsley**

⅓ cup pitted **black olives**, chopped

Kosher salt and **pepper**

BURGERS:

2 pounds **ground chicken**, **veal**, or **turkey**

1 tablespoon **dried herbes de Provence**

2 teaspoons **fennel seeds**

2 teaspoons grated **lemon** zest

2 cloves **garlic**, pasted (see Tip, page 138) or grated

1 tablespoon **EVOO** (extra-virgin olive oil)

4 slices deli-sliced **Gruyère** or **Swiss cheese**

4 **crusty rolls**, split and lightly toasted

INDIAN-SPICED PATTIES with YOGURT SAUCE

SERVES 4

In a large bowl, combine the chicken or lamb with the curry paste (or seasoning blend) and cinnamon; season with salt and mix thoroughly. Score the mixture into 4 equal portions and form them into patties slightly thinner at the center than at the edges for even cooking and to ensure a flat surface (burgers plump as they cook).

Heat the EVOO, 1 turn of the pan, in a large skillet over medium-high heat. Cook the burgers, flipping once, 10 minutes for medium lamb burgers (adjust the cooking time for rarer or more well-done burgers) and 10 to 12 minutes, or until the juices run clear, for chicken burgers.

While the burgers are cooking, in a small bowl, stir together the yogurt, garlic, lemon juice, cilantro, and mint. Season the lettuce and tomatoes with a little salt.

Place the burgers on the roll bottoms or on one side of a naan and top with yogurt sauce, lettuce, and tomato. Set the roll tops in place or fold the naans over the burgers.

1¼ pounds **ground chicken** or **lamb**

2 tablespoons **mild** or **hot curry paste** or seasoning blend (see Tip, page 94)

A pinch of **ground cinnamon**

Kosher salt

1 tablespoon **EVOO** (extra-virgin olive oil)

1 cup **Greek yogurt**

1 clove **garlic**, grated or pasted (see Tip, page 138)

Juice of ½ **lemon**

A small handful of **cilantro**, finely chopped

A small handful of **mint leaves**, finely chopped

4 leaves **Bibb** or **Boston lettuce**, chopped

2 **tomatoes**, sliced

4 **brioche rolls** or grilled **naan breads**

TIP: Naan is a type of fluffy flat bread typical of India. It is traditionally made by rolling out rounds of yeast dough and sticking them to the inside of a tandoor oven, where they cook at very high heat. Large supermarket chains often carry one or more varieties of naan—so check them out!

MARSALA BURGERS

SERVES 4

Heat 1 tablespoon EVOO, 1 turn of the pan, and the butter in a medium skillet over medium-high heat. Add the sliced mushrooms and cook until deep brown, 10 to 12 minutes, stirring them frequently. Season the mushrooms with salt and pepper after they brown. Add the Marsala and cook it down to glaze the mushrooms with its flavor. Remove from the heat.

While the mushrooms are cooking, preheat the broiler and make the burgers: In a large bowl, combine the chicken or veal, shallot, sage, parsley, chopped garlic, and Worcestershire sauce; season with salt and pepper and mix thoroughly. Score the meat into 4 equal portions and form them into patties slightly thinner at the center than at the edges for even cooking and to ensure a flat surface (burgers plump as they cook).

Heat 1 tablespoon EVOO, 1 turn of the pan, in a grill pan or large cast-iron or other large skillet over medium-high heat. Cook the burgers, flipping once, 10 to 12 minutes, or until the juices run clear. Top the burgers with cheese during the last minute or two of cooking, tenting the pan with aluminum foil, if you like, to help melt the cheese.

While the burgers are cooking, brown the split rolls under the broiler and rub them lightly with the garlic halves. Drizzle the rolls with EVOO. Place a burger on a roll bottom and top with a pile of Marsala mushrooms. Set the roll tops in place.

2 tablespoons **EVOO** (extra-virgin olive oil), plus more for drizzling

2 tablespoons **butter**, cut into small pieces

4 large **portobello mushrooms caps**, gills scraped off (see Tip, page 225), thinly sliced

Kosher salt and **pepper**

½ cup **Marsala, dry** or **sweet**

1½ pounds **ground chicken** or **veal**

1 **shallot**, finely chopped or grated

2 to 3 tablespoons finely chopped **fresh sage**

A handful of **flat leaf parsley**, finely chopped

3 cloves **garlic**, 2 finely chopped, 1 peeled and halved

1 tablespoon **Worcestershire sauce**

⅓ pound **Italian Fontina cheese**, sliced or shredded

4 **crusty rolls**, split

TIP: Salting the mushrooms before they brown will draw out the liquids, slowing the browning process.

RACHEL PATTY MELTS

SERVES 4

No, I did not misspell my name. A Rachel is a Reuben patty melt made with turkey rather than beef, topped with sauerkraut and Russian-style dressing. SOOOOOOOOOO good!

Make the burgers: In a large bowl, combine the turkey, grated onion (grate it right over the bowl so the juices fall into the meat), Worcestershire sauce, parsley, and poultry seasoning; season with salt and pepper and mix thoroughly. Score the mixture into 4 equal portions and form them into patties slightly thinner at the center than at the edges for even cooking and to ensure a flat surface (burgers plump as they cook).

Heat the EVOO, 1 turn of the pan, in a large nonstick skillet over medium-high heat. Cook the burgers, flipping once, 10 to 12 minutes, or until the juices run clear. Transfer to a plate, wipe the pan clean, and set aside.

While the burgers are cooking, make the dressing: Stir the sour cream, lemon juice, hot sauce, relish, and ketchup together in a small bowl; season with salt and pepper.

Butter 1 side of each slice of bread. Make the sandwiches with the buttered sides facing out. Spread some of the dressing on half the bread slices and top with a slice of cheese, a few forkfuls of sauerkraut, a burger, and another slice of cheese. Slather the unbuttered side of the remaining bread slices with mustard and set the top slices of bread, buttered side up, into place. Reheat the skillet over medium-low heat and grill the sandwiches, turning once, until crisp and golden and the cheese melts, about 5 minutes total.

BURGERS:

1½ pounds **ground turkey** (mix of dark and white meat; see page x)

2 to 3 tablespoons grated **onion**

1 tablespoon **Worcestershire sauce**

2 tablespoons finely chopped **flat-leaf parsley**

1½ tablespoons **poultry seasoning**

Kosher salt and coarsely ground **pepper**

1 tablespoon **EVOO** (extra-virgin olive oil)

DRESSING:

1 cup **sour cream**

1 tablespoon fresh **lemon** juice

1 teaspoon **hot sauce**, such as Tabasco

2 tablespoons **dill relish**

¼ cup good-quality **ketchup**, such as Heinz Organic

SANDWICH FIXINGS:

4 tablespoons (½ stick) **butter**, softened

8 slices **marble rye** or **pumpernickel bread**

8 slices deli-sliced **Emmentaler Swiss cheese**

1 (1-pound) package **sauerkraut**, rinsed and drained

Spicy brown mustard

BUFFALO TURKEY BURGERS with BLUE CHEESE DRESSING

SERVES 4

In a large bowl, combine the turkey, poultry seasoning, grill seasoning, garlic, scallions, and celery; mix thoroughly. Score into 4 equal portions and form them into patties slightly thinner at the center than at the edges for even cooking and to ensure a flat surface (burgers plump as they cook). Drizzle the patties with oil.

Heat a large nonstick skillet over medium-high heat. Cook the burgers, flipping once, 10 to 12 minutes, or until the juices run clear. Remove to a plate. Wipe the pan clean and reduce the heat to low. Melt the butter in a pan and stir in the hot sauce. Return the burgers to the skillet and turn to coat in the hot sauce–butter mixture.

Mix the sour cream or ranch dressing with the blue cheese crumbles and season with salt and pepper.

Place the burgers on the roll bottoms, and top with lettuce and blue cheese sauce. Set the roll tops in place.

1½ pounds **ground turkey breast**

1½ teaspoons **poultry seasoning**

1 tablespoon **grill seasoning**, such as McCormick Montreal Steak Seasoning

2 cloves **garlic**, chopped

4 **scallions**, whites and greens, finely chopped

1 rib **celery**, from the heart, with greens, finely chopped

Vegetable oil, for drizzling

2 tablespoons **butter**

¼ cup **hot sauce**, such as Frank's RedHot

1 cup **sour cream, reduced-fat sour cream**, or **ranch dressing**

½ cup **blue cheese crumbles**

Kosher salt and **pepper**

4 **crusty rolls**, split

Leaf lettuce

CALIFORNIA TURKEY CLUB BURGERS

SERVES 4

Preheat the oven to 425°F.

Arrange the bacon on a slotted broiler pan or a cooling rack set over a baking sheet and cook until crisp, about 12 minutes. Break each piece of bacon in half and reserve.

While the bacon is getting crispy, make the burgers: In a large bowl, combine the ground turkey, grated onion (grate it right over the bowl so the juices fall into the meat), garlic, parsley, paprika, and lemon zest; season with salt and pepper and mix thoroughly. Score the mixture into 4 equal portions and form them into thin patties about ¼ inch thick, slightly thinner at the center than at the edges for even cooking and to ensure a flat surface (burgers plump as they cook). Heat the EVOO, 2 turns of the pan, in a large nonstick skillet over medium-high heat. Cook the burgers, flipping once, about 10 minutes, or until the juices run clear.

While the burgers are cooking, blend the avocado in a food processor or blender along with the cream, lemon juice, mustard, and a little salt and pepper until smooth and thick.

Spread a little of the avocado smear on 2 slices of toast. Top each with a burger. Top that with a slice of red tomato, a little more avocado smear, another piece of toast, more avocado smear, a second burger, yellow tomato, 2 slices bacon, Bibb lettuce, and more avocado smear. Top with the remaining 2 slices of toast. Stick the top of each sandwich with 4 toothpicks, just shy of each corner. Cut each club burger into 4 triangles; the toothpicks will help hold everything together.

4 slices **center-cut bacon**

1 pound **ground turkey breast**

½ small **yellow onion**, grated

1 large clove **garlic**, finely chopped

A handful of **flat-leaf** parsley leaves or **cilantro**, chopped

1 tablespoon **sweet paprika** or **smoked sweet paprika**

Grated zest and juice of 1 **lemon**

Kosher salt and **pepper**

2 tablespoons **EVOO** (extra-virgin olive oil)

1 **avocado**, flesh cut into chunks

2 tablespoons **heavy cream** or **half-and-half**

1 tablespoon **yellow mustard**

6 slices **white bread**, toasted

2 slices from 1 small **red beefsteak tomato**

2 slices from 1 small **yellow beefsteak tomato**

2 leaves **Bibb lettuce**

8 toothpicks or sandwich picks (get something fun and fancy if you feel like it)

COBB-STYLE TURKEY BURGER CLUB with GREEN RANCH DRESSING

SERVES 4

I prefer a thicker, meatier bacon as opposed to a thinner slice. My favorite is from Oscar's Smokehouse in Warrensburg, New York.

Preheat the oven to 375°F.

Arrange the bacon on a slotted broiler pan or a cooling rack set over a baking sheet and bake until crisp, about 15 minutes.

Meanwhile make the burgers: Heat a drizzle of EVOO in a large skillet over medium-high heat. Add the onion and garlic and cook until softened, about 5 minutes. Place in a large bowl and cool. Wipe out the skillet and reserve.

Once the onion is cool, add the turkey and thyme; season with salt and pepper and mix thoroughly. Score the mixture into 4 equal portions and form each into 2 thin patties (a total of 8 patties). Top half of the patties with a mound of blue cheese, then sandwich together with another thin patty. Press the edges of the patties together and shape them into burgers slightly thinner at the center than at the edges for even cooking and to ensure a flat surface (burgers plump as they cook). Drizzle the burgers with EVOO. Return the skillet to medium-high heat and, when hot, cook the burgers, flipping once, 10 to 12 minutes, or until the juices run clear.

While the burgers are cooking, make the green ranch dressing: Puree the avocado flesh, lemon juice, sour cream, buttermilk, chives, garlic, Tabasco sauce, and a pinch of salt and pepper in a blender.

Place the burgers on the roll bottoms and top with lettuce, tomato, and bacon. Slather the roll tops with green ranch dressing and set the tops in place.

8 slices good-quality **bacon** (see headnote)

STUFFED BURGERS:

EVOO (extra-virgin olive oil), for drizzling

½ small **onion**, finely chopped

2 cloves **garlic**, finely chopped

1½ pounds **ground turkey breast**

2 tablespoons **fresh thyme**, finely chopped

Kosher salt and **pepper**

¾ cup **blue cheese crumbles**

GREEN RANCH DRESSING:

1 **avocado**

Juice of 1 **lemon**

½ cup **sour cream**

½ cup **buttermilk**

3 tablespoons finely chopped **chives**

1 clove **garlic**, grated

1 teaspoon **Tabasco sauce**

4 **club rolls** or **brioche rolls**, split

Tender lettuce leaves, such as **butter, red-** or **green-leaf**, or **Boston lettuce**

4 slices **tomato**, about ½ inch thick

CRANBERRY BOG TURKEY BURGERS

SERVES 4

Heat the butter in a medium skillet over medium heat. Add the apple, celery, onion, and poultry seasoning, and season with salt and pepper. Cook until softened, 6 to 7 minutes. Transfer to a large bowl and cool.

Add the turkey to the cooled apple mix; season with salt and pepper and mix thoroughly. Score the mixture into 4 equal portions and form them into patties slightly thinner at the center than at the edges for even cooking and to ensure a flat surface (burgers plump as they cook). Heat a drizzle of oil in a large skillet or grill pan over medium-high heat. Cook the burgers, flipping once, 10 to 12 minutes, or until the juices run clear.

In a small bowl, mix together the cranberry sauce and mayo or soy mayo. Spread the toasted muffin halves with cran-mayonnaise. Place the burgers on the muffin bottoms and top with Bibb lettuce. Set the muffin tops in place.

2 tablespoons **butter**

1 small **McIntosh** or **Honeycrisp apple**, peeled, cored, and finely chopped

1 rib **celery**, from the heart, finely chopped

1 small **white onion**, chopped

1 rounded teaspoon **poultry seasoning**

Kosher salt and **pepper**

1½ pounds **ground turkey**

Vegetable oil, for drizzling

1 cup prepared **whole-berry cranberry sauce**

½ cup **mayo** or **soy mayo**

4 **sandwich-size sourdough English muffins**, split and toasted

8 leaves **Bibb lettuce**

CURRIED TURKEY BURGERS

SERVES 4

In a large bowl, combine the turkey, curry powder or spice mix, Worcestershire sauce, garlic, and grated onion (grate it right over the bowl so the juices fall into the meat); season with salt and pepper and mix thoroughly. Score the mixture into 4 equal portions and form them into patties slightly thinner at the center than at the edges for even cooking and to ensure a flat surface (burgers plump as they cook).

Heat the oil, 1 turn of the pan, over medium-high heat in a large nonstick skillet. Melt the butter into the oil. Cook the burgers, flipping once, 10 to 12 minutes, or until the juices run clear.

Place the burgers on the roll bottoms and top with Bibb lettuce, tomato, and red onion. Slather the roll tops with mango chutney and set them in place.

1½ pounds **ground turkey** or **turkey breast** (see page x)

2 tablespoons **curry powder** or curry spice mix (see Tip)

2 tablespoons **Worcestershire sauce**

2 cloves **garlic**, grated

¼ **onion**, grated

Kosher salt and **pepper**

1 tablespoon **vegetable oil**

1 tablespoon **butter**

4 **crusty rolls**, split

Bibb lettuce

Sliced **tomato**

Thinly sliced **red onion**

Major Grey's mango chutney

TIP: If you don't have curry powder or paste, stir together 1 teaspoon each of ground cumin, ground turmeric, paprika, and ground coriander, and a pinch each of ground cinnamon and ground cardamom.

HAWAII BURGERS

SERVES 4

Heat a large skillet or griddle over medium-high heat.

In a large bowl, combine the turkey, ginger, tamari, garlic, scallions, and sesame oil; season with salt and pepper and mix thoroughly. Score the mixture into 4 equal portions and form them into patties slightly thinner at the center than at the edges for even cooking and to ensure a flat surface (burgers plump as they cook).

Add the vegetable oil, 1 turn of the pan, to the hot skillet. Cook the burgers, flipping once and brushing them with hoisin sauce, 10 to 12 minutes, or until the juices run clear. While the burgers cook, grill the pineapple rings alongside the burgers or in a separate skillet or grill pan.

Place the burgers on the bun or roll bottoms and top with pineapple rings, lettuce, and red onion. Set the roll or bun tops in place.

1½ pounds **ground turkey** or **turkey breast**

1-inch piece **fresh ginger**, peeled and grated

3 tablespoons **tamari** or **soy sauce**

2 cloves **garlic**, grated or finely chopped

2 **scallions**, whites and greens, finely chopped

2 teaspoons **dark sesame oil**

Kosher salt and **pepper**

1 tablespoon **vegetable oil**

½ cup **hoisin sauce**

4 slices **fresh pineapple**

4 **fresh-baked buns** or **rolls**, such as **brioche** or other soft rolls, split

Bibb or **leaf lettuce**

Thinly sliced **red onion**

TIP: Precut pineapple rings are sometimes available in the produce section of supermarkets.

CARIBBEAN BURGERS with MANGO SALSA

SERVES 4

Make the burgers: Place the ground meat of choice in a large bowl. Combine the allspice, thyme, cinnamon, nutmeg, cayenne, and brown sugar in a small bowl. Sprinkle evenly over the meat. Add the basil or cilantro and lots of salt and black pepper and mix thoroughly. Score the mixture into 4 equal portions and form them into large patties slightly thinner at the center than at the edges for even cooking and to ensure a flat surface (burgers plump as they cook).

Heat 2 tablespoons EVOO, 2 turns of the pan, in a large nonstick skillet over medium-high heat. Add the burgers and cook, flipping once, 10 to 12 minutes, or until the juices run clear.

While the burgers are cooking, make the mango salsa: In a small bowl, combine the mango, bell pepper, jalapeño, cucumber, and lime juice; season with salt to taste.

Place the burgers on the roll bottoms and top with Bibb lettuce and lots of salsa. Set the roll tops in place.

BURGERS:

2 pounds **ground chicken, pork,** or **turkey breast**

1½ teaspoons **ground allspice**

1 teaspoon **dried thyme leaves** or **ground thyme**

½ teaspoon **ground cinnamon**

½ teaspoon freshly grated **nutmeg**

½ teaspoon **cayenne pepper**

1 tablespoon **light** or **dark brown sugar**

5 to 6 fresh **basil** leaves or 2 tablespoons chopped **cilantro**

Kosher salt and black **pepper**

2 tablespoons **EVOO** (extra-virgin olive oil), plus more for drizzling

SALSA:

1 **mango**, peeled and cut into ¼-inch dice

1 small **red bell pepper**, seeded and cut into ¼-inch dice

1 **jalapeño chile**, seeded and finely chopped

¼ **seedless cucumber**, peeled and cut into ¼-inch dice

Juice of 1 **lime**

4 **cornmeal-dusted kaiser rolls**, split and toasted

Bibb lettuce leaves

HUNGARIAN TURKEY BURGERS with SMOKED GOUDA

SERVES 4

Make the burgers: Heat a large skillet or grill pan over medium-high heat.

In a large bowl, combine the turkey, garlic, grated onion (grate it right over the bowl so the juices fall into the meat), chile, parsley, Worcestershire sauce, and paprika; season with salt and pepper and mix thoroughly. Score the mixture into 4 equal portions and form them into patties slightly thinner at the center than at the edges for even cooking and to ensure a flat surface (burgers plump as they cook). Drizzle the patties with EVOO.

Cook the burgers, flipping once, 10 to 12 minutes, or until the juices run clear. Top the burgers with cheese for the last minute or two of cooking, tenting the skillet with aluminum foil, if you like, to help melt the cheese.

While the burgers are cooking, make the sauce: Stir the grated shallot, sour cream, and dill together in small bowl. Season with salt and pepper.

Place the burgers on the roll bottoms and top with watercress, radishes, pickles, and some of the sour cream sauce. Set the roll tops in place.

BURGERS:

1½ pounds **ground turkey** or **turkey breast** (see page x)

2 cloves **garlic**, grated or pasted (see Tip, page 138)

3 to 4 tablespoons grated **onion**

1 **fresh red chile**, such as Fresno, seeded and finely chopped

A handful of **flat-leaf parsley**, finely chopped

2 tablespoons **Worcestershire sauce**

2 tablespoons **sweet paprika** or **smoked sweet paprika**

Kosher salt and **pepper**

EVOO (extra-virgin olive oil), for drizzling

4 slices **smoked Gouda cheese**

SAUCE:

1 small **shallot**, grated or minced

1 cup **sour cream**

¼ cup finely chopped **fresh dill**

4 **crusty rolls** or **burger rolls** of your choice, split

Watercress leaves

Sliced **radishes**

Bread-and-butter pickle slices

JERK BURGERS

SERVES 4

Heat a large skillet over medium-high heat.

In a large bowl, combine the chicken or pork, scallions, chile, ginger, garlic, thyme, allspice, cumin, coriander, paprika, nutmeg, and brown sugar; season with salt and lots of pepper and mix thoroughly. Score the mixture into 4 equal portions and form them into patties slightly thinner at the center than at the edges for even cooking and to ensure a flat surface (burgers plump as they cook).

Drizzle EVOO into the hot skillet. Cook the burgers, flipping once, 10 to 12 minutes, or until the juices run clear. Squeeze lime juice over the patties before removing them from the heat.

Place the burgers on the roll bottoms and garnish with the toppings of choice before setting the roll tops in place.

1½ pounds **ground chicken** or **pork**

4 **scallions**, whites and greens, finely chopped

1 **serrano** or **jalapeño chile**, seeded and minced

1-inch piece **fresh ginger**, peeled and grated

3 to 4 cloves **garlic**, grated or chopped

2 tablespoons **fresh thyme**, finely chopped

1 teaspoon **ground allspice**

1 teaspoon **ground cumin**

1 teaspoon **ground coriander**

1 teaspoon **sweet paprika**

¼ teaspoon freshly grated **nutmeg**

1 tablespoon **light brown sugar**

Kosher salt and **pepper**

EVOO (extra-virgin olive oil) or **vegetable oil**, for drizzling

Juice of 1 **lime**

4 crusty **plain** or **cornmeal-dusted kaiser rolls**, split

TOPPINGS:

Grilled or **fresh pineapple** rings

Bottled hot pepper rings

Lettuce leaves

Sliced **red onion**

Fruit chutney or **salsa**

CUBANO BURGERS

SERVES 4

Pulse the ham in a food processor until finely minced and transfer to a large bowl Add the turkey, garlic, chile, scallions, and cilantro; season with salt and pepper and mix thoroughly. Score the mixture into 4 equal portions and form patties slightly thinner at the center than at the edges for even cooking and to ensure a flat surface (burgers plump as they cook). Drizzle the patties with oil.

Heat a large nonstick skillet over medium-high heat. Cook the burgers, flipping once, 10 to 12 minutes, or until the juices run clear. Top each burger with 2 slices Swiss cheese during the last minute or two of cooking, tenting the skillet with aluminum foil, if you like, to help melt the cheese.

Place the burgers on the roll bottoms and top with pickles and hot pepper rings. Slather the bun tops with lots of mustard and set the tops in place. Serve with plantain chips on the side.

$\frac{1}{3}$ pound deli-sliced **smoked ham,** chopped

$1\frac{1}{2}$ pounds **ground turkey breast**

2 cloves **garlic,** minced

1 **Fresno chile pepper,** seeded and finely chopped

2 **scallions,** whites and greens, finely chopped

2 tablespoons chopped **cilantro**

Kosher salt and **pepper**

Vegetable oil or **olive oil,** for drizzling

8 slices deli-sliced **Swiss cheese** (about $\frac{1}{3}$ pound)

4 **Portuguese rolls** (slightly sweet) or crusty **kaiser rolls,** split

2 large **dill pickles,** thinly sliced lengthwise

Bottled hot pepper rings, drained

Yellow mustard

1 (12-ounce) bag store-bought **plantain chips**

TIP: You can find bottled sliced hot pepper rings (usually banana peppers although the label might not say so) near the pickles and olives in the supermarket.

CHICKEN OR TURKEY BURGERS with CAESAR PESTO

SERVES 4

Make the pesto: Combine the romaine, pecorino, mustard, anchovy paste, Worcestershire sauce, lemon juice, garlic, pine nuts, and pepper in a food processor. Add ¼ cup EVOO and pulse to a thick sauce, streaming in a little more EVOO if necessary. Transfer the pesto to a serving bowl and keep at room temperature.

Preheat the broiler with a rack in the center of the oven.

Make the burgers: In a large bowl, combine the chicken or turkey, Worcestershire sauce, garlic, coriander, and poultry seasoning; season with salt and pepper and mix thoroughly. Score the mixture into 4 equal portions and form them into patties slightly thinner at the center than at the edges for even cooking and to ensure a flat surface (burgers plump as they cook).

Heat the EVOO, 2 turns of the pan, in a large skillet over medium-high heat. Cook the burgers, flipping once, 10 to 12 minutes, or until the juices run clear.

While the burgers are cooking, prepare the rolls. Stir the butter and garlic together in a small bowl. Broil the rolls until lightly toasted. Brush the rolls with garlic butter and top with a generous sprinkle of pecorino and a few grinds of pepper. Turn off the oven and return the rolls to the oven for a few minutes to set the cheese while the oven cools.

Place the burgers on the roll bottoms, slather the burgers with pesto, and top with romaine. Set the roll tops in place.

CAESAR PESTO:

1 cup packed stemmed and coarsely chopped dark **romaine lettuce** leaves

A big handful of grated **pecorino cheese**

1 tablespoon **Dijon mustard**

1 rounded teaspoon **anchovy paste**

1 teaspoon **Worcestershire sauce**

Juice of 1 **lemon**

1 large clove **garlic**, grated or pasted (see Tip, page 138)

3 tablespoons **pine nuts**, toasted

Coarsely ground **pepper**

¼ to ⅓ cup **EVOO** (extra-virgin olive oil)

BURGERS:

1½ pounds **ground chicken** or **turkey** (white, dark, or a blend; see page x)

1 tablespoon **Worcestershire sauce**

1 large clove **garlic**, grated or pasted

1½ teaspoons **ground coriander**

1½ teaspoons **poultry seasoning**

Kosher salt and coarsely ground **pepper**

2 tablespoons **EVOO** (extra-virgin olive oil)

CROUTON ROLLS:

3 tablespoons **butter**, softened

1 large clove **garlic**, crushed

4 **ciabatta rolls** or other **crusty rolls**, split

Grated **pecorino Romano cheese**

Romaine lettuce leaves

SPINACH-ARTICHOKE BURGERS

SERVES 4

Preheat the broiler or toaster oven.

Heat a large skillet or griddle over medium-high heat.

In a large bowl, combine the chicken or turkey, Parmigiano-Reggiano, grated garlic, spinach, artichoke hearts, thyme, and nutmeg; season with salt and pepper and mix thoroughly. Score the mixture into 4 equal portions and form them into patties slightly thinner at the center than at the edges for even cooking and to ensure a flat surface (burgers plump as they cook).

Add 2 tablespoons EVOO, 2 turns of the pan, to the hot skillet. Cook the burgers, flipping once, 10 to 12 minutes, or until the juices run clear. Top the burgers with cheese for the last minute or two of cooking, tenting the skillet with aluminum foil, if you like, to help melt the cheese.

While the burgers are cooking, toast the rolls, then rub the cut sides with the halved garlic. Drizzle the rolls with EVOO and season with salt and pepper.

Place the burgers on the roll bottoms and set the roll tops in place.

1½ pounds **ground chicken** or **turkey**

A couple of handfuls of grated **Parmigiano-Reggiano cheese**

4 cloves **garlic**, 3 grated or finely chopped, 1 halved

1 (10-ounce) package **frozen chopped spinach**, thawed and wrung dry in a kitchen towel

1 cup **artichoke hearts** (defrosted if frozen or drained if bottled), finely chopped

2 tablespoons **fresh thyme leaves**

A few grates of **nutmeg**

Kosher salt and **pepper**

2 tablespoons **EVOO** (extra-virgin olive oil), plus more for drizzling

4 slices **fresh mozzarella** or **mild provolone cheese**

4 **ciabatta** or other **crusty rolls**, split

ONION-AND-MUSHROOM-SMOTHERED TURKEY BURGERS with SWISS

SERVES 4

Make the onions and mushrooms: Melt the butter in a skillet over medium-high heat. Add the mushrooms and cook until browned, about 5 minutes. Add the onion and thyme; season with salt and pepper. Stir and cook until softened, 8 to 10 minutes. Add the flour and stir 1 minute. Add the wine and stir until reduced by half. Stir in the stock and stir until thickened, 2 to 3 minutes. Keep warm.

Make the burgers: Heat a large skillet over medium-high heat.

In a large bowl, combine the turkey, diced Swiss cheese, poultry seasoning, mustard, and parsley; season with salt and pepper and mix thoroughly. Score the mixture into 4 equal portions and form them into patties slightly thinner at the center than at the edges for even cooking and to ensure a flat surface (burgers plump as they cook).

Add 2 tablespoons EVOO, 2 turns of the pan, to the hot skillet. Cook the burgers, flipping once, 10 to 12 minutes, or until the juices run clear. Top the burgers with sliced Swiss cheese for the last minute or two of cooking, tenting the skillet with aluminum foil, if you like, to help melt the cheese.

Place the burgers on muffin halves and smother with the onion and mushroom gravy.

ONION AND MUSHROOMS:

2 tablespoons **butter**

½ pound **button mushrooms**, thinly sliced

1 large **onion**, sliced

2 tablespoons **fresh thyme**, finely chopped

Kosher salt and **pepper**

2 tablespoons **flour**

½ cup **dry white wine**

1 cup **chicken stock**

BURGERS:

1½ pounds **ground turkey** or **turkey breast** (see page x)

¼-pound block **Swiss cheese**, **Emmentaler**, or **Jarlsberg**, cut into ¼-inch dice

2 teaspoons **poultry seasoning**

2 rounded tablespoons **Dijon mustard**

¼ cup **flat-leaf parsley** leaves, finely chopped

2 tablespoons **EVOO** (extra-virgin olive oil), plus more for drizzling

4 slices deli-sliced **Swiss cheese**

2 **sandwich-size English muffins**, split, toasted, and buttered

OPEN-FACE TURKEY BURGERS with POTPIE GRAVY

SERVES 4

Make the burgers: In a large bowl, combine the turkey, chives, dill, parsley, grated onion (grate it right over the bowl so the juices fall into the meat), and mustard; season with salt and pepper and mix thoroughly. Score the mixture into 4 equal portions and form them into patties slightly thinner at the center than at the edges for even cooking and to ensure a flat surface (burgers plump as they cook).

Heat the EVOO, 2 turns of the pan, in a large nonstick skillet over medium-high heat. Cook the burgers, flipping once, 10 to 12 minutes, or until the juices run clear.

While the burgers are cooking, make the gravy: Melt the butter in a small saucepan over medium heat. Add the shallots, carrots, and celery, and season with salt and pepper. Cook until softened, 7 to 8 minutes. Sprinkle with the flour, stir 1 minute, then whisk in the stock. Let cook until thickened, 5 to 6 minutes, then stir in the peas and heat through. (The burgers will probably finish cooking before the gravy is finished; just transfer them to a plate to rest.)

Place the burgers on muffin halves and pour the potpie gravy over the top.

BURGERS:

2 pounds **ground turkey** or **turkey breast** (see page x)

¼ cup chopped **chives**

¼ cup chopped **fresh dill**

¼ cup chopped **flat-leaf parsley**

3 to 4 tablespoons grated **onion**

2 tablespoons **Dijon mustard**

Kosher salt and **pepper**

2 tablespoons **EVOO** (extra-virgin olive oil)

POTPIE GRAVY:

3 tablespoons **butter**

2 large **shallots**, chopped

2 **carrots**, peeled and finely chopped

2 ribs **celery**, finely chopped

3 tablespoons **flour**

2 cups **chicken stock**

½ cup **frozen peas**

2 **sandwich-size English muffins**, split, toasted, and lightly buttered

TURKEY TIKKA BURGERS with INDIAN CORN

SERVES 4

These delish ears of corn would also go nicely with Indian-Spiced Patties with Yogurt Sauce (page 85), Curried Turkey Burgers (page 94), or Indian Lamb Sliders (page 161).

Make the corn: Cook the corn in a large pot of boiling water for 5 minutes. Drain the corn and melt the butter in the still-warm pot. Stir the coriander and curry powder or spice mix into the butter. Season with salt. Add the corn and toss to coat.

Make the burgers: Heat a large skillet over medium-high heat.

In a large bowl, combine the turkey, scallions, ginger, garlic, chile, cilantro, curry powder or spice mix, and yogurt; season with salt and pepper and mix thoroughly. Score the mixture into 4 equal pieces and form them into patties slightly thinner at the center than at the edges for even cooking and to ensure a flat surface (burgers plump as they cook).

Add the oil, 1 turn of the pan, to the hot skillet. Cook the burgers, flipping once, 10 to 12 minutes, or until the juices run clear.

Place the burgers on the roll bottoms and top with lettuce, tomato, onion, and cucumber. Spread the roll tops with mango chutney and set in place. Serve the spiced corn on the side.

INDIAN CORN:

4 large **ears corn**, husked

6 tablespoons **butter**

2 tablespoons **ground coriander**

2 tablespoons **curry powder** or curry spice mix (see Tip, page 94)

Kosher salt

BURGERS:

1½ pounds **ground turkey**

4 **scallions**, whites and greens, finely chopped

2-inch piece **fresh ginger**, peeled and grated

4 cloves **garlic**, finely chopped

1 **Fresno chile pepper**, finely chopped

¼ cup chopped **cilantro**

2 tablespoons **curry powder** or curry spice mix

½ cup **plain yogurt**

Pepper

1 tablespoon **vegetable oil** or **olive oil**

4 **crusty rolls**, split

TOPPINGS:

Bibb or **leaf lettuce** leaves

Sliced **vine-ripened tomato**

Sliced **red onions**

Sliced **cucumber**

Major Grey's mango chutney

MIDDLE EASTERN LAMB BURGERS with BABA GHANOUSH

SERVES 4

Make the baba ghanoush: Preheat the oven to 400°F.

Cut a few slits into the skin of the eggplant and set on a cooling rack set over a baking sheet. Roast until tender, 20 to 25 minutes. Let stand until cool enough to handle. Remove the skin and stem.

Put the flesh of the eggplant in a food processor along with the garlic, tahini, lemon juice, and a drizzle of EVOO. Puree until smooth. Season the baba ghanoush with salt and pepper.

Make the burgers: In a large bowl, combine the lamb, parsley, coriander, cumin, turmeric, and cinnamon; season with salt and pepper and mix thoroughly. Score the mixture into 4 equal portions and form them into patties slightly thinner at the center than at the edges for even cooking and to ensure a flat surface (burgers plump as they cook).

Heat the EVOO, 1 turn of the pan, in a large nonstick skillet over medium-high heat. Cook the burgers, flipping once, 10 minutes for medium (adjust the timing for rarer or more well-done burgers).

Place the burgers on the roll bottoms and top with lettuce leaves. Slather each roll top with the baba ghanoush and set the tops in place.

BABA GHANOUSH:

1 small **eggplant**

2 cloves **garlic**, grated

¼ cup **tahini paste**

Juice of 1 **lemon**

EVOO (extra-virgin olive oil)

Kosher salt and **pepper**

BURGERS:

1½ pounds **ground lamb**

¼ cup finely chopped **flat-leaf parsley**

1 tablespoon **ground coriander**

2 teaspoons **ground cumin**

2 teaspoons **ground turmeric**

A pinch of **ground cinnamon**

1 tablespoon **EVOO** (extra-virgin olive oil)

4 **crusty rolls**, split and lightly toasted

4 leaves **romaine lettuce**

TIP: Extra eggplant puree is great with pita chips.

LAMB BURGERS with WALNUT and FETA CHEESE SAUCE

SERVES 4

Make the sauce: Toast the walnuts in a skillet over medium heat until fragrant. Place the toasted nuts in a food processor with the milk, feta, oregano, and pepper. Process into a smooth sauce.

Make the burgers: Heat a large skillet over medium-high heat.

In a large bowl, combine the lamb, parsley, mint, and garlic; season with salt and pepper and mix thoroughly. Score the mixture into 4 equal portions and form them into patties slightly thinner at the center than at the edges for even cooking and to ensure a flat surface (burgers plump as they cook).

Add the EVOO, 1 turn of the pan, to the hot skillet. Cook the burgers, flipping once, 10 minutes for medium (adjust the timing for rarer or more well-done burgers).

Place the burgers on the roll bottoms and top with chopped lettuce or spinach and lots of walnut-feta sauce. Set the roll tops in place.

WALNUT-FETA SAUCE:

3 to 4 tablespoons **walnuts**

1/3 cup **milk**

3/4 cup **feta crumbles**

1 teaspoon **dried oregano**

Pepper

BURGERS:

1 1/2 pounds **ground lamb**

1/4 cup chopped **flat-leaf parsley**

1/4 cup finely chopped **mint**

4 cloves **garlic**, finely chopped

Kosher salt

1 tablespoon **EVOO** (extra-virgin olive oil)

4 **ciabatta** or other **crusty rolls**, split

Chopped **lettuce** or **spinach** leaves

THE GYRO BURGER

SERVES 4

Start the tzatziki: Sprinkle the grated cucumber with a generous amount of salt and let drain in a strainer for 20 minutes.

Make the burgers: Heat a large skillet or griddle pan over medium-high heat.

In a large bowl, combine the lamb or chicken, parsley, oregano, thyme, grated onion (grate it right over the bowl so the juices fall into the meat), garlic, coriander, red pepper flakes, cinnamon, and lemon zest; season with salt and pepper and mix thoroughly. Score the mixture into 4 equal portions and form them into patties slightly thinner at the center than at the edges for even cooking and to ensure a flat surface (burgers plump as they cook).

Add the EVOO, 2 turns of the pan, to the hot skillet. Cook the lamb burgers, flipping once, 10 minutes for medium (adjust the timing for rarer or more well-done burgers). Cook the chicken burgers, flipping once, 10 to 12 minutes, or until the juices run clear.

While the burgers are cooking, finish the tzatziki: Squeeze excess water out of the cucumber. Put the drained cucumber, yogurt, cumin, garlic, lemon juice, dill, and pepper in a food processor and pulse to combine. Adjust the seasoning with salt, if necessary, and pepper.

Place the burgers on the roll bottoms and top with lettuce, tomato, red onion, pepperoncini rings, and a dollop of tzatziki. Set the roll tops in place.

TZATZIKI:

½ **seedless cucumber**, peeled and grated

Kosher salt

1 cup **regular** or **2% Greek yogurt**

A pinch of **ground cumin**

1 large clove **garlic**, grated or minced

Juice of ½ **lemon**

2 tablespoons finely chopped **fresh dill**

Pepper

BURGERS:

2 pounds **ground lamb** or **chicken**

¼ cup finely chopped **flat-leaf parsley**

2 tablespoons chopped **fresh oregano**, or 2 teaspoons **dried oregano**

2 tablespoons chopped **fresh thyme**

¼ cup grated **onion**

4 cloves **garlic**, grated or pasted (see tip, page 138)

1 tablespoon **ground coriander**

2 teaspoons **crushed red pepper flakes**

A pinch of **ground cinnamon**

Finely grated zest of 1 **lemon**

2 tablespoons **EVOO** (extra-virgin olive oil)

4 **crusty rolls**, split

Romaine lettuce leaves

Thinly sliced **tomatoes**

Sliced **red onions**

Sliced bottled **pepperoncini** (hot Greek peppers)

SHISH KA BURGERS

SERVES 4

Heat 3 tablespoons EVOO, 3 turns of the pan, in a large skillet over medium-high heat. Add the mushrooms and cook until browned, 7 to 8 minutes. Add the bell pepper and onion, season with salt and pepper, and cook until tender-crisp, 5 to 7 minutes more. Add the sherry to deglaze the pan.

Heat a large skillet or griddle over medium-high heat. In a large bowl, combine the lamb or beef, parsley, garlic, and Worcestershire sauce; season with salt and pepper and mix thoroughly. Score the mixture into 4 equal portions and form them into patties slightly thinner at the center than at the edges for even cooking and to ensure a flat surface (burgers plump as they cook).

Add the remaining 1 tablespoon EVOO, 1 turn of the pan, to the hot skillet. Cook the burgers, flipping once, 10 minutes for medium (adjust the timing for rarer or more well-done burgers).

Place the burgers on the roll bottoms and top with mushrooms, pepper, and onion. Set the roll tops in place.

4 tablespoons **EVOO** (extra-virgin olive oil)

4 **portobello mushroom caps**, gills scraped off (see Tip, page 225), sliced

1 **green bell pepper**, seeded and sliced

1 **onion**, thinly sliced

Kosher salt and **pepper**

¼ cup **dry sherry**

1½ pounds **ground lamb** or **beef chuck**

¼ cup finely chopped **flat-leaf parsley**

4 cloves **garlic**, grated or finely chopped

3 tablespoons **Worcestershire sauce**

4 **crusty rolls**, split

BERBER BURGERS

SERVES 4

Make the eggplant: Preheat the oven to 450°F.

Poke the eggplant with the tip of a sharp knife in a few places and set on a cooling rack set over a baking sheet. Finely chop 2 large cloves of garlic and reserve. Cut the tip off the remaining head of garlic to expose the cloves; drizzle the cut side of the garlic with EVOO and season with salt and pepper. Finely chop the rosemary and press the garlic head into it to coat. Wrap the garlic head in foil and roast with the eggplant until the garlic is soft and golden and the eggplant is tender, about 35 minutes. Let the eggplant and garlic cool.

Squeeze the garlic pulp into a food processor. Cut open the eggplant and scoop the flesh into the food processor; discard the skin. Puree the garlic and eggplant with the mint and lemon juice; season with salt and pepper.

Make the burgers: In a large bowl, combine the lamb with the reserved chopped garlic, the parsley, chives, paprika or harissa, coriander, and cumin; season with salt and pepper and mix thoroughly. Score the mixture into 4 equal portions and form them into patties slightly thinner at the center than at the edges for even cooking and to ensure a flat surface (burgers plump as they cook). Heat a drizzle of EVOO in a large nonstick or cast-iron skillet over medium-high heat. Cook the burgers, flipping once, 8 minutes for rare, 10 minutes for medium. Top the burgers with the cheese during the last minute or two of cooking, tenting the skillet with aluminum foil, if you like, to help melt the cheese.

Place the burgers on the roll bottoms or on one side of the flatbreads. Top with the eggplant puree, lettuce, tomato, and onion. Set the roll tops in place or fold the flatbread over the burger.

EGGPLANT:

1 small **eggplant**

1 head **garlic**

EVOO (extra-virgin olive oil), for drizzling

Kosher salt and **pepper**

1 sprig **fresh rosemary**

A handful of **fresh mint** leaves

Juice of 1 small **lemon**

BURGERS:

1½ pounds **ground lamb**

3 tablespoons finely chopped **flat-leaf parsley**

2 tablespoons finely chopped **chives**

2 teaspoons **smoked sweet paprika** for mild burgers, or 1 tablespoon **harissa** (see Tip) for spicy burgers

1½ teaspoons **ground coriander**

1½ teaspoons **ground cumin**

EVOO (extra-virgin olive oil), for drizzling

4 slices deli-sliced **Emmentaler cheese**

4 **brioche rolls**, split, or **Mediterranean flatbreads**

Red- or **green-leaf lettuce** leaves

Sliced **tomato**

Thinly sliced **red onion**

TIP: Harissa is a thick hot sauce (sometimes with a smoky flavor) that is popular in North African cuisine.

PORTOBELLO BURGERS with SPINACH PESTO

SERVES 4

Make the spinach pesto: Place the spinach in a food processor with the walnuts, cheese, garlic, and nutmeg; season with salt and pepper. Turn on the processor and stream in enough EVOO to form a thick pesto.

Make the portobellos: Brush the portobello caps with a damp towel to clean them. In a large plastic food storage bag, combine the EVOO, Worcestershire sauce, balsamic vinegar, and rosemary. Add the mushroom caps and slush around to coat with seasonings.

Heat a grill pan or large skillet over medium-high heat. Shake the marinade off the mushrooms and cook the caps, turning once, 10 to 12 minutes, or until well browned on both sides. Season with salt and pepper. Top the caps with the mozzarella, remove the pan from the heat, and tent loosely with aluminum foil. Let stand 1 to 2 minutes to melt the cheese.

Place the mushrooms on the roll bottoms and top with pesto, a mound of baby spinach, and a few slices of red onion. Set the roll tops in place.

SPINACH PESTO:

2 packed cups **baby spinach**

¼ cup **walnut pieces**, toasted

¼ cup grated **pecorino Romano** or **Parmigiano-Reggiano cheese** (a generous handful)

1 clove **garlic**, grated or pasted (see Tip, page 138)

A few grates of **nutmeg**

Kosher salt and **pepper**

¼ to ⅓ cup **EVOO** (extra-virgin olive oil)

PORTOBELLO CAPS:

4 large **portobello mushroom caps**

¼ cup **EVOO** (extra-virgin olive oil)

2 tablespoons **Worcestershire sauce**

2 tablespoons **balsamic vinegar**

2 tablespoons finely chopped **rosemary**

½ pound **fresh mozzarella** or **smoked fresh mozzarella**, thinly sliced

4 **crusty rolls**, split

Baby spinach leaves

Thinly sliced **red onions**

FALAFEL BURGERS

SERVES 6

These patties are more tender in texture than a traditional falafel, with the same great flavors.

Preheat the oven to 300°F.

Make the burgers: Pat the chickpeas dry with paper towels and place them in a food processor. Add the onion, garlic, parsley, 3 tablespoons flour, chili powder, coriander, cumin, and turmeric; season with salt and pepper. Process until fairly smooth; the mixture should be very thick so you can form it into patties; if it is not, add the remaining 1 tablespoon flour.

Heat the oil in a large nonstick skillet or griddle over medium heat. Form the bean mixture into 6 large patties of even thickness. Cook the burgers, flipping once, for 6 minutes.

While the burgers are cooking, make the sauce: Scoop the tahini paste into a medium bowl. Whisk in 3 tablespoons water, the lemon zest, and the lemon juice; season with salt and pepper.

Cut open an edge of each pita to form a big pocket, then wrap them in foil and place them in the oven to warm for 3 minutes or so.

Open up the pitas and spoon a couple of tablespoons of tahini sauce into each. Stuff some shredded lettuce, cucumber, pepperoncini, and tomatoes into each pita. Then slide in a burger. Pass extra tahini sauce at the table.

FALAFEL BURGERS:

2 (15-ounce) cans **chickpeas**, rinsed and drained

1 small **red onion**, chopped

2 cloves **garlic**, grated or finely chopped

A large handful of **flat-leaf parsley** leaves

3 to 4 tablespoons **flour**

1 tablespoon **chili powder**

1 tablespoon **ground coriander**

1 tablespoon **ground cumin**

1½ teaspoons **ground turmeric**

Kosher salt and **pepper**

¼ cup **vegetable oil**

TAHINI SAUCE:

½ cup **tahini paste**

Grated zest and juice of 2 **lemons**

6 **sandwich-size pita pockets**

1 to 1½ cups shredded **romaine lettuce**

½ **seedless cucumber**, sliced

¼ to ½ cup (depending on how hot you like it) sliced bottled **pepperoncini** (hot Greek peppers)

2 **vine-ripened tomatoes**, sliced

MEDITERRANEAN VEGGIE BURGERS with
Provolone and Italian Ketchup
SERVES 6

Make the ketchup: In a small saucepan, combine all ketchup ingredients and bring to a bubble. Turn the heat to low, and simmer until thickened to the consistency of ketchup, 15 to 20 minutes.

Meanwhile, make the burgers: Heat 1 tablespoon EVOO, 1 turn of the pan, in a skillet over medium to medium-high heat. Add the carrot, onion, and fresh mushrooms and sauté until tender. Add the thyme and garlic, season with salt and pepper, and cook a minute or two more. Turn off the heat and cool.

Put the dried mushrooms in a food processor. Process to finely chop, then add the lentils, quinoa or couscous, chickpeas, nuts, and currants. Season with salt and pepper and add the cooked vegetables. Pulse the ingredients until well combined. Add the egg and pulse a few more times. Form 6 patties of even thickness.

Heat the remaining 2 tablespoons EVOO, 2 turns of the pan, in a large skillet over medium-high heat. Cook the burgers 5 to 6 minutes without turning, then flip and cook 2 to 3 minutes on the second side. Top the burgers with cheese for the last minute or two of cooking, tenting the skillet with aluminum foil, if you like, to help melt the cheese.

Place the burgers on roll bottoms, then top with the dressed arugula and the Italian ketchup. Set the roll tops in place.

TIP: For a vegan burger, omit the egg and cheese (or use an egg or cheese substitute), but be gentle when flipping the burgers.

ITALIAN KETCHUP:

1 cup or 1 (8-ounce) can **tomato sauce**

3 tablespoons good-quality **balsamic vinegar**

1 clove **garlic**, grated

1½ teaspoons **light brown sugar**

1 teaspoon **dried oregano**

Kosher salt and coarsely ground **pepper**

VEGGIE BURGERS:

3 tablespoons **EVOO** (extra-virgin olive oil)

1 small **carrot**, chopped

1 small **onion**, chopped

12 **fresh cremini mushrooms**, chopped

2 tablespoons chopped **fresh thyme**

4 cloves **garlic**, finely chopped

A small handful of **dried porcini mushrooms** or **mixed dried mushrooms**

2½ cups cooked **brown lentils**

1½ cups cooked **quinoa** (nuttier) or cooked **couscous** (softer)

1 cup **canned chickpeas**, rinsed and drained

¼ cup **pine nuts** or **sliced almonds**, toasted

¼ cup **dried currants** or chopped **raisins**

1 large **egg**

6 slices deli-sliced **provolone cheese**

6 **ciabatta** or other **crusty rolls**, split and lightly toasted

Arugula, dressed lightly with **lemon** juice and **EVOO**

EVERYTHING BAGEL SALMON BURGERS

SERVES 4

Make the burgers: Pulse the salmon in a food processor until finely chopped; it should look like coarse-ground beef or turkey. Transfer the salmon to a large bowl and mix in the poppy seeds, sesame seeds, onion flakes, garlic flakes, and dill; season with salt and pepper. Score the mixture into 4 equal portions and form them into patties of even thickness.

Heat a drizzle of EVOO in a large skillet over medium-high heat. Cook the burgers for 3 minutes on each side for a pink center, 4 to 5 minutes on each side for fully cooked.

While the burgers are cooking, make the sauce: In a bowl, mix together the cream cheese and the scallions. Fold in the sour cream and lemon juice.

Place the burgers on the roll bottoms and top with lettuce, tomato, and red onion. Slather the roll tops with cream cheese sauce and set in place.

BURGERS:

1½ pounds skinless **salmon fillets**, cut into large chunks

2 tablespoons **poppy seeds**

2 tablespoons **sesame seeds**

2 tablespoons **dehydrated onion flakes**

2 tablespoons **garlic flakes**

¼ cup finely chopped **fresh dill**

Kosher salt and **pepper**

EVOO (extra-virgin olive oil), for drizzling

CREAM CHEESE SAUCE:

½ cup (4 ounces) **cream cheese**, softened

3 to 4 **scallions**, whites and greens, finely chopped

½ cup **sour cream**

1 tablespoon fresh **lemon** juice

4 **poppy seed kaiser rolls**, split and toasted

Green-leaf lettuce leaves

Sliced **beefsteak tomato**

Sliced **red onion**

SALMON BURGERS
with TARTAR SAUCE

SERVES 4

Make the sauce: In a small bowl, mix together the mayo, pickles, capers, dill, lemon juice, hot sauce, and Worcestershire sauce; season with salt and pepper.

Make the burgers: Pulse the salmon with ¼ cup of the tartar sauce in a food processor until finely chopped and combined. Transfer the salmon mixture to a bowl and mix in the cracker crumbs and Old Bay. Score the mixture into 4 equal portions and form them into patties of even thickness.

Heat the oil, 2 turns of the pan, in a large skillet over medium-high heat. Cook the burgers, turning occasionally, 6 to 8 minutes, for barely pink centers, 2 minutes more for fully cooked burgers.

Place the burgers on the roll bottoms and top with lettuce, tomato, and onion. Slather the roll tops with tartar sauce and set them in place.

TARTAR SAUCE:

1 cup **mayo** or **vegan mayo**

3 tablespoons finely chopped **gherkins** or **cornichons**

2 tablespoons **capers**, chopped

3 tablespoons finely chopped **fresh dill**

1 tablespoon fresh **lemon** juice

1 teaspoon **hot sauce**

1 teaspoon **Worcestershire sauce**

Kosher salt and **pepper**

SALMON BURGERS:

1½ pounds skinless **salmon fillets**, cut into 2-inch cubes

A handful of **cracker crumbs** or **fine dry breadcrumbs**

2 teaspoons **Old Bay seasoning**

2 tablespoons **olive oil**

4 crusty **burger rolls**, split

Shredded lettuce

Sliced **tomato**

Sliced **red onion**

OPEN-FACE SALMON BURGERS with HONEY MUSTARD

SERVES 4

In a small bowl, stir together the mustard and honey.

Pulse the salmon in a food processor until finely chopped; it should look like coarse-ground beef or turkey. Transfer the salmon to a bowl and add 2 tablespoons of the honey-mustard, the chives, Old Bay, and lemon zest; season with salt and pepper and mix thoroughly. Score the mixture into 4 equal portions and form them into patties of even thickness.

Heat the EVOO, 1 turn of the pan, in a large skillet or griddle over medium-high heat. Cook the burgers for 3 minutes on each side for a pink center, 4 to 5 minutes on each side for fully cooked.

Place the burgers on a muffin half and spoon some of the remaining honey-mustard over each. Top with cucumbers, red onion, and watercress.

½ cup **Dijon mustard**

3 tablespoons **honey**

1½ pounds skinless **salmon fillets**, cut into large chunks

¼ cup finely chopped **chives**

1 tablespoon **Old Bay seasoning**

2 teaspoons grated **lemon** zest

Kosher salt and **pepper**

1 tablespoon **EVOO** (extra-virgin olive oil)

2 **sandwich-size sourdough English muffins**, split, toasted, and buttered

Thinly sliced **cucumbers**

Thinly sliced **red onion**

Watercress leaves

GARLIC-GINGER SALMON BURGERS with WASABI MAYO

SERVES 4

Pulse the salmon in a food processor until finely ground; it should look like coarse-ground beef or turkey. Transfer the salmon to a bowl and add the garlic, ginger, tamari, scallions, and sesame oil; season with salt and pepper and mix thoroughly. Score the mixture into 4 equal portions and form them into patties of even thickness.

Heat the oil, 1 turn of the pan, in a large skillet over medium-high heat. Cook the burgers, flipping once, 6 minutes for medium-rare and up to 10 minutes for fully cooked.

While the burgers are cooking, make the mayo: Stir the wasabi paste, mayo, and lime juice together in a small bowl.

Place the burgers on the roll bottoms; top with lettuce, pickled ginger, and cucumber. Slather the roll tops with the mayo and set in place.

1½ pounds skinless **salmon fillets**, cut into large chunks

3 cloves **garlic**, finely chopped or grated

1-inch piece **fresh ginger**, peeled and grated

3 tablespoons **tamari** or **soy sauce**

3 to 4 **scallions**, whites and greens, finely chopped

2 teaspoons **dark sesame oil**

Sea salt and **pepper**

1 tablespoon **vegetable oil**

2 teaspoons **wasabi paste**

½ cup **mayo** or **vegan mayo**

Juice of 1 **lime**

4 **sesame kaiser rolls**, split and toasted

Bibb lettuce leaves

Pickled ginger slices

Sliced **seedless cucumber**

FRENCH TUNA BURGERS

SERVES 4

Pulse the tuna in a food processor until finely chopped. Transfer the tuna to a bowl and add the parsley, rosemary, thyme, lemon zest, fennel seeds, and red pepper flakes; season with salt and pepper and mix thoroughly. Score the mixture into 4 equal portions and form them into patties of even thickness.

Puree the olives, capers, vinegar, anchovies, and 4 tablespoons EVOO in a food processor to make a tapenade.

Heat the remaining 1 tablespoon EVOO, 1 turn of the pan, in a large nonstick skillet over medium-high heat. Cook the burgers, flipping once, 6 minutes for medium rare and up to 10 minutes for fully cooked.

Place the burger on the roll bottoms; top with lettuce, tomato, and onion. Spread the olive tapenade on the roll tops and set in place.

$1\frac{1}{2}$ pounds skinless **tuna steaks**, trimmed of dark meat and cut into large chunks

$\frac{1}{4}$ cup finely chopped **flat-leaf parsley**

2 tablespoons finely chopped **fresh rosemary**

2 tablespoons finely chopped **fresh thyme**

1 teaspoon grated **lemon** zest

1 teaspoon **fennel seeds**

1 teaspoon **crushed red pepper flakes**

Kosher salt and pepper

$\frac{1}{2}$ cup pitted **niçoise olives**

3 tablespoons **capers**

1 tablespoon **white wine vinegar**

4 **anchovy fillets**

5 tablespoons **EVOO** (extra-virgin olive oil), plus more for drizzling

4 **crusty rolls**, split

8 leaves **green-leaf lettuce**

Sliced **tomato**

Thinly sliced **red onion**

SICILIAN-STYLE TUNA or SWORDFISH BURGERS

SERVES 4

Pulse the fish cubes in a food processor until finely chopped. Transfer to a large bowl and add the garlic and red pepper flakes; season with salt and pepper and mix thoroughly. Score the mixture into 4 equal portions and form them into patties of even thickness.

Grate the zest from the lemon. In a shallow bowl, mix together ¼ cup of the parsley, the lemon zest, and panko. Press the burgers in the seasoned crumbs to coat them completely.

Heat a thin layer of EVOO in a large skillet over medium to medium-high heat. Cook tuna burgers, turning once, 8 minutes, or until golden brown and slightly pink at the center. Cook swordfish burgers, turning once, 10 to 12 minutes, or until cooked through. Squeeze the juice of ½ lemon over the patties just before removing them from the skillet.

In a medium bowl, combine the remaining ¼ cup parsley, the tomatoes, capers, red onion, and basil. Drizzle with EVOO and season with salt and pepper.

Place the burgers on the roll bottoms and top with tomato relish. Set the roll tops in place.

1½ pounds skinless **tuna** or **swordfish steaks**, trimmed of any dark-colored meat and cut into 2-inch cubes

4 cloves **garlic**, grated or finely chopped

1 teaspoon **crushed red pepper flakes**

Kosher salt and **pepper**

1 **lemon**

½ cup finely chopped **flat-leaf parsley**

1½ cups **panko breadcrumbs**

EVOO (extra-virgin olive oil) or vegetable oil, for shallow frying and drizzling

2 **vine-ripened** or **plum tomatoes**, seeded and chopped

3 tablespoons **capers**

¼ cup finely chopped **red onion**

A small handful of **basil** leaves, thinly sliced

4 **ciabatta rolls** or other **crusty rolls**, split

FRESH TUNA FRENCH-STYLE CHEESEBURGERS

SERVES 4

Some people call fennel pollen the "spice of angels." It has a flavor that is sweet and intense. If you can't find fennel pollen, you may substitute ground fennel seeds.

Heat 1 tablespoon EVOO, 1 turn of the pan, in a small skillet over medium heat. Add the chopped shallot and garlic and cook 1 minute to soften. Season with salt and pepper. Cool completely.

Pulse the tuna in a food processor until finely ground. Transfer to a bowl and add the cooled shallot and garlic, the herbes de Provence (or fresh herbs), fennel pollen, and celery seeds; season with salt and pepper and mix thoroughly. Score the mixture into 4 equal portions and form them into patties of even thickness.

Heat the remaining 1 tablespoon EVOO, 1 turn of the pan, in a large skillet over medium-high. Cook the burgers, turning once, 6 minutes for medium-rare and up to 10 minutes for fully cooked. Top the burgers with cheese after they are flipped, tenting the pan with aluminum foil, if you like, to help melt the cheese.

While the burgers are cooking, combine the mustard or Dijonnaise and capers in a small bowl.

Place the burgers on the roll bottoms and top with toppings of choice. Slather the mustard-caper sauce on the roll tops and set in place.

2 tablespoons **EVOO** (extra-virgin olive oil)

1 large **shallot**, finely chopped

2 cloves **garlic**, finely chopped

Kosher salt and **pepper**

1½ pounds skinless **tuna steak**, dark meat trimmed, cut into large chunks

1 tablespoon **herbes de Provence**, or 3 tablespoons chopped **mixed fresh herbs**, such as parsley, sage, rosemary, and thyme

1 teaspoon **fennel pollen** (see headnote)

1 teaspoon **celery seeds**

⅓ pound **Gruyère cheese**, sliced or shredded

½ cup **Dijon mustard** or **Dijonnaise**

2 tablespoons nonpareil **capers** or chopped capers

4 **brioche rolls**, split

TOPPINGS:

Celery leaves

Torn **flat-leaf parsley, basil,** or **tarragon leaves**

Sliced **tomato**

Sliced **cornichons**

Sliced **shallot**

SHRIMP BURGERS

SERVES 4

Pulse half the shrimp in a food processor and grind them up. Transfer the ground shrimp to a bowl. Add the remaining whole shrimp to the ground shrimp. Put the empty food processor bowl back in place and add the celery, onion, bell pepper, garlic, and parsley; pulse-grind the mixture until finely chopped. Add the vegetable mixture to the shrimp along with the Old Bay, chili powder, cayenne, and lemon zest; season with salt and pepper and mix thoroughly.

Heat the EVOO, 2 turns of the pan, in a large non-stick skillet over medium to medium-high heat. Use a large metal ice cream scoop to scoop 4 mounds of shrimp-burger mixture into the pan. Gently pat down the mounds to form burgers. Fry the burgers until they firm up and the shrimp turn whitish-pink, 3 to 5 minutes on each side.

While the burgers are cooking, in a small bowl, mix together the mayo and chili sauce.

Place the burgers on the muffin bottoms and top with lettuce. Slather the muffin tops with sauce and set in place.

1 pound raw peeled small or extra small **shrimp**

1 small rib **celery**, from the heart

½ small **yellow onion**, cut into chunks

½ small **green bell pepper**, seeded and cut into pieces

1 clove **garlic**

A handful of **flat-leaf parsley** leaves

1 tablespoon **Old Bay seasoning**

1 teaspoon **chili powder**

½ teaspoon **cayenne pepper**

Grated zest of 1 **lemon**

Kosher salt and **pepper**

2 tablespoons **EVOO** (extra-virgin olive oil)

¼ cup **mayo**

¼ cup **chili sauce** (such as Heinz), **salsa**, or **taco sauce**

4 **sandwich-size English muffins**, plain or sourdough flavor, split and toasted

Bibb lettuce leaves or chopped **iceberg lettuce**

TIP: This shrimp burger mixture is looser than most burger mixes. Using a scoop to form the patties right in the pan cuts down on mess.

SLIDERS

BEEF, PORK (and 1 LAMB!) SLIDERS

131 Bife de Chorizo Sliders

132 Beer and Beef Chili Sliders on Bacon Biscuits with Tomatillo Ketchup

135 Bistro Sliders à la Rachael

136 BL(FG)T Sliders

139 Bourbon Barbecue Sliced Steak Sliders

141 Brooklyn Beer Chili Sliders with Smoky BBQ Sauce, Oil-and-Vinegar Slaw, and Sweet 'n' Spicy Pickles

143 Jalapeño Popper Sliders

144 Green and Red Chili Nacho Sliders

146 Mac 'n' Cheese-Burger Sliders

147 Slider Salad with Yellow Mustard Vinaigrette

148 Pimiento Cheese Sliders

149 Poblano Popper Super-Sliders

150 South by Southwest 7-Layer Sliders

152 Cheeseburger Egg Rolls with Russian Dressing Dipper

153 St. Paddy's–Style Reuben Sliders

154 Sliced Steak Soft Taco Sliders with Guaca-Salsa

156 Chorizo Sliders

157 BBQ "Bun"-Mi Sliders

158 Mexican Pulled Pork Sliders

160 I'll Have What Charlie's Having Sliders

161 Indian Lamb Sliders with Green Raita Sauce and Red Onions

CHICKEN AND TURKEY SLIDERS

162 Satay Sliders

163 Chicken and Biscuit Sliders with Spicy Orange-Maple Drizzle and Crunchy Oil-and-Vinegar Slaw

165 Fried Chicken and Biscuit Sliders with Smoky Chard

166 Buffalo Turkey Sliders

167 Deluxe Turkey Club Sliders

168 Club Burger Sliders with Avocado-Ranch Dressing

SEAFOOD SLIDERS

171 Black Sesame and Panko–Crusted Tuna Sliders

173 5-Spice Tuna Sliders with Hoisin

BIFE DE CHORIZO SLIDERS

MAKES 8 SLIDERS

This is my take on the classic Argentinean dish *bife de chorizo*. Top this slider with chimichurri, the condiment of all condiments in Argentina!

Make the chimichurri: Pulse together the garlic, herbs, and vinegar in a food processor until finely chopped. With the machine on, pour in the EVOO. Remove to a bowl.

Make the sliders: Pulse-chop the chorizo in the food processor until finely ground. Heat a griddle, large skillet, or grill pan over medium-high heat. In a large bowl, combine the beef and chorizo; season with salt and pepper and mix thoroughly. Score the mixture into 4 equal portions, then form each portion into 2 patties slightly thinner at the center than at the edges for even cooking and to ensure a flat surface (burgers plump as they cook). Drizzle with EVOO.

Cook the sliders 3 minutes, then flip and cook 2 minutes on the second side for medium (adjust the timing for rarer or more well-done sliders).

Place the sliders on the roll bottoms and top with lots of chimichurri, diced tomatoes, and chopped onions. Set the roll tops in place.

CHIMICHURRI:

2 large cloves **garlic**, grated or minced

½ cup chopped **flat-leaf parsley**

2 to 3 tablespoons chopped **mixed fresh herbs**—your choice, but try to use at least three of these: **oregano, thyme, rosemary,** and **sage**

3 tablespoons **white wine vinegar**

⅓ cup **EVOO** (extra-virgin olive oil)

SLIDERS:

½ pound **Spanish chorizo**, casings removed

1 pound **lean ground beef chuck**

Kosher salt and **pepper**

EVOO (extra-virgin olive oil), for drizzling

8 **brioche dinner rolls** or 8 **slider rolls**, split

Diced, seeded **plum tomatoes**

Finely chopped **onion**

BEER and BEEF CHILI SLIDERS ON BACON BISCUITS with TOMATILLO KETCHUP

MAKES 8 SLIDERS

2 poblano chiles

BISCUITS:

8 slices **bacon**, chopped

1 (8-ounce) box **Jiffy buttermilk biscuit mix**

1 cup shredded **sharp yellow cheddar cheese**

¼ cup chopped **chives**

¼ cup **yellow mustard**

2 tablespoons **honey**

KETCHUP:

6 **tomatillos**, husked, rinsed, and coarsely chopped

1 small **red onion**, chopped

2 cloves **garlic**, chopped

Kosher salt and **pepper**

2 tablespoons **cilantro** leaves

1 teaspoon grated zest plus the juice of 1 **lime**

Preheat the broiler.

Halve the poblanos and seed them. Place them skin side up on a baking sheet and blacken them under broiler with the oven door ajar to let steam escape. (Or leave the poblanos whole and char them over an open flame on a stovetop burner.) Change the oven setting to 425°F. Place the charred peppers in a bowl, cover with plastic wrap, and cool. When cool enough to handle, peel (and seed if charred whole).

Meanwhile, make the biscuits: Cook the bacon in a medium skillet over medium-high heat until crisp, about 7 minutes. Drain the bacon, reserving about 2 tablespoons of the bacon fat.

In a large bowl, combine the biscuit mix with ½ cup water and stir until a dough forms. Mix in the cheddar, chives, mustard, honey, bacon, and reserved bacon fat. Spoon 8 equal mounds (2 to 2½ inches high) of the biscuit dough onto a baking sheet and bake until golden, 10 minutes. Let cool on the pan for 2 minutes, then transfer to a rack to cool completely. Split.

While the biscuits are cooling, make the ketchup: In a medium saucepan, combine the tomatillos, onion, and garlic; season with salt and pepper. Cook over medium-high heat until the onion and tomatillos have mellowed, 10 to 12 minutes. Cool a little. Puree the tomatillo mixture, roasted poblanos, cilantro, lime zest, and lime juice in a food processor; season with salt and pepper.

Make the sliders: In a large bowl, combine the beef, beer, Worcestershire sauce, chili powder, grill seasoning, paprika, cumin, coriander, and oregano. Score the mixture into 4 equal portions, then form each portion into 2 patties about ½ inch thick and slightly thinner at the center than at the edges for even cooking and to ensure a flat surface (burgers plump as they cook). Drizzle the patties with EVOO.

Heat a large nonstick skillet or grill pan over medium-high heat. Cook the sliders, flipping once, 5 minutes for medium-rare (adjust the timing for rarer or more well-done sliders).

Top each biscuit bottom with a little shredded lettuce, a slider, and some tomatillo ketchup. Set the biscuit tops in place and secure with toothpicks.

SLIDERS:

1½ pounds **ground beef chuck**

½ cup **beer**

¼ cup **Worcestershire sauce**

2 tablespoons **chili powder**

2 tablespoons **grill seasoning**, such as McCormick Montreal Steak Seasoning

1 tablespoon **smoked sweet paprika**

1 tablespoon **ground cumin**

1 tablespoon **ground coriander**

1 teaspoon **dried oregano**

EVOO (extra-virgin olive oil), for drizzling

Shredded lettuce

BISTRO SLIDERS À LA RACHAEL

MAKES 12 SLIDERS

Serve with a spinach or green salad with Dijon vinaigrette.

Get started on the Oven Fries. While the fries are in the oven for the first time, make the Fry Dipper and the onion topping.

Make the onion topping: Melt the butter in a skillet over medium heat. Add the onions, garlic, and thyme and season with salt and pepper. Cook 30 minutes, stirring occasionally. Be careful not to brown the onions too fast—you want them to be very soft and caramel in color. Deglaze with the sherry, then stir in enough stock to keep the onions wet. Reduce the heat to low and keep warm.

While the fries are in the oven for the second time, make the sliders: Season the beef with salt and pepper and mix thoroughly. Score the mixture into 4 equal portions, then form each portion into 3 patties, making them thinner at the center than at the edges for even cooking and to ensure a flat surface (burgers plump as they cook). Drizzle the patties with EVOO.

Heat a cast-iron pan or griddle over medium-high heat. Cook the sliders, turning once, 5 to 6 minutes for medium-rare, a few minutes longer for medium-well. Top the sliders with cheese for the last minute or two of cooking, tenting the pan with aluminum foil, if you like, to help melt the cheese.

Place the sliders on the roll bottoms and top with onions, fries, and horseradish fry dipper. Set the roll tops in place.

Double-Baked Crazy-Crisp Oven Fries (page 244)

Horseradish and Sour Cream Fry Dipper (page 271)

FRENCH ONION TOPPING:

2 tablespoons **butter**

2 large **onions**, thinly sliced

2 cloves **garlic**, finely chopped

½ teaspoon **ground thyme**

Kosher salt and **pepper**

¼ cup **dry sherry**

About ½ cup **beef stock**

SLIDERS:

2 pounds **ground beef chuck**

EVOO (extra-virgin olive oil), for drizzling

12 (2-inch square) slices deli-sliced **Gruyère** or **Swiss cheese**

12 **brioche dinner rolls** or other **slider rolls**, split

BL(FG)T SLIDERS

MAKES 8 SLIDERS

I've added the crunchy goodness of a fried green tomato to this BLT burger slider—get it? BL(FG)T?

Preheat the oven to 375°F with a rack in the center position.

Arrange the bacon on a slotted broiler pan or a cooling rack set over a baking sheet and bake until crisp, 15 to 18 minutes. Let cool.

Meanwhile, make the FGT: Trim the tops and bottoms of the tomatoes and cut into 4 slices each, no more than ½ inch thick. Salt the sliced tomatoes on each side and drain on a doubled paper towel for a few minutes, then season with a little pepper.

Line up 3 shallow bowls on the counter: Spread some flour out in one; beat the eggs (or whites) in the second; and mix the breadcrumbs, cornmeal, Parmesan, and parsley together in the third. Coat the tomato slices in the flour, then in egg, and finally in the breadcrumb mixture, pressing to make sure the coating sticks. Heat ⅛ inch of oil in a large skillet over medium to medium-high heat. Cook the tomato slices until golden and crisp, a few minutes on each side. Cool on a cooling rack.

Make the sliders: Heat a large griddle or skillet over medium-high heat. In a large bowl, combine the beef,

(CONTINUED ON PAGE 138)

8 slices smoky **bacon**, halved crosswise

FGT:

2 **green** or very firm **underripe tomatoes**

Kosher salt and **pepper**

Flour

2 large **eggs** or **egg whites**

½ cup **fine dry breadcrumbs**

⅓ cup **cornmeal**

⅓ cup grated **Parmesan cheese**

A handful of **flat-leaf parsley**, finely chopped

Canola oil or **light olive oil**, for shallow frying

SLIDERS:

1½ pounds **ground beef chuck**

3 to 4 tablespoons grated **onion**

2 tablespoons **hot sauce**, such as Frank's RedHot

2 tablespoons **Worcestershire sauce**

Canola oil or **light olive oil**, for drizzling

grated onion (grate it right over the bowl so the juices fall in the meat), hot sauce, and Worcestershire sauce; season with salt and pepper and mix thoroughly. Score the mixture into 4 equal portions, then form each portion into 2 patties slightly thinner at the center than at the edges for even cooking and to ensure a flat surface (burgers plump as they cook). Drizzle the patties with a little oil. Cook the sliders a couple of minutes on each side, or until done to your taste.

While the sliders are cooking, make the sauce: In a small bowl, stir together the sour cream, garlic, chives, and lemon juice; season with salt, pepper, and a dash or two of hot sauce, if you like.

Place the sliders on the roll bottoms and top with 2 pieces of bacon, lettuce, a slice of fried green tomato, and sour cream sauce. Set the roll tops in place.

SOUR CREAM SAUCE:

1 cup **sour cream**

1 clove **garlic**, grated or pasted (see Tip)

A few tablespoons minced **chives**

Juice of ½ **lemon**

Hot sauce (optional)

8 **slider rolls** or **brioche dinner rolls**, split

Tender lettuce leaves, such as Bibb or butter

TIP: To make "pasted" garlic, first give your garlic a rough chop and then sprinkle with a little bit of coarse salt. Hold your knife at a 45-degree angle (almost horizontal to the cutting board) and chop while mashing the garlic and salt together at the same time.

BOURBON BARBECUE SLICED STEAK SLIDERS

MAKES 12 SLIDERS

Make the BBQ sauce: Combine all the sauce ingredients in a medium skillet and bring to a low bubble. Simmer gently 20 minutes to reduce.

Meanwhile, make the steaks: Drizzle the steaks lightly with vegetable oil and season with salt and pepper. Bring to room temperature.

Heat a large cast-iron skillet, griddle, or grill pan over medium-high to high heat. Cook the steaks 4 minutes on each side for medium-rare (adjust the timing for rarer or more well-done steaks). Transfer to a cutting board and let rest 5 to 10 minutes.

Thinly slice the meat on an angle against the grain and add to the skillet with the BBQ sauce. Stir in ½ cup beef stock and warm through. If the mixture is too thick for you, add more beef stock a little at a time.

Spoon the sliced steak and sauce over the roll bottoms. Set the tops in place.

BOURBON BBQ SAUCE:

2 shots good-quality **bourbon**

1 cup good-quality **ketchup**, such as Heinz Organic

2 large cloves **garlic**, finely chopped

2 tablespoons **dark brown sugar**

2 tablespoons **dark amber maple syrup**

2 tablespoons **Worcestershire sauce**

2 tablespoons **cider vinegar**

1 teaspoon **ground cumin**

Pinch of **ground cloves** or **allspice**

Coarsely ground **pepper**

STEAKS:

1½ pounds **flat iron steaks** or **flank steak**

Vegetable oil, for drizzling

Kosher salt and **pepper**

½ to ¾ cup **beef stock**

12 soft **slider rolls**, split

BROOKLYN BEER CHILI SLIDERS with Smoky BBQ Sauce, Oil-and-Vinegar Slaw, and Sweet 'n' Spicy Pickles

MAKES 12 SLIDERS

I fell in love with this burger when I created it for the Brooklyn Block Party I threw one summer—and I've been in love with it ever since. It has my almost-famous smoky BBQ sauce and my sweet 'n' spicy pickles, which I can eat on just about anything. I also served it up to more than three thousand people at the 2012 Burger Bash at the South Beach Wine and Food Festival!

Make the pickles: Bring the vinegar, 1/3 cup water, the sugar, salt, peppercorns, garlic, and bay leaves to a boil in a small saucepan. Reduce the heat to low and simmer 5 minutes.

Put the chile, cucumbers, onion, and dill in a small food storage container and sprinkle in the mustard seeds and coriander seeds. Pour the hot brine over the pickles. Cool, cover, and chill overnight, shaking every once in a while.

When you are ready to make the sliders, make the slaw: In a bowl, combine the cabbage, onion, vinegar, and oil; season with celery salt and salt and pepper. Toss until the cabbage is coated.

Make the BBQ sauce: In a small saucepan, combine all sauce ingredients and cook over medium-low heat to thicken and combine flavors, 15 to 20 minutes.

(CONTINUED ON NEXT PAGE)

SWEET 'N' SPICY PICKLES:

2 cups **white balsamic** or **cider vinegar**

1/2 cup **sugar**

2 teaspoons **sea salt**

1 teaspoon **black peppercorns**

1 large clove **garlic**, halved

2 **bay leaves**

1 small **fresh red chile**, such as Fresno, sliced

4 **Kirby cucumbers**, sliced 1/8 to 1/4 inch thick

1/2 small **red onion**, thinly sliced

A few sprigs **fresh dill**

1 teaspoon **mustard seeds**

1 teaspoon **coriander seeds**

OIL-AND-VINEGAR SLAW:

1/2 pound **red cabbage**, shredded

1/2 small **red onion**, very thinly sliced

3 tablespoons **cider vinegar**

3 tablespoons **vegetable oil**

Celery salt

Kosher salt and **pepper**

Meanwhile, make the sliders: Heat a large cast-iron pan, griddle, or grill pan over medium-high to high heat. In a large bowl, combine the beef, Worcestershire sauce, marjoram, thyme, chile powder, and beer; season with grill seasoning or with salt and pepper and mix thoroughly. Divide into 4 equal portions, then form each portion into 3 equal patties thinner at the center than at the edges for even cooking and to ensure a flat surface (burgers plump as they cook). Drizzle the patties with oil. Cook the sliders for a few minutes on each side, or until done to your taste. Baste liberally with the barbecue sauce during the last minute of cooking.

Place the sliders on the roll bottoms and top with a little slaw and a slice of pickle. Set the roll tops in place. Pass the rest of the pickles at the table.

SMOKY BBQ SAUCE:

1 cup good-quality **ketchup**, such as Heinz Organic

2 large cloves **garlic**, finely chopped

2 tablespoons **dark brown sugar**

2 tablespoons **dark amber maple syrup**

2 tablespoons **Worcestershire sauce**

1½ tablespoons **cider vinegar**

1 teaspoon **smoked sweet paprika**

Coarsely ground **pepper**

CHILI SLIDERS:

2 pounds **ground beef chuck**

¼ cup **Worcestershire sauce**

1 teaspoon **dried marjoram** or **Mexican oregano**

1 teaspoon **dried thyme**

2 tablespoons **ancho chile powder**

½ cup **Brooklyn Ale** or other **beer** of choice

Grill seasoning, such as McCormick Montreal Steak Seasoning, or **kosher salt** and **coarsely ground pepper**

Vegetable oil or **olive oil**, for drizzling

12 **slider rolls**, split

JALAPEÑO POPPER SLIDERS

MAKES 12 SLIDERS

Cut the tops off the jalapeños and, using an apple corer or fork handle, scoop out the seeds. Slice the chiles into $1/8$- to $1/4$-inch rings.

Heat 1 tablespoon oil, 1 turn of the pan, in a small skillet over medium-high heat. Add the jalapeño and Fresno chiles to the pan and toss for a couple of minutes to char the edges. The chiles should remain tender-crisp.

While the chiles are cooking, in a small bowl, stir together the cream cheese, onion, garlic, cumin, and cilantro; season with salt and pepper. Set aside.

Season the beef with salt and pepper and mix thoroughly. Score the mixture into 4 equal portions, then form each portion into 3 patties thinner at the center than at the edges for even cooking and to ensure a flat surface (burgers plump as they cook). Drizzle the patties with oil.

Heat a grill pan, large nonstick skillet, or griddle over medium-high heat. Cook the sliders for 2 to 3 minutes. Flip the sliders and top with a spoonful of the cream cheese mixture, setting the mixture in place by topping with a slice of cheddar. Cook for 2 to 3 minutes more (or until done to your taste), tenting the pan with aluminum foil, if you like, to melt the cheddar.

Place the sliders on the roll bottoms and top with the charred chile slices. Set the roll tops in place.

3 large **jalapeño chiles**

1 tablespoon **EVOO** (extra-virgin olive oil) or **vegetable oil**, plus more for drizzling

1 **Fresno chile pepper**, cut into $1/8$- to $1/4$-inch slices

8 ounces **cream cheese**, softened

2 tablespoons grated **yellow onion**

1 large clove **garlic**, grated or minced

$1/2$ teaspoon **ground cumin**

A small handful of **cilantro** leaves, finely chopped

Kosher salt and **pepper**

2 pounds **coarse-ground beef chuck** (see Tip, page 6)

12 (2-inch square) slices **sharp yellow cheddar** or **smoked yellow cheddar cheese**

12 (3-inch) **brioche dinner rolls** or cornmeal-topped **dinner rolls**, split

GREEN and RED CHILE NACHO SLIDERS

MAKES 8 SLIDERS

You can find Mexican cheeses that are great for melting, such as *queso blanco* or Chihuahua cheese, in the refrigerated Latin foods section of your grocery store.

Preheat the broiler.

Make the red chile paste: Process the chiles, onion, garlic, cilantro, and bay leaves to a paste in a food processor. Scrape into a bowl and reserve. Return the processor bowl to the base. Do not rinse.

Make the green chile sauce: Halve the poblanos and seed them. Place them skin side up on a baking sheet and blacken them under the broiler with the oven door ajar to let steam escape. (Or leave the poblanos whole and char them over an open flame on a stovetop burner.) Place the charred peppers in a bowl, cover with plastic wrap, and cool. When cool enough to handle, peel and seed the peppers.

Meanwhile, heat a good drizzle of oil in a skillet over medium-high heat. Add the tomatillos, onion, and garlic and cook until the onions are tender, 8 to 10 minutes. Transfer the onions and tomatillos to the food processor bowl and add the peeled poblanos, cilantro, cumin, honey or agave nectar, and lime juice. Process until smooth and season with salt.

Make the sliders: Heat a griddle or large cast-iron skillet over medium-high heat. In a large bowl, combine the beef, pork, and red chile paste; season with salt and pepper and mix thoroughly. Score the mixture into 4 equal portions, then form each portion into 2 patties thinner at the center than at the edges for even cooking and to ensure a flat surface (burgers plump as they cook). Add a drizzle of oil to the hot pan. Cook the sliders about 3 minutes on each side, or until done to your taste.

RED CHILE PASTE:

2 **fresh red chiles**, such as Fresno, sliced

1 small **red onion**, coarsely chopped

2 large cloves **garlic**

Generous handful of **cilantro** leaves

2 **fresh bay leaves**

GREEN CHILE SAUCE:

2 large **poblano chiles**

Vegetable oil, for drizzling

5 to 6 **tomatillos**, husked, rinsed, and coarsely chopped

1 small **onion**, chopped

2 cloves **garlic**, chopped or sliced

Small handful of **cilantro** leaves, chopped

1 teaspoon **ground cumin**

2 teaspoons **honey** or **agave nectar**

Juice of 1 **lime**

Kosher salt

While the sliders are cooking, heat the refried beans in a small skillet over medium heat with a splash of water to thin them out a bit.

While still in the pan, top the burgers with the green chile sauce and a few chips each. Top the chips with refried beans and shredded cheese and a pickled jalapeño slice or two. Tent the pan with foil to help melt cheese and cook for 1 minute.

Place the sliders on the roll bottoms. Set the tops in place

SLIDERS:

1 pound **ground beef chuck**

½ pound **ground pork**

Pepper

Vegetable oil, for drizzling

1 (16-ounce) can **spicy vegetarian refried beans**

Good-quality **tortilla chips**

1 cup shredded mild **Mexican melting cheese** (see headnote), **Monterey Jack**, or **cheddar cheese**

Pickled jalapeño slices

8 **slider** or **brioche dinner rolls**, split

MAC 'N' CHEESE-BURGER SLIDERS

MAKES 12 SLIDERS

Bring a medium pot of water to a boil.

Meanwhile, make the sliders: In a large bowl, combine the beef, Worcestershire sauce, parsley, garlic, onion (grate it right over the bowl so the juices fall into the meat); season with some salt and lots of pepper and mix thoroughly. Score the mixture into 4 equal portions, then form each portion into 3 patties slightly thinner at the center than at the edges for even cooking and to ensure a flat surface (burgers plump as they cook). Drizzle the patties with EVOO.

Make the mac 'n' cheese: Salt the pasta water, add the pasta, and undercook by a minute or so from package directions, just shy of al dente. Drain and reserve.

While the pasta is cooking, melt the butter in a medium saucepan over medium heat, then sprinkle in the flour and whisk 30 seconds. Whisk in the milk and season the sauce with the nutmeg, salt, and pepper. Bring to a bubble and cook to thicken, 3 to 4 minutes. Stir the cheeses into the sauce to melt, then turn off the heat and stir in the mustard. Fold in the drained reserved macaroni.

Heat a cast-iron skillet or large griddle over medium-high heat. Cook the sliders for 3 minutes on each side for medium (adjust the timing time for rarer or more well-done sliders).

Place the sliders on the bun bottoms and top with mac 'n' cheese and a dot of ketchup or some Bacon Tomato Jam, if you wish. Secure the bun tops with toothpicks and anchor a pickle slice atop the burgers for a cheeky presentation.

SLIDERS:

2 pounds **ground beef chuck**

¼ cup **Worcestershire sauce**

A scant handful of **flat-leaf parsley**, very finely chopped

2 cloves **garlic**, minced, very finely chopped, or pasted (see Tip, page 138)

3 to 4 tablespoons grated **onion**

Kosher salt and coarsely ground **pepper**

EVOO (extra-virgin olive oil), for drizzling

MAC 'N' CHEESE:

½ pound small **elbow macaroni, ditalini**, or small **whole wheat elbow macaroni**

2 tablespoons **butter**

2 tablespoons **flour**

1¼ cups **milk**

A few grates of **nutmeg**

1 cup shredded **sharp yellow** or **white cheddar cheese**

½ cup shredded **Gruyère** or **Swiss cheese**

¼ cup grated **Parmigiano-Reggiano cheese** (about a handful)

1 rounded tablespoon **Dijon mustard**

12 **slider rolls** or **brioche dinner rolls**, split

Good-quality **ketchup**, such as Heinz Organic (optional)

Bacon Tomato Jam (optional; page 274)

Bread-and-butter or **dill pickle slices**

SLIDER SALAD with YELLOW MUSTARD VINAIGRETTE

MAKES 12 SLIDERS

There are many flavors of sharp cheddar in today's markets to choose from, so go plain or go wild! Among the choices out there in sharp cheddars: 5-peppercorn, smoked, dill, garlic and herb, roasted garlic, horseradish, chipotle, habanero, jalapeño—on and on!

Make the sliders: In a large bowl, combine the beef, grated onion (grate it right over the bowl so the juices fall into the meat), Worcestershire sauce, and grill seasoning (or salt and pepper); mix thoroughly. Score the mixture into 4 equal portions, then form each portion into 3 patties slightly thinner in the center than at the edges for even cooking and to ensure a flat surface (burgers plump as they cook). Drizzle the patties with EVOO. Heat a grill pan or large nonstick skillet over medium-high heat. Cook the sliders for 3 minutes on each side for medium (adjust the timing for rarer or more well-done sliders). Top the sliders with the cheddar slices during the last minute or two of cooking, tenting the skillet loosely with aluminum foil, if you like, to help melt the cheese.

While the burgers are cooking, make the salad and dressing: In a large bowl, combine the romaine, pickles, and tomatoes and toss. Arrange the salad on a serving platter or plates. In a small bowl, whisk together the mustard and vinegar, then stream in the EVOO. Add the chives and pimientos or bell pepper to the dressing and stir to combine.

Arrange the cheeseburger sliders over the salad and drizzle the dressing over the salad and sliders.

SLIDERS:

2 pounds **ground beef chuck**

3 to 4 tablespoons grated **onion**

¼ cup **Worcestershire sauce**

1 rounded tablespoon **grill seasoning**, such as McCormick Montreal Steak Seasoning, or **kosher salt** and coarsely ground **pepper**

EVOO (extra-virgin olive oil), for drizzling

¾-pound brick **sharp cheddar cheese**, cut into ¼-inch slices

SALAD AND DRESSING:

5 to 6 cups chopped **hearts of romaine** lettuce

1 cup sliced **pickles** (sweet, half-sour, or dill)

1 cup **cherry** or **grape tomatoes**, halved

3 tablespoons **yellow mustard**, such as French's

2 tablespoons **cider vinegar**

½ cup **EVOO** (extra-virgin olive oil)

2 to 3 tablespoon finely chopped **chives**

3 tablespoons drained bottled **pimientos** or ¼ **red bell pepper**, seeded and finely chopped

PIMIENTO CHEESE SLIDERS

MAKES 8 SLIDERS

Preheat the oven to 350°F.

Trim the crusts off the bread or use a biscuit cutter or empty can to cut into 3-inch slider-size rounds. Arrange the bread on a baking sheet and bake until lightly toasted and golden, 8 to 10 minutes.

Make the sliders: Heat a griddle pan or large cast-iron skillet over medium-high heat. In a large bowl, combine the beef, garlic, grated onion (grate it right over the bowl so the juices fall into the meat), paprika, and beer; season with salt and pepper and mix thoroughly. Score the mixture into 4 equal portions, then form each portion into 2 patties slightly thinner at the center than at the edges for even cooking and to ensure a flat surface (burgers plump as they cook). Drizzle the patties with oil. Cook the sliders for 3 to 4 minutes on each side, or until done to your taste.

While the sliders are cooking, make the sauce: Melt the butter in a saucepan over medium heat. Whisk in the flour and cook for 1 minute. Whisk in the milk and bring to a bubble. Cook until thickened, about 3 minutes; season with salt and pepper. Melt the cheddar into the sauce and stir in the mustard, hot sauce, and pimientos.

Place the sliders on 8 toast slices and top with the pimiento cheese sauce. Set the remaining pieces of toast on top and garnish with pickle slices, securing the pickles in place with toothpicks.

16 slices good-quality **white bread**

SLIDERS:

1½ pounds **ground beef chuck**

2 to 3 cloves **garlic**, grated or finely chopped

3 to 4 tablespoons grated **onion**

1 tablespoon **sweet paprika** or **smoked sweet paprika**

½ cup **lager beer**

Kosher salt and **pepper**

Olive oil or **vegetable oil**, for drizzling

PIMIENTO CHEESE SAUCE:

2 tablespoons **butter**

2 tablespoons **flour**

1 cup **milk**

1 cup shredded **sharp yellow cheddar cheese**

1 tablespoon **yellow mustard**

Several drops of **hot sauce**

3 tablespoons well-drained chopped **pimientos**

8 slices good-quality **dill pickle chips** or **bread-and-butter pickles**

POBLANO POPPER SUPER-SLIDERS

MAKES 8 SLIDERS

Preheat the broiler.

Halve the poblanos and seed them. Place them skin side up on a baking sheet and blacken them under the broiler with the oven door ajar to let steam escape. (Or leave the poblanos whole and char them over an open flame on a stovetop burner.) Place the charred peppers in a bowl, cover with plastic wrap, and cool. When cool enough to handle, peel and seed the chiles, then purée them in a food processor.

While the peppers are cooling, make the pickled onions: Toss the red onion rings in a small bowl with the lime juice and season with salt and pepper. Add a little EVOO and toss to coat.

In another bowl, make the avocado sauce: Mash together the avocado flesh, sour cream, cilantro, and chile. Stir in the lime juice and season with salt.

Make the sliders: In a large bowl, combine the beef, pork, puréed poblano, coriander, cumin, paprika, cinnamon, beer, and Worcestershire sauce; season with salt and lots of pepper and mix thoroughly. Score the mixture into 4 equal portions, then form each portion into 2 patties slightly thinner at the center than at the edges for even cooking and to ensure a flat surface (burgers plump as they cook). Heat a drizzle of EVOO in a large nonstick skillet or griddle over medium-high heat. Cook the sliders, turning once, 7 minutes for medium-rare (adjust the timing for rarer or more well-done sliders). Top the sliders with the cheese during the last minute or two of cooking, folding the slices to fit the patties and tenting the skillet loosely with foil, if you like, to help melt the cheese.

Place the sliders on the roll bottoms and top with the pickled onions and avocado sauce. Set the roll tops in place.

2 large **poblano chiles**

PICKLED ONIONS:

1 small **red onion**, thinly sliced into rings

Juice of 1 **lime**

Kosher salt and **pepper**

EVOO (extra-virgin olive oil), for drizzling

AVOCADO SAUCE:

1 small **avocado**

½ cup **sour cream**

A handful of **cilantro leaves**, finely chopped

1 **jalapeño** or **Fresno chile**, seeded and finely chopped

Juice of 1 **lime**

SLIDERS:

¾ pound **ground beef chuck**

¾ pound **ground pork**

1½ teaspoons **ground coriander**

1½ teaspoons **ground cumin**

1½ teaspoons **smoked sweet paprika**

A pinch of **ground cinnamon**

⅓ cup **beer**, such as Negra Modelo

2 tablespoons **Worcestershire sauce**

8 (2-inch-square) slices deli-sliced **pepper jack**, **hot-pepper cheddar**, or **sharp yellow cheddar cheese**

8 **slider rolls** (white, potato, or whole-wheat), split

SOUTH BY SOUTHWEST 7-LAYER SLIDERS

MAKES 12 SLIDERS

I created this one for my Feedback event at South by Southwest Music Festival in Austin, Texas. It is one of my best sliders, and definitely the tallest!

Heat the beans and a small splash of water in a small skillet over medium-low heat. Keep warm.

Make the sliders: In a large bowl, combine the beef, beer, grated onion (grate it right over the bowl so the juices fall into the meat), garlic, grill seasoning, chile powder, and paprika. Score the mixture into 4 equal portions, and form each portion into 3 patties slightly thinner at center than at the edges for even cooking and to ensure a flat surface (burgers plump as they cook). Drizzle the patties with EVOO.

Make the guacamole, salsa, and spicy sour cream: In a small bowl, mash the avocado flesh with half the red onion, jalapeños, and cilantro; all of the lime zest and lime juice; and the garlic. Season the guacamole with salt. In another small bowl, toss the tomatoes with the mustard and the remaining half of the red onion, jalapeños, and cilantro; season the salsa with salt. In another small bowl, stir together the sour cream, hot sauce, and cumin.

Heat a large skillet or grill pan over medium-high heat. Cook the sliders, flipping once, 6 minutes for medium (adjust the timing for rarer or more well-done sliders). During the last minute of cooking, top each slider with 2 squares of pepper jack, tenting the pan with aluminum foil, if you like, to help melt the cheese.

Top the roll bottoms with small spoonfuls of refried beans. Place the sliders on the beans and top with some lettuce, guacamole, salsa, spicy sour cream, and a sprinkling of olives. Set the roll tops in place. Serve the sliders with any remaining toppings.

1 cup canned **spicy vegetarian refried beans**

SLIDERS:

2 pounds **ground beef chuck**

1 cup **beer**

¼ cup grated **onion**

2 cloves **garlic**, grated or finely chopped

1½ tablespoons **grill seasoning**, such as McCormick Montreal Steak Seasoning

1 tablespoon **pure chile powder**, preferably chipotle

1 tablespoon **smoked sweet paprika**

EVOO (extra-virgin olive oil), for drizzling

GUACAMOLE, SALSA, AND SPICY SOUR CREAM:

1 **avocado**

½ small **red onion**, finely chopped

2 **jalapeño chiles**, seeded and finely chopped

3 tablespoons finely chopped **cilantro**

1 teaspoon grated zest plus juice of 2 **limes**

1 clove **garlic**, grated or finely chopped

Kosher salt

2 **yellow tomatoes**, seeded and chopped

¼ cup **yellow mustard**

1 cup **sour cream**

1 tablespoon **hot sauce**

1 teaspoon **ground cumin**

6 slices deli-sliced **pepper jack cheese,** quartered

12 **slider rolls,** split

1 cup shredded **romaine lettuce**

½ cup **pimiento-stuffed green olives,** chopped

CHEESEBURGER EGG ROLLS with RUSSIAN DRESSING DIPPER

MAKES 12 TO 14 ROLLS

These aren't exactly sliders but I couldn't leave them out—I mean, how much fun is a cheeseburger inside an egg roll?

Preheat the oven to 375°F.

Make the egg rolls: Heat a drizzle of EVOO in a skillet over medium-high heat. Add the onion and cook until tender, 5 to 7 minutes. Add the beef and brown, 5 to 6 minutes, crumbling it with a wooden spoon as it cooks. Season with salt and pepper. Drain the fat from the pan and transfer the beef mixture to a medium bowl and let cool. Once cool, mix in the cheddar, Worcestershire sauce, mustard, and ketchup.

To form the egg rolls, brush water around the edges of one of the wrappers and put the wrapper on your work surface with one of the corners pointing toward you. Place a few tablespoons of the beef mixture in the center of the wrapper. Fold the two side corners over the filling, then fold the corner nearest you over those. Roll the egg roll away from you into a neat little package. Place on a cooling rack set over a baking sheet. Repeat with the remaining wrappers and filling.

Coat the egg rolls lightly with cooking spray and sprinkle with sesame seeds. Bake until browned, 20 to 25 minutes.

While the egg rolls are baking, make the dipper: In a medium bowl, mix together the sour cream, relish, and ketchup; season with salt and pepper.

Serve the egg rolls hot with Russian dressing dipper.

CHEESEBURGER EGG ROLLS:

EVOO (extra-virgin olive oil), for drizzling

½ red onion, chopped

¾ pound ground sirloin or chuck

Kosher salt and pepper

1 cup grated sharp yellow cheddar cheese

1 tablespoon Worcestershire sauce

1 tablespoon grainy Dijon mustard or other mustard of choice

1 tablespoon good-quality ketchup, such as Heinz Organic

12 to 14 egg roll wrappers

All-natural cooking spray

Sesame seeds

RUSSIAN DRESSING DIPPER:

1 cup sour cream

2 rounded tablespoons dill relish

¼ cup good-quality ketchup, such as Heinz Organic

ST. PADDY'S–STYLE REUBEN SLIDERS

MAKES 12 SLIDERS

Make the potato-kraut: Heat a liberal drizzle of oil in a medium skillet over medium to medium-high heat. Add the potatoes, season with salt and pepper, and cook 5 to 6 minutes. Add the sauerkraut and stir. Add the beer and simmer 5 minutes more.

Make the sliders: In a large bowl, combine the beef and grated onion (grate it right over the bowl so the juices fall into the meat); season with salt and pepper. Pulse the corned beef in a food processor to grind it up. Add to the beef along with the mustard and mix thoroughly. Score the mixture into 4 equal portions and form each portion into 3 patties slightly thinner at the center than at the edges for even cooking and to ensure a flat surface (burgers plump as they cook). Drizzle the patties lightly with oil.

Heat a large skillet or griddle over medium-high heat. Cook the sliders 3 minutes on each side, or until done to your taste. Cut or fold the Swiss cheese slices to fit the sliders and place them over the sliders for the last minute or two of cooking, tenting the pan with aluminum foil, if you like, to help melt the cheese.

In a small bowl, stir together the sour cream, ketchup, relish, and Worcestershire sauce. Place the sliders on the roll bottoms or half the toasts and top with the potato-kraut and a generous dollop of the sour cream mixture. Set the roll tops or remaining toasts in place.

POTATO-KRAUT:

EVOO (extra-virgin olive oil) or **vegetable oil**, for drizzling

4 **baby Yukon gold potatoes**, cut into ¼-inch dice

Kosher salt and **pepper**

1 (1-pound) package **sauerkraut**, rinsed and drained

½ cup **lager beer**

SLIDERS:

1 pound **ground beef chuck**

3 tablespoons grated **onion**

½ pound **cooked corned beef**, chopped

3 tablespoons **grainy mustard**

⅓ pound deli-sliced **Swiss cheese**

½ cup **sour cream**

3 tablespoons good-quality **ketchup**, such as Heinz Organic

2 tablespoons **dill relish**

1 teaspoon **Worcestershire sauce**

12 **slider rolls** or **party-size rye bread slices**, toasted

SLICED STEAK SOFT TACO SLIDERS with GUACA-SALSA

MAKES 8 SLIDERS

Bring the steak to room temp. Rub with oil and season with chile powder and grill seasoning or salt and pepper.

Make the guaca-salsa: In a blender or food processor, combine the avocado flesh, lime juice, tomatillos, onion, jalapeño, garlic, honey or sugar, cilantro, mint, thyme, and salt. Process until almost smooth.

Heat a grill pan or large nonstick skillet over medium-high heat. Cook the steak(s), turning occasionally, 10 to 12 minutes, or until done to your taste. Transfer to a cutting board to rest 5 to 10 minutes. Wipe the drippings from the pan and turn the heat to low under the pan. When the meat has rested, slice it very thinly against the grain.

Coat the tortillas with cooking spray and char them lightly, a few seconds on each side, in the skillet or over stove burners.

To form each slider, spread a little guaca-salsa on a tortilla and top with a thin, even layer of sliced steak. Fold the tortilla into quarters, forming a triangle-shaped slider.

STEAK:

4 small (6- to 7-ounce) **flat iron steaks** or 1½ to 1¾ pounds **flank steak**

Vegetable oil, for rubbing the steak

1½ tablespoons **ancho chile powder** (or **chipotle** for heat)

1 tablespoon **grill seasoning**, or **kosher salt** and **pepper**

GUACA-SALSA:

1 large or 2 small **avocados**

Juice of 2 **limes**

2 **tomatillos**, husked and coarsely chopped

½ small **red onion**, coarsely chopped

1 **jalapeño chile**, seeded and coarsely chopped

1 large clove **garlic**, grated or pasted

2 teaspoons **honey** or a sprinkle of **sugar**

A small handful of **cilantro** leaves

Leaves from a few sprigs **mint**

Leaves from a few sprigs **thyme**

A generous sprinkle of **sea salt**

8 (8-inch) **flour tortillas**

All-natural cooking spray

CHORIZO SLIDERS

MAKES 8 SLIDERS

Make the sliders: Pulse-chop the chorizo in a food processor to very small crumbles. Transfer to a large bowl; add the ground pork, parsley or cilantro, and smoked paprika; season with salt and pepper and mix thoroughly. Score the mixture into 4 equal portions and form each portion into 3 patties slightly thinner at the center than at the edges for even cooking and to ensure a flat surface (burgers plump as they cook). Drizzle the patties with EVOO. Heat a skillet or grill pan over medium-high heat. Cook the sliders 3 minutes on each side, or until done to your taste. Pile some shredded cheese on top of the sliders for the last minute of cooking, tenting the pan with aluminum foil, if you like, to help melt the cheese.

While the sliders are cooking, make the avocado sauce: Place the avocado flesh in a food processor with the lemon juice, garlic, and sour cream or crema; season with salt. Process until very smooth.

Place the sliders on the roll bottoms and top with tomato, onion, lettuce, and avocado sauce. Set the roll tops in place.

SLIDERS:

½ pound **Spanish chorizo**, casings removed and coarsely chopped

1 pound **ground pork**

A handful of **flat-leaf parsley** or **cilantro**, finely chopped

½ tablespoon **smoked sweet paprika**

Kosher salt and **pepper**

EVOO (extra-virgin olive oil), for drizzling

½ pound **Manchego** or **cheddar cheese**, shredded

AVOCADO SAUCE:

1 **avocado**

Juice of 1 **lemon**

1 large clove **garlic**, pasted (see Tip, page 138) or grated

About ¼ cup **sour cream** or **Mexican crema**

8 **slider rolls** or **brioche dinner rolls**, split

Sliced **plum tomatoes**

Sliced **red onion**

Chopped **lettuce**

BBQ "BUN"-MI SLIDERS

MAKES 8 SLIDERS

Make the vegetables: In a small bowl, combine the carrots, cucumber, and radishes. Heat ½ cup water, the sugar, vinegar, and salt in a small saucepan, stirring to dissolve the sugar and salt. Pour the hot dressing over the vegetables and let cool while you get the sliders and sauce together.

Make the BBQ sauce: Combine the hoisin, honey, soy sauce, and sriracha in a small saucepan and heat until warm.

Make the sliders: Pulse the bologna in a food processor until very finely chopped and transfer to a large bowl. Add the ground pork, grated onion (grate directly over the mixing bowl so the juices fall into the meat), garlic, and ginger; season with a little salt and lots of pepper and mix thoroughly. Score the mixture into 4 equal portions and form each portion into 2 patties slightly thinner at the center than at the edges for even cooking and to ensure a flat surface (burgers plump as they cook). Lightly drizzle the patties with oil.

Heat a large skillet or grill pan over medium-high heat. Cook the sliders 3 to 4 minutes on each side, or until done to your taste. Liberally brush the burgers with BBQ sauce in the last minute or so of cooking.

While the sliders are cooking, drain the vegetables, return them to the bowl, and add the cilantro, mint, and micro greens or pea shoots. Toss together.

Place the sliders on the baguette or roll bottoms and top with the vegetable mixture. Set the tops in place.

VEGETABLES:

2 **carrots**, cut into matchsticks

⅓ to ½ **seedless cucumber**, cut into matchsticks

4 or 5 large **radishes**, cut into matchsticks

¼ cup **sugar**

¼ cup **white wine vinegar** or **rice vinegar**

1 scant teaspoon **sea salt**

Cilantro and **mint** leaves

A handful of **micro greens** or **pea shoots**

BBQ SAUCE:

⅓ cup **hoisin sauce**

¼ cup **honey**

3 tablespoons **soy sauce** or **tamari**

2 tablespoons **sriracha** or other **chili sauce**

SLIDERS:

¼ pound **bologna**, coarsely chopped

1½ pounds **ground pork**

3 tablespoons finely grated **onion**

2 cloves **garlic**, finely chopped

1½-inch piece **fresh ginger**, peeled and grated or finely chopped

Sea salt and **pepper**

Vegetable oil, for drizzling

8 (3-inch) lengths of **baguette** or **French rolls**, split

MEXICAN PULLED PORK SLIDERS

MAKES 24 SLIDERS

I could eat pickled red onions by the handful. They are great on tacos, burgers, or just about anything, for that matter. For the best flavor, pickle the onions at least a day before making the sliders.

Make the pickled onions: Layer the sliced chiles, bay leaves, and red onion rings in a plastic food storage container. Bring the vinegar and ½ cup water up to a bubble in a small saucepan. Add 1 tablespoon salt, the coriander seeds, and sugar. Pour the brine over the onions. Cool to room temperature, then refrigerate.

Make the pulled pork: Season the pork generously with salt and pepper and let sit at room temperature for 30 minutes.

Preheat the oven to 325°F.

Pat the pork dry with a paper towel. Heat the EVOO, 3 turns of the pan, in a large Dutch oven or heavy-bottomed pot over medium-high heat. Cook the pork until golden brown, about 5 minutes per side. Transfer the pork to a plate. Stir the onion and garlic into the pan. Season with the cumin, oregano, and salt and pepper and cook, stirring, 5 to 6 minutes. Deglaze the pan with the beer, scraping up any bits stuck to the bottom of the pot. Stir in the chicken stock and orange juice, return the pork to the pan, and bring the liquid to a simmer. The liquid should come about two-thirds of the way up the meat. (If it doesn't, add more stock.) Cover and braise in the oven until the meat is tender and falls apart when you touch it, 2½ to 3 hours. Turn the pork halfway through cooking.

PICKLED ONIONS:

1 **fresh red chile**, such as Fresno, or 1 **jalapeño**, thinly sliced into rings

2 **bay leaves**, fresh or dried

2 small **red onions**, thinly sliced

1 cup **white wine vinegar** or **white balsamic vinegar**

Kosher salt

1 teaspoon **coriander seeds**

1 tablespoon **sugar**

PULLED PORK:

1 (3- to 4-pound) **boneless pork shoulder**

Pepper

3 tablespoons **EVOO** (extra-virgin olive oil)

1 large **onion**, sliced

3 cloves **garlic**, coarsely chopped

2 tablespoons **ground cumin**

1 tablespoon **dried Mexican oregano**

1 (12-ounce) bottle **Mexican beer**, such as Dos Equis

2 cups **chicken stock**

Juice of 1 **orange**

Juice of 2 **limes**

When the pork is done, transfer it carefully to a plate and let stand until cool enough to handle. Pull the meat apart with 2 forks or shred with a carving knife.

While the pork is cooling, simmer the braising liquid over medium heat until reduced by half. Add the lime juice. Gently stir the shredded pork back into the reduced liquid.

Using tongs, lift the shredded pork onto the roll bottoms. Top with pickled jalapeños, pickled red onions, and cheese. Set the roll tops in place.

24 **small rolls**, such as **brioche dinner rolls** or **slider rolls**, split

1 cup **pickled jalapeño slices** or **hot pepper rings**

1 cup **queso fresco**, crumbled, or 2 cups shredded **Monterey Jack cheese**

I'LL HAVE WHAT CHARLIE'S HAVING SLIDERS

MAKES 8 SLIDERS

My good friend Charlie made me these sliders one night for dinner. He hit the nail on the head with this one! Come on, pastrami IN a burger? You'll need a 3-inch round cookie cutter or an empty 4-ounce can to cut rounds of bread for these sliders.

16 slices **rye** or **whole-grain bread**

½ pound good-quality lean **pastrami**, coarsely chopped

1 pound **ground pork**

1 teaspoon **sweet paprika**

1 teaspoon **granulated garlic**

3 tablespoons grated **onion**

Kosher salt and coarsely ground **pepper**

EVOO (extra-virgin olive oil) or **vegetable oil**, for drizzling

2 to 3 **pickled tomatoes**, sliced

Grainy Dijon mustard

2 whole **half-sour, garlic,** or **dill pickles,** sliced into rounds

Preheat the oven to 325°F.

Place a cooling rack over a baking sheet. Using a 3-inch cookie cutter or empty can, cut bread rounds from the bread and arrange on the rack. Toast until light golden, 7 to 8 minutes.

Pulse the pastrami in a food processor until very finely chopped. Transfer to a large bowl and add the ground pork, paprika, garlic, and grated onion (grate it right over the bowl so the juices fall into the meat); season with a little salt and lots of pepper and mix thoroughly. Score the mixture into 4 equal portions and form each portion into 2 patties slightly thinner at the center than at the edges for even cooking and to ensure a flat surface (burgers plump as they cook). Heat a drizzle of EVOO in a large nonstick skillet or griddle over medium-high heat. Cook the sliders 3 to 4 minutes on each side, or until done to your taste.

Place the sliders on half the toast rounds and top each with a slice of pickled tomato. Slather lots of grainy mustard on the remaining toast rounds and set in place on top of the tomatoes. Arrange pickle slices on top and secure them with toothpicks.

TIP: Reserve bread trimmings in the freezer for another use like breadcrumbs or stuffing.

INDIAN LAMB SLIDERS with GREEN RAITA SAUCE and RED ONIONS

MAKES 8 SLIDERS

Make the green raita: Process the yogurt, cilantro, mint, garlic, and lime juice in a food processor until smooth. Season with salt and pepper. Transfer to a small serving dish and reserve.

Make the pickled onions: Separate the red onion into rings and place them in a small bowl. Toss with the lime juice and a drizzle of EVOO; season with salt and pepper.

Make the sliders: In a large bowl, combine the lamb, grated onion (grate it right over the bowl so the juices fall into the meat), garlic, chile, ginger, and curry powder or curry mix; season with salt and pepper and mix thoroughly. Score the mixture into 4 equal portions and form each portion into 2 patties, thinner at the center than at the edges for even cooking and to ensure a flat surface (burgers plump as they cook).

Heat a drizzle of EVOO in a large skillet or a griddle over medium-high heat and melt the butter into it. Cook the sliders, flipping once, 6 minutes, or until done to your taste.

Place the sliders on the roll bottoms and top with chopped lettuce or spinach, pickled onions, and green raita. Set the roll tops in place.

GREEN RAITA:

1 cup plain **Greek yogurt**

A handful of **cilantro** leaves

A handful of **mint** leaves

1 clove **garlic**, grated or pasted (see Tip, page 138)

Juice of 1 **lime**

Kosher salt and **pepper**

PICKLED ONIONS:

4 (¼-inch-thick) slices small **red onion**

Juice of 1 **lime**

EVOO (extra-virgin olive oil), for drizzling

SLIDERS:

1½ pounds **ground lamb**

3 tablespoons grated **onion**

2 large cloves **garlic**, grated or finely chopped

1 **fresh red chile**, such as Fresno, seeded and finely chopped

1-inch piece **fresh ginger**, peeled and grated or minced

2 tablespoons **curry powder** or curry spice mix (see Tip, page 94)

EVOO (extra-virgin olive oil), for drizzling

1 tablespoon **butter**

8 small soft **potato rolls** or **slider rolls**

Chopped **lettuce** or **spinach** leaves

SATAY SLIDERS

MAKES 8 SLIDERS

Make the relish: Bring the vinegar, ¼ cup water, and the sugar to a bubble in a small saucepan over medium-high heat, stirring to dissolve the sugar. Combine the mint, cucumber, and onion in a bowl. Pour the hot vinegar over the veggies, stir to combine, and let stand, stirring occasionally, while you make the sliders.

Make the sliders: In a large bowl, combine the chicken or pork, tamari or soy sauce, peanut butter, garlic, ginger, and chives; season with pepper and mix thoroughly. Score the mixture into 4 equal portions and form each portion into 2 patties thinner at the center than at the edges for even cooking and to ensure a flat surface (burgers plump as they cook).

Heat the oil, 1 turn of the pan, in a large skillet over medium-high heat. Cook the sliders 2 to 3 minutes on each side, or until the juices run clear.

Place a little shredded cabbage or lettuce on the roll bottoms and top with the sliders and some drained cucumber relish. Set the roll tops in place.

CUCUMBER RELISH:

½ cup **rice vinegar**

¼ cup **sugar**

¼ cup **fresh mint** leaves, finely chopped

½ **seedless cucumber**, cut into ¼-inch dice

¼ cup finely chopped **red onion** (about 1 small)

SLIDERS:

1½ pounds **ground chicken** or **pork**

3 tablespoons **tamari** or **soy sauce**

¼ cup **smooth peanut butter**, softened in a microwave for 20 seconds on high

2 large cloves **garlic**, finely chopped or grated

1-inch piece **fresh ginger**, peeled and finely chopped or grated

A handful of finely chopped **chives**

Pepper

1 tablespoon **vegetable oil**

1 cup shredded **cabbage** or **iceberg lettuce**

8 **slider rolls**, split

CHICKEN and BISCUIT SLIDERS with Spicy Orange-Maple Drizzle and Crunchy Oil-and-Vinegar Slaw

MAKES 8 SLIDERS

If you're making your own biscuits, bake them now. You'll need eight 3-inch biscuits.

Make the slaw: In a small bowl, combine the coleslaw mix and red onion. Add the vinegar, oil, and celery salt; season with salt and pepper and toss to coat the veggies with dressing.

Make the chicken: Season the chicken with salt and pepper. Stir the chicken and buttermilk together in a small bowl and let sit for 30 minutes.

Place the flour, mustard, and poultry seasoning in a paper sack.

Fill a countertop fryer with oil, or pour a few inches of oil into a large Dutch oven. Heat the oil to 350° to 375°F. The oil is ready for frying when bubbles stream out rapidly from the handle of a wooden spoon inserted into the oil.

While the frying oil is heating, make the drizzle: Stir the maple syrup, orange zest, and sriracha together in a small saucepan. Warm over low heat.

When the frying oil is ready, add the chicken pieces to the sack of seasoned flour. Fold the top down and shake the bag. Shake any excess flour off the chicken pieces and add them to the hot frying oil. Fry the chicken thighs 7 to 8 minutes (a minute or two less for breasts), until deeply golden and the juices run clear when the chicken is poked. Remove from the oil with a skimmer or tongs and cool on a cooling rack.

Place the chicken on the biscuit bottoms and top with a spoonful of the spicy orange-maple drizzle and some slaw. Set the biscuit tops in place.

8 **buttermilk biscuits**, homemade (from scratch or from a mix) or good-quality store-bought, warmed and split

OIL-AND-VINEGAR SLAW:

½ pound **coleslaw mix** or ¼ head **green cabbage**, shredded

½ small **red onion**, very thinly sliced

3 tablespoons **cider vinegar**

2 tablespoons **vegetable oil**

1 teaspoon **celery salt**

Kosher salt and **pepper**

FRIED CHICKEN:

1½ to 2 pounds boneless, skinless **chicken thighs** or **breasts**, trimmed into 8 (3- to 4-ounce) pieces to fit the biscuits

2 cups **buttermilk**

1½ cups **flour**

1 tablespoon **dry mustard**

1 tablespoon **poultry seasoning**

Vegetable oil for frying

ORANGE-MAPLE DRIZZLE:

½ cup **dark amber maple syrup**

Grated zest of 1 **orange** or a curl of zest

1 tablespoon **sriracha**

FRIED CHICKEN and BISCUIT SLIDERS with SMOKY CHARD

MAKES 8 SLIDERS

If you're making your own biscuits, bake them now. You'll need eight 3- to 4-inch biscuits.

Make the chicken: Season the chicken with salt and pepper. In a small bowl, mix the sour cream with the chives and garlic. Coat the chicken with the sour cream mixture. Place the flour, mustard, poultry seasoning, onion powder, paprika, ginger, and cayenne in a paper sack.

Fill a countertop fryer with oil or pour a few inches of oil into a large Dutch oven. Heat the oil to 350° to 375°F. The oil is ready for frying when bubbles stream out rapidly from the handle of a wooden spoon inserted into the oil.

While the frying oil is heating, make the smoky chard: Heat a drizzle of oil in a skillet over medium-high heat. Add the bacon and cook until crisp, about 3 minutes. Add the shredded chard and toss to wilt. When the chard is wilted, douse it with the vinegar and season with the nutmeg and pepper. Reduce the heat to a simmer and tightly cover. Cook 8 to 10 minutes, then turn off the heat.

When the frying oil is ready, add the chicken pieces to the sack of seasoned flour. Fold the top down and shake the bag. Shake any excess flour off the chicken pieces and add them to the hot frying oil. Fry the chicken thighs 7 to 8 minutes (a minute or two less for breasts), until deeply golden and cooked through and the juices run clear when the chicken pieces are poked. Remove from the oil with a skimmer or tongs and cool on a cooling rack.

Dress the chicken with a drizzle of honey and a few dashes of hot sauce on each piece. Place the chicken on the biscuit bottoms, top with the chard, and set the biscuit tops in place.

Fried Chicken and Biscuit Sliders with Smoky Chard; Parsnip Oven Fries (page 256).

8 **buttermilk biscuits**, homemade or store-bought, warmed and split

FRIED CHICKEN:

1½ to 2 pounds boneless, skinless **chicken thighs** or **breasts**, trimmed into 8 (3- to 4-ounce) pieces to fit the biscuits

Kosher salt and **pepper**

1 cup **sour cream**

¼ cup finely chopped **chives**

2 cloves **garlic**, grated or pasted (see Tip, page 138)

1½ cups **flour**

1 tablespoon **dry mustard**

1 tablespoon **poultry seasoning**

1 tablespoon **onion powder**

1 tablespoon **sweet paprika** or **smoked sweet paprika**

1½ teaspoons **ground ginger**

1 teaspoon **cayenne pepper**

Vegetable oil for frying

SMOKY CHARD:

Vegetable oil

4 slices thick-cut **smoky bacon**, chopped

1 bundle **Swiss chard**, stemmed and shredded

2 tablespoons **cider vinegar** or **wine vinegar**

A few grates of **nutmeg**

Honey

Hot sauce

BUFFALO TURKEY SLIDERS

MAKES 8 SLIDERS

Make the blue cheese sauce: In a small bowl, combine the sour cream, blue cheese, and milk or cream; season with salt and pepper and set aside.

Make the sliders: Heat 1 tablespoon oil, 1 turn of the pan, in a small skillet over medium-high heat. Add the celery, carrot, onion, and garlic; season with salt and pepper. Cook until tender, 4 to 5 minutes. Transfer to a large bowl and cool.

Add the turkey and Old Bay to the cooled vegetables; season with salt and pepper and mix thoroughly. Score the mixture into 4 equal portions and form each portion into 2 patties slightly thinner at the center than at the edges for even cooking and to ensure a flat surface (burgers plump as they cook). Heat the remaining 1 tablespoon oil, 1 turn of the pan, in a large skillet or griddle over medium-high heat. Cook the sliders 3 to 4 minutes on each side, or until the juices run clear.

While the sliders are cooking, melt the butter in a small saucepan over low heat. When the butter is melted, stir in the hot sauce and remove from the heat.

Turn the cooked sliders in the hot sauce mixture to coat. Place the sliders on the roll bottoms and top with lettuce and a dollop of blue cheese sauce. Set the roll tops in place.

BLUE CHEESE SAUCE:

1 cup **reduced-fat sour cream**

⅓ pound **blue cheese**, crumbled

A splash of **milk** or **cream**

Kosher salt and **pepper**

SLIDERS:

2 tablespoons **vegetable oil**

1 rib **celery**, very finely chopped

1 **carrot**, grated or very finely chopped

½ cup grated or very finely chopped **onion**

2 cloves **garlic**, grated or chopped

1½ pounds **ground turkey breast**

1 rounded tablespoon **Old Bay seasoning**

4 tablespoons (½ stick) **butter**

¼ cup **hot sauce**, such as Frank's RedHot

8 **slider rolls** or **small potato rolls**

2 cups chopped **lettuce**, such as romaine

DELUXE TURKEY CLUB SLIDERS

MAKES 12 SLIDERS

Preheat the oven to 375°F. Arrange the bacon on a slotted broiler pan or a cooling rack set over a baking sheet and bake until crisp, 15 to 17 minutes. Break the slices in half and set aside.

While the bacon is cooking, make the ranch dressing: In a small bowl, stir together the sour cream, lemon juice, hot sauce, and herbs; season with salt and pepper.

Make the sliders: Heat a griddle or large cast-iron pan over medium-high heat.

In a large bowl, combine the turkey, garlic, grated onion (grate it right over the bowl so the juices fall into the meat), coriander, and cumin; season with salt and pepper and mix thoroughly. Score the mixture into 4 equal portions and form each portion into 3 patties slightly thinner at the center than at the edges for even cooking and to ensure a flat surface (burgers plump as they cook). Drizzle a little EVOO into the heated pan and cook the sliders, flipping once, 6 to 7 minutes, or until the juices run clear.

Place the sliders on the roll bottoms and top with bacon, lettuce, tomato, radish, and some ranch dressing. Set the roll tops in place.

12 slices **bacon**

RANCH DRESSING:

1½ cups **sour cream** (for thinner dressing, use 1 cup sour cream and ½ cup **buttermilk**)

2 tablespoons fresh **lemon** juice

2 tablespoons **hot sauce**

¼ cup finely chopped mixed fresh herbs: **dill**, **parsley**, and **chives**

Kosher salt and **pepper**

SLIDERS:

2 pounds **ground turkey**

4 cloves **garlic**, pasted (see Tip, page 138) or minced

3 to 4 tablespoons grated **onion**

2 teaspoons **ground coriander**

2 teaspoons **ground cumin**

EVOO (extra-virgin olive oil), for drizzling

12 **slider rolls**, such as **brioche dinner rolls**, split

Shredded or chopped **romaine** or **iceberg lettuce**

Sliced **vine-ripened tomatoes** or **plum tomatoes**

Thinly sliced **radishes**

CLUB BURGER SLIDERS with AVOCADO-RANCH DRESSING

MAKES 8 SLIDERS

Preheat the oven to 375°F. Arrange the bacon on a slotted broiler pan or a cooling rack set over a baking sheet and bake until crisp, 15 to 17 minutes. Cool the bacon and break the slices in half. (Leave the oven on for toasting the bread.)

Using a 3-inch round cookie cutter, cut out rounds of bread (or trim 1 inch of crust all the way around the bread slices to form small squares); save the trimmings (see Tip, page 160). Arrange the bread on a baking sheet.

Make the sliders: Heat a skillet or griddle over medium-high heat.

In a large bowl, combine the turkey, grated onion (grate it right over the bowl so the juices fall into the meat), hot sauce, and poultry seasoning; season with salt and pepper and mix thoroughly. Score the mixture into 4 equal portions and form each portion into 2 patties slightly thinner at the center than at the edges for even cooking and to ensure a flat surface (burgers plump as they cook). Add the oil, 1 turn of the pan, to the hot skillet. Cook the sliders, flipping once, 6 minutes, or until the juices run clear.

While the sliders are cooking, lightly toast the bread rounds in the oven and make the avocado dressing: Puree the avocado flesh, sour cream, lemon juice, garlic, chives, dill, and parsley in a food processor; season with salt and pepper.

Place the sliders on 8 toasts and top with crisscrossed bacon, lettuce, tomato, and avocado-ranch dressing. Set the top toasts in place.

8 slices thick-cut **bacon**

16 slices good-quality **white** or **whole wheat bread**

SLIDERS:

1½ pounds **ground turkey**

¼ cup grated **onion**

1 tablespoon **hot sauce**

1 tablespoon **poultry seasoning**

Kosher salt and **pepper**

1 tablespoon **vegetable oil**

AVOCADO-RANCH DRESSING:

1 **avocado**

½ cup **sour cream**

Juice of 1 **lemon**

1 clove **garlic**, grated or finely chopped

2 tablespoons finely chopped **chives**

2 tablespoons finely chopped **fresh dill**

2 tablespoons finely chopped **flat-leaf parsley**

Chopped or torn **lettuce**

Sliced **plum tomatoes**

BLACK SESAME and PANKO-CRUSTED TUNA SLIDERS

MAKES 8 SLIDERS

In a small bowl, combine the mustard, honey, and wasabi powder; set aside.

Pulse the tuna in a food processor until coarsely ground. Transfer the tuna to a medium bowl and add the tamari or soy sauce, garlic, and chives; season with pepper and mix thoroughly. Score the mixture into 4 equal portions and form each portion into 2 patties. In a shallow dish, combine the panko and sesame seeds. Coat the patties in the sesame breadcrumbs.

Heat a thin layer of oil in a large skillet over medium-high heat. Cook the sliders 1 to 2 minutes per side, or until golden brown on the outside and still pink at the center (adjust the cooking time for more well-done sliders).

Place the sliders on the roll bottoms and top with lettuce and pickled ginger. Slather the roll tops with wasabi mustard and set them in place.

½ cup **yellow** or **Dijon mustard**

3 tablespoons **honey**

½ to 1 teaspoon **wasabi powder** or **paste** (adjust the heat level to your taste)

1½ pounds skinless **tuna steaks,** trimmed of dark meat and cut into large chunks

3 tablespoons **tamari** or **soy sauce**

3 cloves **garlic,** grated or finely chopped

¼ cup thinly sliced **chives**

Pepper

1 cup **panko breadcrumbs**

3 tablespoons **black sesame seeds**

Vegetable oil, for frying

8 **slider rolls,** such as **brioche dinner rolls,** split

Bibb lettuce

Pickled ginger slices

MY LOVE FOR BURGERS
JOSH OZERSKY

Author of *The Hamburger: A History*

I agree with Rachael about almost everything, but the one thing we disagree on is the most important issue in the world. She and I have a fundamental disagreement about hamburgers. It's more than just a matter of taste. It's a political issue. It may even be a religious issue. Here is the problem: Rachael thinks of our great national sandwich as a vast and malleable concept, one that allows for infinite creativity, variation, and personal expression. I think of it as a round monument, like the Jefferson Memorial, meant to be admired and enjoyed but never for a moment interfered with. The hamburger, in my point of view, is still the center of a chaotic cultural universe; it's the stem cell of all our food. I hate one little thing on it to be different.

Now, this is what you call a major philosophical divide, and it doesn't matter if everyone, including me, knows I'm wrong. Whatever. I'm sure Rachael understands how strongly I feel about the subject, and how irrational my conviction is, and forgives me for it.

I am convinced that hamburgers are supposed to be served on enriched soft white buns, preferably without sesame seeds. They should be made of ground beef, covered with a slice of tangerine-colored American cheese, and either a little onion or a little pickle, and your choice of ketchup, mustard, or preferably neither.

I envy Rachael's ability to take classic dishes and tweak them in small but important ways that make them better. To take just one example, she made a double-bacon beer-braised cheeseburger that was as luxurious as a hot tub. I never could have thought of it. I'm too hidebound, dogmatic, and inflexible. Sure, I would like to be more like Rachael—who wouldn't?—but it's not going to happen. But at least I can be friends with her, and eat her burgers, even though I pretend that I don't believe in them. She knows better, anyway. The clean plate tells the tale.

Meet Josh Ozersky.

5-SPICE TUNA SLIDERS with HOISIN

MAKES 8 SLIDERS

Pulse the tuna in a food processor until coarsely ground. Transfer the tuna to a medium bowl and add the 5-spice powder, garlic, ginger, tamari, and chives; season with salt and pepper and mix thoroughly. Score the mixture into 4 equal portions, then form each portion into 2 small patties.

Heat the oil, 1 turn of the pan, in a large skillet over medium-high heat. Cook the sliders 1 to 2 minutes per side, or until browned on the outside and still pink at their center (adjust the timing for more well-done sliders). Brush liberally with hoisin sauce after turning.

Place the sliders on the roll bottoms and top with pickled ginger and cucumber. Set the roll tops in place.

1½ pounds **skinless tuna steaks,** trimmed of dark meat and cut into large chunks

1½ teaspoons **Chinese 5-spice powder**

3 cloves **garlic**, finely chopped or grated

1-inch piece **fresh ginger**, peeled and grated

2 tablespoons **tamari** or **soy sauce**

¼ cup finely chopped **chives**

Kosher **salt** and **pepper**

1 tablespoon **vegetable oil**

Hoisin sauce

8 **slider rolls**, split

Pickled ginger slices

Thinly sliced **seedless cucumber**

SANDWICHES AND DOGS

BEEF, PORK, and CHICKEN SANDWICHES

177 Sliced Steak Reubens with Horseradish Russian Dressing

179 The Best Sandwich I Ever Made (and My Husband Ever Tasted)

181 Red Wine and Garlic Marinated Sliced Steak Sandwiches

182 Chicagoan-Italian Roast Beef Heroes

184 Schnitzel-wich with Garlic Butter and Hot Relish

185 Portland Pork Schnitzel-wiches with Pinot-Blackberry Gravy

186 Albondigas Subs: Spicy Spanish Meatball Subs

188 Pulled Pork with Broccoli Rabe Subs

189 Italian Sliced Chicken and Pork Hoagies

191 Pork Schnitzel Sandwiches with Chunky Apple and Onion Chutney

192 Bourbon BBQ Pulled Chicken Sandwiches and Green Apple Slaw

SEAFOOD and VEGGIE SANDWICHES

194 Fishwiches

196 Tex-Mex Beer-Battered Fishwiches with Avocado Sauce

197 Niçoise-Style Pan Bagnats

198 Big, Beefy Mushroom Cheddar Melts

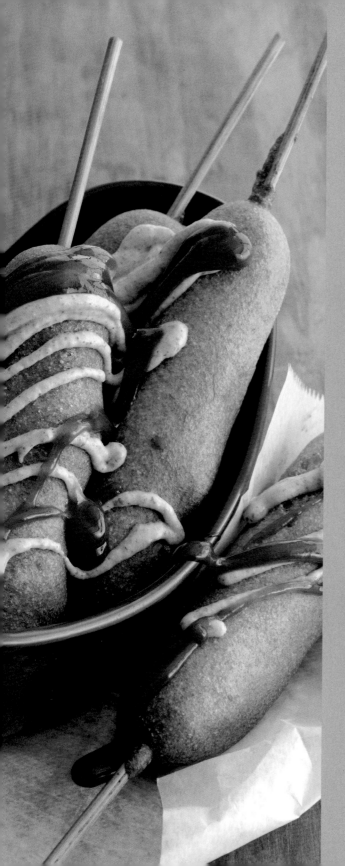

HOT DOGS and SAUSAGES

199 Cubano Dogs

200 Hot and Sweet Pepper Dogs

201 Michigan Dogs with Cheese Sauce

203 Pigs in Ponchos: Quesadilla-Wrapped Franks and Beans

204 Firecracker Deviled Corn Dogs

206 Coney Chili Dogs

207 Jalapeño Popper Dogs

208 Pigs in a Blanket with the Works

209 Reuben Dogs

211 Kielbasa Chili Dogs

212 Creole Andouille Dawgs

213 7-Layer Chili Dog Dip

SLICED STEAK REUBENS with HORSERADISH RUSSIAN DRESSING

SERVES 4

Season the flank steak with salt, pepper, and Old Bay. Let the seasoned steak come to room temp.

Heat a grill pan or heavy griddle over medium-high to high heat. Drizzle the pan with a little oil. Cook the steak for 12 minutes, turning occasionally. Remove the steak to a cutting board to rest 10 minutes. Reserve the grill pan. When the steak has rested, slice it thinly against the grain.

Meanwhile, make the Russian dressing: In a small bowl, stir together the sour cream, ketchup, relish, and horseradish; season with salt and pepper. Squeeze the sauerkraut to remove excess liquid. Heat the sauerkraut in a small saucepan over medium heat.

Butter 1 side of each slice of bread and spread mustard on the other side. To build the sandwiches, place all the bread buttered side down. Stack 2 cheese slices on half of the bread, then top with some watercress, sauerkraut, sliced steak, and Russian dressing. Flip the remaining bread slices, buttered side up, onto the sandwiches. Grill the sandwiches, turning once, 4 minutes per side, or until the cheese is melted and the bread is golden. Serve with chips and pass extra sauerkraut and/or dressing at the table.

$1\frac{1}{2}$ to 2 pounds **flank steak**

Kosher salt and cracked **pepper**

1 tablespoon **Old Bay seasoning**

Vegetable oil

1 cup **sour cream**

3 tablespoons good-quality **ketchup**, such as Heinz Organic

2 tablespoons **dill relish**

1 tablespoon **prepared horseradish**

1 (1-pound) package **sauerkraut**, rinsed and drained

8 slices **pumpernickel bread**

Softened **butter**, for the bread

Grainy mustard

8 slices deli-sliced **Emmentaler Swiss cheese**

A small bundle of **watercress**, trimmed of thick stems

Salt-and-vinegar potato chips

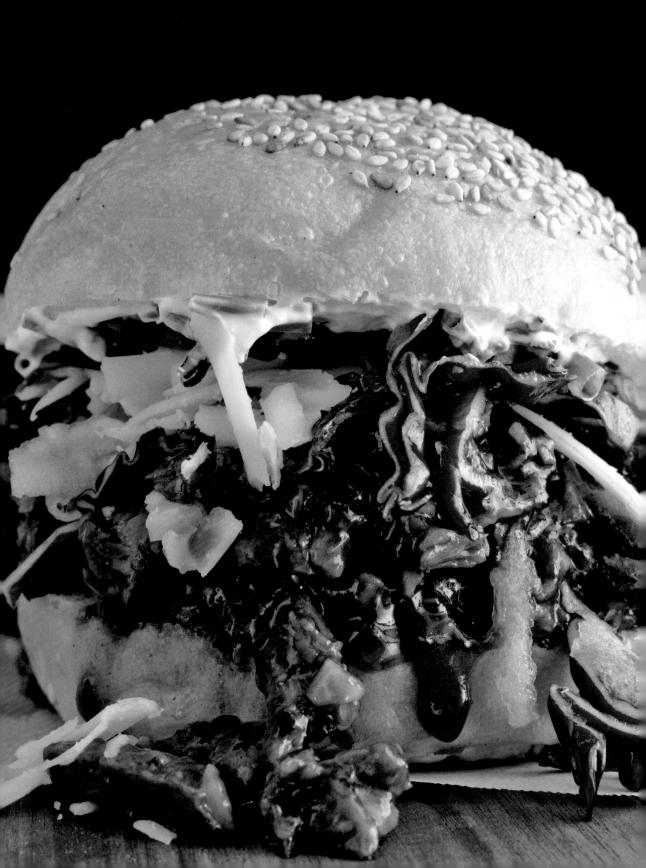

THE BEST SANDWICH I EVER MADE (and MY HUSBAND EVER TASTED)

aka The 7-Hour Smoked Brisket Sandwich with Smoky BBQ Sauce, Sharp Cheddar, Red Cabbage Slaw, and Horseradish Sauce

SERVES 8 WITH LEFTOVERS

Smokers are all the rage these days and I get it! Whether it's sweet and tangy smoked honey and lemon chicken or 7-hour brisket, our smokers—small and large—make the food too tender for words.

Make the rub: In a small bowl, combine the rub ingredients.

Generously coat the brisket with lots of black pepper on all sides, then the spice rub, massaging the spices into the meat. Cover with plastic wrap and let sit overnight in the fridge.

Preheat a smoker to 250°F and set up for cooking over indirect heat by placing coals and a couple of handfuls of wood chips (apple or cherry chips are nice) to one side. Place the brisket fat side up on the grate on the opposite side from the coals and cook for 4 hours.

Remove the brisket from the smoker and slather with the grated onion. Using a double layer of foil, create a pouch/packet around the brisket. Add the apple juice and beer and tightly seal the foil pouch. Place the brisket back in the smoker for another 2 hours, adding a handful of chips and 12 or so coals. After 2 hours, open the lid and let the brisket sit in the packet for another hour.

While the brisket finishes cooking, make the Smoky BBQ Sauce, Horseradish Sauce, and Red Cabbage Slaw.

Thinly slice the brisket against the grain on a large cutting board. Add some BBQ sauce to the brisket slices and give everything a rough chop to combine.

(CONTINUED ON FOLLOWING PAGE)

SPICE RUB:

3 tablespoons **smoked sea salt** or **kosher salt**

2 tablespoons **light brown sugar**

3 tablespoons **sweet paprika**

1 tablespoon **mustard seeds**

1 tablespoon **garlic powder**

2 teaspoons **ground coriander**

2 teaspoons **ground cumin**

2 teaspoons **ground ginger**

1½ teaspoons **cayenne pepper**

1 (8-pound) **brisket**, fat trimmed to ⅛ inch on top

Pepper

1 **red onion**, grated

½ cup **apple juice** or **cider**

½ cup **lager beer**, at room temperature

Smoky BBQ Sauce, Horseradish Sauce, and **Red Cabbage Slaw** (recipes follow)

8 seeded **sourdough** or **kaiser rolls**, split

Coarsely grated **extra-sharp cheddar cheese**

Pile the roll bottoms with brisket and top with a sprinkle of cheddar and some slaw. Slather the roll tops with horseradish sauce and set the tops in place.

SMOKY BBQ SAUCE

MAKES ABOUT 2 CUPS

Combine all ingredients in a small saucepan. Bring to a simmer and cook at a low bubble for 15 to 20 minutes.

1 cup good-quality ketchup, such as Heinz Organic

2 large cloves garlic, finely chopped

2 tablespoons dark brown sugar

2 tablespoons dark amber maple syrup

2 tablespoons Worcestershire sauce

1½ tablespoons cider vinegar

½ cup beef stock

1 teaspoon smoked sweet paprika

Coarsely ground pepper

HORSERADISH SAUCE

MAKES ABOUT 1 CUP

In a small bowl, stir together all ingredients. Refrigerate until needed.

1 cup sour cream

1 tablespoon heavy cream

1 tablespoon sliced chives

1 to 2 tablespoons prepared horseradish, to taste

Kosher salt and pepper

RED CABBAGE SLAW

MAKES ABOUT 3 CUPS

Mix all ingredients together in a bowl until the cabbage is coated with dressing. Refrigerate until needed.

2 cups packed shredded red cabbage

½ cup grated red onion (1 small or ½ medium)

1 Granny Smith apple, peeled and grated

3 tablespoons vegetable oil

2 tablespoons cider vinegar

1 teaspoon superfine sugar

Kosher salt and pepper

RED WINE and GARLIC MARINATED SLICED STEAK SANDWICHES

SERVES 4 TO 6

Pat the beef dry and season with kosher salt and a liberal amount of pepper. Whisk up the wine, garlic, rosemary, and EVOO, then pour into a large (2-gallon) plastic food storage bag. Add the beef and seal the bag, pushing out most of the air. Lay the bag flat and rub with your hands to distribute the marinade, bathing the beef evenly in it. Refrigerate for several hours.

Bring the beef to room temperature. Preheat the broiler and set the rack one level up from the center of the oven.

Shake off the excess marinade and place the beef on a broiler pan. Broil 5 minutes on each side for rare; 12 minutes total for a pink center (or medium). Let the steak rest 5 to 10 minutes, then thinly slice against the grain.

Dress the sliced steak with a squeeze of lemon juice, a pinch of sea salt, some parsley, and a drizzle of EVOO. Pile the seasoned beef into the warm, crusty bread.

1½ to 2 pounds **flank steak** or **top round** (used for, and sometimes labeled as, London broil), 1 inch thick

Kosher salt and coarsely ground **pepper**

½ cup **dry red wine**

6 cloves **garlic**, finely chopped

2 tablespoons finely chopped **rosemary**

⅓ cup **EVOO** (extra-virgin olive oil), plus more for drizzling

Small wedges of **lemon**

Fine sea salt

Chopped **flat-leaf parsley**

Baguettes, cut into 6- to 8-inch lengths, or **crusty sub rolls**, split open like a book and warmed

CHICAGOAN-ITALIAN ROAST BEEF HEROES

MAKES 10 HOAGIES

If making homemade giardiniera, make it 2 days ahead.

Preheat the oven to 325°F.

Heat 1 tablespoon EVOO, 1 turn of the pan, in a large Dutch oven over high heat. Pat the roast dry and season liberally with salt and pepper. Add to the pan and brown evenly on all sides. Transfer to a plate. Wipe the pan out and reduce the heat to medium. Heat 2 tablespoons EVOO, 2 turns of the pan, in the pan. Add the 2 chopped onions, the garlic, bay leaves, thyme, rosemary, and oregano. Stir and cook 5 to 6 minutes to soften the vegetables. Add the wine, deglaze the pan, and boil until the wine is reduced, about 5 minutes. Stir in the stock and tomatoes. Return the roast to the pot, cover, and bake until tender, 3 to 3½ hours.

Carefully remove the roast to a cutting board and let rest. Discard the thyme sprigs and bay leaves. Stir the sauce and place over medium-high heat until reduced by half. When the sauce is reduced, slice the meat thinly against the grain and return to the sauce.

While the sauce is reducing, heat the remaining 1 tablespoon EVOO, 1 turn of the pan, in a large skillet over medium to medium-high heat. Add the cubanelle or bell peppers and the 1 sliced onion and season with salt and pepper. Cook, stirring occasionally, until softened, 10 to 15 minutes.

Open a hoagie roll, fill with beef, and top with provolone, sautéed peppers and onions, and giardiniera. Close up the rolls.

3 cups **giardiniera** (Italian hot pickled vegetables), store-bought or homemade (recipe follows)

HEROES:

4 tablespoons **EVOO** (extra-virgin olive oil)

1 (3- to 3½-pound) **beef chuck roast**, at room temperature

Kosher salt and coarsely ground **black pepper**

3 **onions**, 2 chopped and 1 thinly sliced

6 cloves **garlic**, sliced

2 large **fresh bay leaves**

A small handful of **thyme** sprigs

2 sprigs **fresh rosemary**

1½ teaspoons **dried oregano** or **marjoram**

1½ cups **dry red wine**

4 cups **beef stock**

1 (15-ounce) can **diced tomatoes**

4 **cubanelle** or 2 **bell peppers**, seeded, halved, and thinly sliced

10 Italian-style **hoagie rolls** or Italian **bread** cut into 8-inch lengths, split open like a book

1 pound deli-sliced **provolone cheese** (sliced, not shaved!)

GIARDINIERA

MAKES ABOUT 4 CUPS

Place the salt in a bowl large enough to hold all the vegetables. Add the bell or cubanelle pepper, chiles, cauliflower, carrots, and celery. Pour in enough cold water to cover. Stir to dissolve the salt and cover. Make sure the vegetables are covered with liquid. Refrigerate for at least 2 days or up to 1 week before using.

Before serving, whisk up a dressing of garlic, oregano, celery seeds, vinegar, and oil. Drain the vegetables and toss with the dressing and olives.

¼ cup **kosher salt**

1 small **red bell pepper** or **green cubanelle pepper**, quartered, seeded, and cut into ½-inch slices

2 **small finger peppers, Fresno chiles,** or **banana chile peppers**, sliced into thin rings

2 cups **cauliflower** florets, blanched

2 **carrots**, cut into ¼-inch-thick slices

2 to 3 ribs **celery**, with leafy tops, chopped into 1-inch pieces

2 large cloves **garlic**, grated or minced

1 teaspoon **dried oregano** or **marjoram**

1 teaspoon **celery seeds**

¼ cup **white balsamic** or **white wine vinegar**

¼ cup **EVOO** (extra-virgin olive oil)

1 cup **Sicilian green olives**, pitted and chopped

SCHNITZEL-WICH with GARLIC BUTTER and HOT RELISH

SERVES 4

Pulse-chop the giardiniera in a food processor until coarsely chopped (like a relish).

Pound the veal very thin (about ⅛ inch) and season with salt and pepper. Line up 3 shallow bowls on the counter: Spread the flour out in one, beat the eggs in the second, and mix together the breadcrumbs and nutmeg in the third. Coat the veal in the flour, then in egg, and finally in the breadcrumb mixture, pressing to make sure the coating sticks.

Heat a thin layer of oil in a large skillet. Add as many cutlets as will fit in the pan without crowding and cook, turning once, over medium heat, until golden, 4 to 6 minutes. Repeat with the rest of the cutlets if necessary. Drain on a cooling rack.

Wipe out the pan and return to the heat. Add the butter and heat until foaming. Add the garlic and stir 1 to 2 minutes. Add the parsley and lemon juice; remove from the heat.

Place the schnitzels on the roll bottoms and top with garlic butter, lettuce, and giardiniera relish. Set the roll tops in place.

HOLSTEINER-STYLE SCHNITZEL-WICH

Top the veal cutlet with 2 crossed anchovy fillets and an egg fried over-easy.

1 cup **giardiniera** (Italian hot pickled vegetables), store-bought or homemade (page 183), drained

4 (5- to 6-ounce) **veal cutlets**

Kosher salt and **pepper**

1 cup **flour**

2 large **eggs**

1 cup **fine dry breadcrumbs**

A few grates of **nutmeg**

EVOO (extra-virgin olive oil) or **vegetable oil**, for frying

4 tablespoons (½ stick) **butter**

4 cloves **garlic**, finely chopped

A handful of **flat-leaf parsley**, finely chopped

Juice of 1 **lemon**

4 **ciabatta rolls**, split

Green-leaf lettuce leaves

PORTLAND PORK SCHNITZEL-WICHES with PINOT-BLACKBERRY GRAVY

SERVES 4

Make the schnitzels: Grind the hazelnuts in a food processor to fine crumbs. Season the cutlets with salt and pepper. Line up 3 shallow bowls on the counter: Spread the flour out in one, beat the eggs in the second, and mix together the breadcrumbs and ground hazelnuts in the third. Coat the cutlets in the flour, then in egg, and finally in the breadcrumb mixture, pressing to make sure the coating sticks.

Preheat the oven to 275°F. Place a cooling rack over a baking sheet to allow heat to circulate around the cutlets while they stay hot and crispy in the oven.

Heat a shallow layer of oil in a large skillet over medium-high heat. Add as many cutlets as will fit in the pan without crowding and cook until golden brown, 2 to 3 minutes on each side. Repeat with the rest of the cutlets if necessary. Place on the cooling rack on the baking sheet and keep warm in the oven.

Make the gravy: Melt the butter in a small saucepan over medium heat. Add the shallot and cook to soften, 2 to 3 minutes. Add the flour and cook, whisking, 1 minute. Whisk in the wine, bring the sauce to a bubble, and cook 1 minute to reduce. Stir in the blackberries and stock, season with salt and pepper, and cook a few minutes until thickened.

Pile the parsley, mint, and thyme on a cutting board and chop them together.

Place the schnitzels on the roll bottoms and slather with some blackberry gravy. Arrange a few pickles on top and sprinkle with the chopped herbs. Set the roll tops in place.

PORK SCHNITZELS:

½ cup **hazelnuts**, skinned, chopped, and toasted

4 (6-ounce) **boneless pork loin cutlets**, pounded to ⅛ inch thick

Kosher salt and **pepper**

Flour

2 large **eggs**

1 cup **fine dry breadcrumbs**

Canola oil or **vegetable oil**, for frying

BLACKBERRY GRAVY:

3 tablespoons **butter**

1 large **shallot**, minced

2 tablespoons **flour**

½ cup **pinot noir** or other **dry red wine**

⅓ cup mashed **blackberries** (preferably fresh but frozen will do)

½ cup **chicken stock**

½ cup **flat-leaf parsley** leaves

¼ cup **mint** leaves

2 to 3 tablespoons **fresh thyme** leaves

4 crusty **ciabatta rolls** or **hoagie rolls**, split

Bread-and-butter pickle slices

ALBONDIGAS SUBS: SPICY SPANISH MEATBALL SUBS

SERVES 4 (MAKES 20 OR 24 SMALL MEATBALLS)

Preheat the broiler.

Make the salsa: Halve the chiles and seed them. Place them skin side up on a baking sheet and blacken them under the broiler with the oven door ajar to let steam escape. (Or leave them whole and char them over an open flame on a stovetop burner.) Place the charred peppers in a bowl, cover with plastic wrap, and cool. When cool enough to handle, peel, seed, and chop the peppers. Switch the oven setting to 400°F.

Heat the EVOO, 2 turns of the pan, in a medium saucepot over medium heat. Add the onion, garlic, and oregano and season with salt and pepper. Cook 8 to 10 minutes, stirring occasionally. Stir in the beer or wine. Add the chopped roasted chiles, tomato sauce, and diced tomatoes and heat through. Reduce the heat to low to keep warm. Just before serving, stir in the Tabasco sauce and lime juice.

Make the meatballs: Toast the nuts in a small skillet over medium heat until golden in color and fragrant. Pulse them in a food processor to fine crumbs and set aside. Wipe out the processor bowl and return it to the base. Grind the chorizo in the processor until finely ground.

In a large bowl, combine the pork, ground almonds, ground chorizo, garlic, grated onion (grate it right over the bowl so the juices fall into the meat), parsley, breadcrumbs, egg yolk, and paprika; season with salt and lots of pepper.

Drizzle liberally with EVOO and mix thoroughly.

WARM FIRE-ROASTED SALSA:

2 medium **poblano** or 4 large **jalapeño chiles**

2 tablespoons **EVOO** (extra-virgin olive oil)

1 **Spanish onion**, finely chopped

3 to 4 large cloves **garlic**, finely chopped

1 teaspoon **dried oregano**

Kosher salt and **pepper**

½ cup **lager beer** (such as Corona) or **white wine**

1 cup or 1 (8-ounce) can **tomato sauce**

1 (28-ounce) can **diced fire-roasted tomatoes**

2 teaspoons **Tabasco sauce**

Juice of 1 **lime**

MEATBALLS (ALBONDIGAS):

¼ cup **sliced almonds**

⅓ pound **Spanish chorizo**, casing removed, coarsely chopped

1 pound **ground pork**

2 cloves **garlic**, minced or finely chopped

3 tablespoons grated **onion**

A generous handful of **flat-leaf parsley**, finely chopped

¼ to ⅓ cup **breadcrumbs** (a generous handful)

1 **egg** yolk, beaten

Score the mixture into 4 equal portions and form each portion into 5 or 6 small meatballs. Arrange the balls on a cooling rack set over a baking sheet as you roll them. Roast 12 to 15 minutes, or until deep golden brown.

Place the meatballs in the sub rolls and top with the salsa and cheese and toppings of your choice.

1 tablespoon **smoked sweet paprika**

EVOO (extra-virgin olive oil), for drizzling

4 crusty **sub rolls** or 4 (6-inch) pieces **baguette**, split open like a book

Shredded **Manchego cheese** or **queso fresco** crumbles

TOPPING OPTIONS:

Chopped **giardiniera** (Italian hot pickled vegetables) or **bottled hot pepper rings**

Sliced or chopped **pimiento-stuffed Spanish olives**

Cilantro or **flat-leaf parsley** leaves

Thinly sliced or chopped **scallions**

TIP: The rack allows the heat to circulate around the meatballs and brown them evenly without turning.

PULLED PORK with BROCCOLI RABE SUBS

MAKES 8 SUBS

Preheat the oven to 325°F.

Butterfly the pork shoulder by cutting a third into and across the meat back in opposite directions to "un-roll" the meat.

Squeeze the lemon into a food processor. Add 4 tablespoons EVOO, 1 chile, the garlic, parsley, rosemary, and thyme. Pulse-chop into a thick sauce.

Season the pork with salt and pepper and slather with the sauce. Roll the meat up and tie it tightly with kitchen twine. Drizzle with EVOO to coat and season liberally with salt and pepper. Heat a large Dutch oven over medium-high heat and brown the meat on all sides. Transfer to a plate. Add the onion and wine to the pan and stir to deglaze. Add the stock and return the pork to the pan. Pour the tomatoes over the top and lightly crush them with your hands. Spoon some of the sauce over the meat. Bring to a bubble, cover the pan, and braise in the oven until very tender, 2½ to 3 hours. (You can also cook the pork on the stovetop at a slow bubble for the same amount of time.) Remove from the oven and let rest 30 minutes. Change the oven setting to broil.

While the meat rests, bring a few inches of salted water to a boil in a large saucepan. Fill a large bowl with ice and water. Boil the broccoli rabe 3 to 4 minutes. Drain and plunge it into ice water; drain well.

Heat the remaining EVOO, 2 turns of the pan, in a large skillet over medium-high heat. Add the remaining 2 chiles, the cubanelles, and bell peppers; season with salt and pepper. Cook, stirring, until tender. Meanwhile, transfer the pork to a cutting board and shred by hand or using 2 forks. Stir the pork back into the sauce to heat.

Cover the insides of the rolls with cheese, and broil to melt. Top with the rabe, peppers, and pork and close up the rolls.

1 (3- to 4-pound) **boneless pork shoulder**

1 **lemon**

6 tablespoons **EVOO** (extra-virgin olive oil), plus more for drizzling

3 **Fresno** or other fresh red **chiles**, thinly sliced

1 head **garlic**, cloves separated and peeled

¼ cup chopped **flat-leaf parsley** (a handful)

3 to 4 tablespoons **fresh rosemary**

3 tablespoons **fresh thyme** leaves

Kosher salt and **pepper**

1 large **onion**, thinly sliced

1½ cups **dry white wine**

2 cups **chicken stock**

1 (28- to 32-ounce) can **San Marzano tomatoes**

2 bundles **broccoli rabe**, trimmed of tough ends

4 **cubanelle peppers**, seeded and sliced

2 **red bell peppers**, seeded and sliced

8 large **Italian sub rolls** or **ciabatta loaves** cut into 8 (8-inch) lengths and split open like a book

4 cups shredded **sharp provolone cheese** or 24 slices deli-sliced **provolone**

TIP: Squeeze the lemon cut side up to prevent the seeds from falling into the processor.

ITALIAN SLICED CHICKEN and PORK HOAGIES

SERVES 4

Preheat the oven to 500°F. Coat the pork tenderloin and chicken in a healthy drizzle of EVOO and season with salt and pepper. Set the pork on a cooling rack over a baking sheet and roast 10 to 12 minutes; lower the temperature to 425°F and cook 15 minutes more; DO NOT OPEN THE OVEN. Remove the roast (internal temp will be 145°F to 155°F). Transfer the pork to a cutting board and let rest.

While the pork is roasting, heat a cast-iron skillet or griddle over medium-high heat. Cook the chicken 12 to 15 minutes, flipping occasionally, until firm but not tight and juices run clear. Transfer to a cutting board to rest.

While the meats are cooking, make the dressing: In a small bowl, combine the chile, garlic, shallot or onion, sugar, vinegar, basil, parsley, and thyme. Squeeze in the juice from the ½ lemon. Whisk in the EVOO in a slow stream, adding salt and pepper to taste and then the mustard, whisking to emulsify.

Pulse-chop the giardiniera in a food processor to a fine relish texture.

When they have rested, slice the pork and chicken very thinly on an angle. Spoon some of the giardiniera onto the bottom halves of the sub rolls. Top with the sliced meat, provolone, lettuce, tomato, and onion. Pour the dressing over the subs and close up the rolls.

1 **pork tenderloin**, well trimmed

1¼ to 1⅓ pounds **boneless, skinless chicken breasts**

EVOO (extra-virgin olive oil), for drizzling

Kosher salt and **pepper**

HOAGIE DRESSING:

1 small **Fresno chile pepper,** seeded and finely chopped

1 large clove **garlic**, grated

1 **shallot**, minced, or 3 tablespoons grated **red onion**

1 rounded teaspoon **superfine sugar**

3 tablespoons **red wine vinegar**

1 tablespoon finely chopped **fresh basil**

1 tablespoon finely chopped **flat-leaf parsley**

2 teaspoons finely chopped **fresh thyme** leaves

½ **lemon**

½ cup **EVOO** (extra-virgin olive oil)

1 rounded tablespoon **Dijon mustard**

1 cup drained **giardiniera** (Italian hot pickled vegetables), store-bought or homemade (page 183)

4 **sub rolls**, or **Italian bread** cut into 8-inch lengths, split

Deli-sliced **provolone**

Chopped **romaine lettuce**

Sliced **tomato**

Thinly sliced **red onion**

PORK SCHNITZEL SANDWICHES with CHUNKY APPLE and ONION CHUTNEY

SERVES 4

Serve this with a simple oil-and-vinegar slaw (see Brooklyn Beer Chili Sliders on page 141).

Make the chutney: Melt the butter in a saucepan over medium to medium-high heat. Add the onion, apples, cinnamon, bay leaves, sugar, and lemon juice; season with salt, pepper, and a light sprinkle of nutmeg. Cook at a bubble to a saucelike consistency, stirring occasionally, 20 to 25 minutes. Douse with the Calvados or brandy. Remove bay leaves.

Preheat the broiler.

Make the schnitzel: Season the pork or chicken with salt and pepper. Line up 3 shallow bowls on the counter: Spread flour out in one, beat the eggs with the half-and-half or milk in the second, and mix together the bread-crumbs, nutmeg, and parsley in the third. Coat the pork in the flour, then in egg, and finally in the breadcrumb mixture, pressing to make sure the coating sticks.

Heat a thin layer of oil in a large skillet over medium heat. Add as many cutlets as will fit in the pan without crowding and cook until crisp and golden, 6 to 8 minutes. Repeat with the rest of the cutlets if necessary. Squeeze lemon juice over the cutlets just before you're ready to build the sandwiches.

Lightly toast the rolls under the broiler. Place the schnitzels on the roll bottoms and top with chutney and cheddar. Return to the broiler until the cheese is melted. Set the roll tops in place.

APPLE AND ONION CHUTNEY:

2 tablespoons **butter**

1 **sweet onion**, finely chopped

5 **apples**, such as Fuji or Honeycrisp, peeled, cored, and chopped

1 **stick cinnamon**

2 **fresh bay leaves**

1 teaspoon **sugar**

1 teaspoon fresh **lemon** juice

Kosher salt and **pepper**

Freshly grated **nutmeg**

1 shot **Calvados** or **apple brandy**

SCHNITZELS:

4 (6-ounce) **boneless pork loin cutlets**, pounded to ¼ inch thick, or the same amount of **chicken breasts**, pounded to ¼ inch thick

Flour

3 large **eggs**

¼ cup **half-and-half** or **milk**

2 cups **fine dry breadcrumbs**

A few grates of **nutmeg**

A handful of **flat-leaf parsley**, finely chopped

Vegetable oil, for frying

Lemon wedges

4 **ciabatta rolls**, split

1 cup shredded **extra-sharp white cheddar cheese**

BOURBON BBQ PULLED CHICKEN SANDWICHES and GREEN APPLE SLAW

SERVES 4

Make the chicken: Place the chicken in a medium pot and add the carrot, onion, orange, and bay leaves. Season with salt and pour in enough water to cover. Cover the pan, bring to a boil, and cook at a low rolling boil for 20 minutes.

Transfer the chicken to a cutting board. When cool enough to handle, remove the skin and bones from the chicken and shred the meat. Strain the broth, return it to the pot, and bring to a boil over high heat to reduce for a few minutes.

Meanwhile, make the BBQ sauce: In a small saucepan, combine all the ingredients for the BBQ sauce and simmer over medium-low heat for 20 minutes.

Make the slaw: In a large bowl, whisk together the lemon juice, vinegar, superfine sugar, salt, onion, and oil; season with pepper. Add the cabbage and apple to the bowl and toss to coat with the dressing.

Add 1 cup of the reduced poaching liquid to the BBQ sauce. Stir in the shredded chicken. Stir and shred the chicken a little more with 2 forks.

Pile the BBQ chicken on the roll bottoms and top with pickles and slaw. Set the roll tops in place.

POACHED CHICKEN:

2 small bone-in, skin-on **chicken breast** halves

2 bone-in, skin-on **chicken thighs**

1 small **carrot**, coarsely chopped

1 small **onion**, quartered

1/2 **orange**, sliced

2 **bay leaves**

Kosher salt

BBQ SAUCE:

1 cup good-quality **ketchup**, such as Heinz Organic

2 shots of **bourbon**

2 large cloves **garlic**, finely chopped

2 tablespoons **Dijon mustard**

2 tablespoons **dark amber maple syrup**

2 tablespoons **dark brown sugar**

2 tablespoons **Worcestershire sauce**

2 tablespoons **cider vinegar**

1 teaspoon **ground ginger**

1 teaspoon coarsely ground **pepper**

1/8 teaspoon freshly grated **nutmeg**

GREEN APPLE SLAW:

Juice of 1 **lemon**

3 tablespoons **cider vinegar**

1 tablespoon **superfine sugar**

1 1/2 teaspoons **kosher salt** or **sea salt**

1/2 **red onion**, grated

1/3 cup **vegetable oil** or **olive oil**

Pepper

½ pound **cabbage**, thinly shredded

1 large **green apple**, peeled and coarsely grated

4 **brioche rolls**, split

Bread-and-butter pickle slices

FISHWICHES

SERVES 6

Make the tartar sauce: In a bowl, combine the mayo with a squirt of lemon juice, the grated shallot or onion, cornichons or pickles, capers, dill, parsley, Worcestershire sauce, and hot sauce. Chill until ready to use.

Make the slaw: In a large bowl, whisk up the shallot, lemon juice, vinegar, sugar, salt, celery seeds, and oil. Add the fennel or carrots and cabbage and toss well. Refrigerate the slaw until ready to serve.

Make the fish: Fill a countertop deep fryer with oil or pour 2½ to 3 inches of oil into a large deep pot. Heat the oil to 375°F. (The oil is ready for frying when bubbles stream out rapidly from the handle of a wooden spoon inserted into the oil.)

While the oil is heating, in a large bowl, whisk together the beer, flour, Old Bay, baking powder, and egg. Season the fish with salt and pepper and dredge lightly in Wondra.

When the oil is hot, dip the fish, 2 pieces at a time, in the batter and fry 4 to 5 minutes until deep golden.

Place the fish on the roll bottoms and top with slaw. Slather the roll tops with tartar sauce and set them in place.

TARTAR SAUCE:

Basic Mayo (page 275) or 1 cup store-bought **mayo**

½ small **lemon**

2 tablespoons grated **shallot** or mild **onion**

3 tablespoons finely chopped **cornichons** or **dill pickles**

2 tablespoons **capers**, chopped

2 tablespoons finely chopped **fresh dill**

2 tablespoons finely chopped **flat-leaf parsley**

1 teaspoon **Worcestershire sauce**

1 teaspoon **hot sauce**

LEMON SLAW:

¼ cup grated **shallot** or **red onion**

Juice of 1 **lemon**

3 tablespoons **white wine vinegar** or **white balsamic vinegar**

2 teaspoons **superfine sugar**

2 teaspoons **kosher salt**

1½ teaspoons **celery seeds**

¼ cup **olive oil** or **vegetable oil**

1 small bulb **fennel**, very thinly sliced, or 2 **carrots**, shredded

1 small head **cabbage** (¾ to 1 pound), quartered, cored, and very thinly shredded

FISH:

Vegetable oil or other light oil, for frying

1 (12-ounce) bottle **lager beer**

2 cups **flour**

2 tablespoons **Old Bay seasoning**

1 teaspoon **baking powder**

1 large **egg**, beaten

2 pounds **cod** or other sustainable white fish fillets, cut into 4- to 5-inch chunks

Pepper

Wondra flour

6 **ciabatta rolls, ciabatta loaves** cut into roll-size pieces, or **brioche rolls**, split, buttered, and grilled

TEX-MEX BEER-BATTERED FISHWICHES with AVOCADO SAUCE

SERVES 4

Fill a countertop fryer with oil or pour a few inches of oil into a large Dutch oven. Heat the oil to 350° to 375°F. (The oil is ready for frying when a 1-inch cube of white bread cooks to golden brown in 40 seconds.)

Make the batter: In a bowl, whisk together the beer, flour, coriander, cumin, paprika, and cayenne; season with salt.

Season the onions: Separate the red onion into rings and douse with the lime juice and season with salt and pepper.

Make the avocado sauce: Grate the garlic directly into the bowl of a food processor or blender. Add the avocado flesh and squeeze in the lemon juice. (Squeeze it cut side up to keep the seeds from falling into the processor.) Add the sour cream, cilantro, chile, and a good pinch of salt. Process or blend to a smooth green sauce. Scrape into a small serving dish and reserve.

Coat the fish pieces in the beer batter and fry in the hot oil to deep golden, 6 to 7 minutes. Drain on a cooling rack and season with a pinch of salt.

Place the fish on the roll bottoms and top with pickles, tomato, lettuce, and lime-pickled red onion. Slather the roll tops with avocado sauce and set in place.

Serve with salt-and-vinegar chips or corn tortilla chips and salsa alongside.

Vegetable oil or other light oil, for frying

BEER BATTER:

1 cup Mexican beer

1 cup flour

1 teaspoon ground coriander

1 teaspoon ground cumin

1 teaspoon sweet paprika

½ teaspoon cayenne pepper

Kosher salt and pepper

ONIONS:

1 small red onion, thinly sliced

Juice of 1 lime

AVOCADO SAUCE:

1 clove garlic

1 avocado

Juice of 1 lemon

1 cup sour cream

A small handful of cilantro

1 large jalapeño or 2 small serrano chiles, seeded and chopped

4 (6-ounce) thick pieces sustainable white fish, such as cod

4 brioche rolls, split

Chopped pickles

4 slices tomato

Sliced lettuce

Salt-and-vinegar potato chips or corn tortilla chips and salsa

NIÇOISE-STYLE PAN BAGNATS

SERVES 4

The longer these sit, the better they get, so make ahead for the beach or a picnic.

In a large bowl, whisk together the lemon juice, shallot, garlic, mustard, herbes de Provence, and fennel pollen. Slowly whisk in the EVOO to combine; season with salt and pepper.

Flake the tuna into the dressing. Add the olives, capers, parsley, celery, and onion and stir to mix. Fill the baguette rolls with the tuna salad and top with hard-boiled egg, tomato, tarragon leaves, and anchovies (if using).

Juice of 2 **lemons**

1 **shallot**, grated or minced

1 clove **garlic**, grated or pasted (see Tip, page 138)

1 tablespoon **Dijon mustard**

1 tablespoon dried **herbes de Provence**

½ teaspoon **fennel pollen** (see page 126) or ground **fennel seeds**

⅓ cup **EVOO** (extra-virgin olive oil)

Kosher salt and **pepper**

2 (6-ounce) cans **imported tuna** or **line-caught American tuna**, drained

¼ cup **niçoise olives**, pitted and chopped

2 tablespoons **capers**

¼ cup coarsely chopped **flat-leaf parsley** leaves

2 ribs **celery**, finely chopped

½ small **red onion**, finely chopped

Baguettes, cut into 4 (10-inch) lengths, split open like a book

4 hard-boiled **eggs**, peeled and chopped

2 **plum tomatoes**, seeded and chopped

Tarragon leaves, stripped from the sprig

Anchovy fillets (optional)

BIG, BEEFY MUSHROOM CHEDDAR MELTS

SERVES 4

In a shallow bowl, whisk together the Worcestershire sauce, sherry, EVOO, and 1 tablespoon pepper. Slice each mushroom cap horizontally into 2 mushroom disks each ½ to ¾ inch thick. You will end up with a total of 8 mushroom rounds. Add the mushroom rounds to the bowl of sauce one at a time, turning each a few times in the sauce to coat it. Season with sea salt and marinate 30 to 45 minutes, turning occasionally in the sauce.

When you are ready to cook the mushrooms, preheat a large nonstick skillet or grill pan over medium-high heat. Cook the mushrooms 2 to 3 minutes on each side to brown them and develop their flavor. While still in the pan, make 4 stacks: mushroom disk, cheese slice, mushroom, cheese. Grill the stacks until the cheese melts, about 1 minute.

Place the stacks on the roll bottoms and top with tomato. Season the tomato with salt and pepper and top with greens. Slather the bun tops with mustard and set them in place. Serve with salt-and-vinegar chips.

¼ cup **Worcestershire sauce**

⅓ cup **dry sherry**

½ cup **EVOO** (extra-virgin olive oil)

Coarsely ground **pepper**

4 large **portobello mushroom** caps, gills scraped off (see Tip, page 225)

Sea salt

8 slices **extra-sharp yellow cheddar cheese**

4 **brioche rolls**, split and lightly toasted

4 thick slices **heirloom tomatoes**

A couple of handfuls of **watercress** or other **spicy greens**

Dijon mustard or other mustard of choice

Salt-and-vinegar potato chips

CUBANO DOGS
MAKES 8 CUBANO DOGS

Preheat the broiler.

Heat a griddle or cast-iron skillet over medium-high heat. Split the dogs or knocks lengthwise and open them up like a book. Grill them up until crispy on both sides.

Arrange the rolls on a baking sheet. Top the rolls with lots of mustard, chopped chiles, ham, and Swiss cheese. Broil just long enough to melt the cheese.

Nestle a dog and pickle spear on top of the melted cheese in each roll.

8 all-natural **pork** or **beef hot dogs** or **knockwursts**

8 **hot dog rolls, soft hoagie rolls**, or 6-inch **sub rolls**, split open like a book

Yellow mustard

1 (4-ounce) can **pickled jalapeños** (hot) or **green chiles** (mild), drained well and finely chopped

8 slices deli-sliced mild **ham**

8 thin slices good-quality **Swiss cheese**

8 **pickle spears**, homemade (recipe follows) or store-bought

SWEET 'N' SPICY PICKLE SPEARS
MAKES 20 OR 24 SPEARS

Bring the vinegar and ½ cup water to a boil in a medium saucepan. Stir in the salt and sugar until dissolved and remove from the heat.

Fit the cucumbers into two Mason jars tall enough to hold the spears standing up. Layer in the garlic, bay leaves, dill, chile pepper, red onion, peppercorns, mustard seeds, and coriander seeds. Pour enough hot brine over the cucumbers to fill the jars. Close the jars. Refrigerate for at least 24 hours or up to a few weeks.

1 cup **cider vinegar**

1 rounded teaspoon **kosher** or **sea salt**

2 rounded tablespoons **sugar**

5 or 6 **Kirby cucumbers**, quartered lengthwise

3 cloves **garlic**, smashed or halved

A few fresh or dried **bay leaves**

A small handful of **fresh dill**

1 **Fresno chile pepper**

¼ **red onion**, sliced

A few **black peppercorns**

1 teaspoon **mustard seeds**

1 teaspoon **coriander seeds**

HOT and SWEET PEPPER DOGS

MAKES 8 PEPPER DOGS

Heat a large griddle over medium-high heat. Bring a few inches of water to a boil in a deep skillet. Reduce the heat, keeping the water at a low boil.

Heat the EVOO, 2 turns of the pan, in a medium skillet over medium heat. Add the garlic and chile and stir 2 minutes. Add the cubanelle pepper, bell peppers, onion, and marjoram or oregano; season with salt and pepper. Cook until very tender, 10 minutes. Stir in the tomato paste, cook 1 minute, then add the stock. Reduce the heat to low to keep the peppers and onions saucy and warm.

Add the dogs to the boiling water and cook 4 to 5 minutes to heat through. Remove the dogs, split them lengthwise, and open them up like a book. Place on the hot griddle long enough to crisp the inside of the dog as well as the casing, a few minutes.

Nestle the dogs in the rolls and top with peppers and onions.

2 tablespoons **EVOO** (extra-virgin olive oil)

2 large cloves **garlic**, finely chopped

1 **fresh red chile**, such as Fresno, seeded and finely chopped

1 **cubanelle pepper**, thinly sliced

2 **red bell peppers**, seeded and very thinly sliced

1 large **onion**, thinly sliced

1 teaspoon **dried marjoram** or **oregano**

Kosher salt and **pepper**

1 tablespoon **tomato paste**

1 cup **chicken stock**

8 all-natural **pork** or **beef hot dogs**

8 bakery **hoagie**, **sub**, or **hot dog rolls**, split open like a book

MICHIGAN DOGS
with CHEESE SAUCE

MAKES 8 MICHIGAN DOGS

Heat a griddle over medium-high heat.

Bring a few inches of water to a boil in a deep skillet. Reduce the heat, keeping the water at a low boil.

Make the Michigan sauce: Heat the EVOO, 1 turn of the pan, in a saucepan over medium-high heat. Add the ground beef and brown, 5 to 6 minutes, crumbling with a wooden spoon as it cooks. Sprinkle with the chili powder, paprika, and coriander; season with salt and pepper. Stir in the tomato paste and cook 1 minute, then add the stock. Reduce the heat to simmering.

Make the cheese sauce: In a small saucepan, melt the butter over medium heat. Add the flour and cook 1 minute. Whisk in the milk, season with salt and pepper, and cook until thickened, 1 to 2 minutes. Melt the cheese into the sauce. Whisk in the mustard and reduce the heat to low.

Add the dogs to the boiling water and cook 4 to 5 minutes to heat through. Remove the dogs, split them lengthwise, and open like a book. Place on the hot griddle long enough to crisp the inside of the dog as well as the casing, a few minutes.

Nestle the dogs in the rolls and top with both the Michigan and the cheese sauces.

MICHIGAN SAUCE:

1 tablespoon **EVOO** (extra-virgin olive oil)

½ pound **ground beef chuck**

1 tablespoon **chili powder**

1½ teaspoons **smoked sweet paprika**

1½ teaspoons **ground coriander**

Kosher salt and **pepper**

1 tablespoon **tomato paste**

1½ cups **beef stock**

CHEESE SAUCE:

2 tablespoons **butter**

2 tablespoons **flour**

1½ cups **milk**

1 cup shredded **yellow cheddar cheese**

½ cup **yellow mustard**

8 large all-natural **pork** or **beef hot dogs**

8 bakery **hoagie**, **sub**, or **hot dog rolls**, split open like a book

PIGS IN PONCHOS: QUESADILLA-WRAPPED FRANKS and BEANS

MAKES 8 PONCHO DOGS

Preheat the broiler.

Halve the poblanos and seed them. Place them skin-side up on a baking sheet and blacken them under the broiler with the oven door ajar to let steam escape. (Or leave the poblanos whole and char them over an open flame on a stovetop burner.) Place the charred peppers in a bowl, cover with plastic wrap, and cool. When cool enough to handle, peel and seed the peppers. Slice 1 pepper and chop the other two.

Make the salsa verde: Heat the oil in a large skillet over medium-high heat. Add the onion, garlic, tomatillos, honey, and cumin; season with salt and pepper. Cook 12 to 15 minutes, stirring frequently, until the onions are tender. Add a splash of water if the sauce thickens into mounds. Squeeze in the lime juice. Transfer to a food processor, add the 2 chopped roasted poblanos and the cilantro, and process until smooth. (Makes about twice as much as you'll need for the pigs.)

Bring a few inches of water to a boil in a deep skillet. Add the dogs and cook 4 to 5 minutes to heat through. Heat the beans with a little water to thin in a small saucepan over medium heat (or in a covered dish in the microwave on high for 3 minutes).

Heat a griddle or grill pan over medium-high heat.

To make the quesadillas, top 8 tortillas with a thin layer of salsa, a swirl of mustard, a few slices of poblano, and lots of cheese. Top with the remaining 8 tortillas. Spread the top tortilla with some beans and set a dog at one end. Wrap and roll the quesadilla around the dog, coat the rolls with cooking spray, and grill a few minutes to brown and crisp the tortillas evenly on all sides and melt the cheese.

3 large **poblano chiles**

2 tablespoons **olive oil** or **vegetable oil**

1 **onion**, chopped

3 to 4 cloves **garlic**, finely chopped

6 to 8 medium to large **tomatillos**, husked, washed, and chopped

1 tablespoon **honey**

1 teaspoon **ground cumin**

Kosher salt and **pepper**

1 **lime**

A small handful of **cilantro** leaves

8 all-natural **pork** or **beef hot dogs**

1 (16-ounce) can **vegetarian spicy refried beans**

16 (8-inch) **flour tortillas**, at room temperature

Yellow mustard, jalapeño mustard, or **honey mustard**

2½ cups shredded **Monterey Jack cheese**

All-natural cooking spray

FIRECRACKER DEVILED CORN DOGS

MAKES 8 CORN DOGS

Fill a countertop fryer with oil or pour 2½ inches of oil into a large Dutch oven. Heat the oil to 350°F. (The oil is ready when a 1-inch cube of white bread cooks to golden brown in 40 seconds.)

Preheat the oven to 275°F and place a cooling rack over a baking sheet (to keep the corn dogs crispy after frying).

Meanwhile, sift the flour, sugar, and baking powder into a bowl. Stir in the mustard, paprika, cayenne (if using hot sauce, add it to the wet ingredients), onion powder, garlic powder, and salt and pepper. Stir in the cornmeal. In a separate bowl, whisk together the egg, 1 cup milk, hot sauce (if using), and 2 tablespoons oil. Stir the wet ingredients into the dry ingredients with a wooden spoon until smooth. Add up to ½ cup more milk, if needed, until the mixture has the consistency of pancake batter.

Pat the dogs dry and skewer them the long way, leaving some of the skewer exposed. Dip the dogs into the batter to coat and fry 2 to 3 at a time to deep golden all over, 4 to 5 minutes. Transfer the cooked dogs to the cooling rack and keep them warm in the oven while frying the rest.

Serve the corn dogs drizzled with mustard or sauce of your choice.

L'IL DEVILS (CORN DOG SLIDERS)

Substitute 20 to 24 pork or beef mini hot dogs for the full-size dogs. Use shorter skewers and fry the mini dogs in batches.

Vegetable oil for deep-frying, plus 2 tablespoons

1 cup flour

2 tablespoons superfine sugar

2 teaspoons baking powder

2 teaspoons dry mustard

2 teaspoons sweet paprika

1 teaspoon cayenne pepper or 1 tablespoon hot sauce

1 teaspoon onion powder or granulated onion

1 teaspoon garlic powder or granulated garlic

Kosher salt and pepper

¾ cup cornmeal

1 large egg

1 to 1½ cups milk

8 all-natural pork or beef hot dogs

8 (8- to 10-inch) bamboo or wooden skewers, trimmed to fit in the pot or fryer

Mustards or sauces of choice (try Chipotle Ketchup, page 276; Moroccan Ketchup, page 277; or Smoky BBQ Sauce, page 180) in squeeze bottles

CONEY CHILI DOGS

MAKES 8 CHILI DOGS

Make the sauce: Heat the oil, 1 turn of the pan, in a medium saucepan over medium-high heat. Add the beef and cook 5 to 6 minutes, crumbling with a wooden spoon as it cooks. Once the meat is browned, add the yellow onion, garlic, and chili powder; season with salt and pepper. Stir in 1 cup water and the tomato paste. Stir to combine, bring to a boil, and reduce the heat to simmering. Whisk in the mustard, Worcestershire sauce, and brown sugar. Cook over low heat until thick, 30 to 40 minutes.

When the sauce is ready, bring a few inches of water to a boil in a deep skillet. Reduce the heat to a low boil, add the dogs, and cook 4 to 5 minutes to heat through.

Nestle the dogs in the rolls, topped with Coney Island sauce and minced white onion.

CONEY ISLAND SAUCE:

1 tablespoon **vegetable oil**

1 pound **ground beef chuck**

1 **yellow onion**, finely chopped

2 cloves **garlic**, minced

2 tablespoons **chili powder**

Kosher salt and **pepper**

1 (6-ounce) can **tomato paste**

2 tablespoons **spicy brown mustard**

2 tablespoons **Worcestershire sauce**

2 tablespoons **light brown sugar**

8 all-natural **pork** or **beef hot dogs**

8 **hot dog rolls**, split open like a book

Minced **white onion**

JALAPEÑO POPPER DOGS

MAKES 8 POPPER DOGS

Try my hot dog salsa as a condiment on your favorite hot dog.

Bring a few inches of water to a boil in a deep skillet. Reduce to a low boil, add the dogs, and cook 4 to 5 minutes to heat through. Serve as is or cook a few minutes on a hot griddle (see Hot and Sweet Pepper Dogs, page 200) if you prefer crispy dogs.

Meanwhile, melt the butter in a saucepan over medium heat. Add the chiles and garlic; season with salt and pepper. Cook 2 to 3 minutes, then sprinkle with flour and cook 1 minute more. Whisk in the milk and cook until thickened, 2 to 3 minutes. Stir the cheeses into the sauce and adjust the salt and pepper to taste.

Nestle the dogs in the rolls, dress with a little mustard, then top with some cheese sauce, pickled jalapeños, and hot dog salsa.

8 all-natural **pork** or **beef hot dogs**

2 tablespoons **butter**

1 small **fresh red chile**, such as Fresno, seeded and finely chopped

2 **fresh jalapeño chiles**, seeded and finely chopped

1 clove **garlic**, finely chopped

Kosher salt and **pepper**

1 rounded tablespoon **flour**

1½ cups **milk**

1 cup grated **pepper jack** or **Monterey Jack cheese**

1 cup grated **extra-sharp yellow cheddar cheese**

8 **hot dog rolls**, split open like a book

Yellow mustard

Sliced **pickled jalapeños**

Hot Dog Salsa (a mix of 2 chopped seeded **tomatoes**; ½ small **onion**, diced; and 1 large **deli pickle**, chopped)

PIGS IN A BLANKET
with THE WORKS

MAKES 30 PIGS IN A BLANKET

Preheat the oven to 400°F.

Unroll all of the crescent dough. Separate the triangles, then cut each into two small triangles.

Lay out the triangle so that one of the points is closest to you. Spread ½ teaspoon brown mustard over the surface of each piece of dough. Place ¾ teaspoon each of the relish, onion, and sauerkraut in the center of each piece of the dough.

Place 1 mini dog on the part of the triangle closest to you and roll the dog and dough over itself, creating a crescent roll, just like it says in the package directions (except yours has a dog with the works in the center). The dog should peek out on both sides of the roll.

Arrange the pigs on a baking sheet and bake 15 to 20 minutes, until golden brown. Serve straight from the oven.

2 (8-ounce) tubes **refrigerated crescent roll dough**

⅓ cup **spicy brown mustard**

½ cup **sweet pickle relish**

1 small **white onion**, minced

½ cup **sauerkraut**, thoroughly drained

1 (12-ounce/30-count) package all-natural **cocktail franks**

REUBEN DOGS

MAKES 8 REUBEN DOGS

This is my spin on the classic Reuben sandwich, turned into a dog!

Make the red cabbage: Heat the EVOO, 2 turns of the pan, in a skillet over medium-high heat. Add the cabbage, onion, apple, caraway seeds, and bay leaves; season with salt and pepper. Cook, stirring frequently, until the cabbage is wilted. Add the brown sugar, cider, and vinegar. Reduce the heat and simmer 30 minutes, stirring occasionally.

Preheat the broiler.

When the cabbage is ready, heat a griddle or grill pan over medium-high heat. Split the wursts lengthwise and open them up like a book. Grill them until crisp on both sides.

Arrange the rolls on a baking sheet. Cover them with mustard and cheese and broil to melt the cheese.

Make the dressing: In a small bowl, stir together the sour cream, ketchup, and relish; season with salt and pepper.

Remove the bay leaves from the cabbage.

Nestle the wursts in the cheesy rolls and top with the dressing and cabbage.

RED CABBAGE:

2 tablespoons **EVOO** (extra-virgin olive oil)

1 pound **red cabbage**, shredded

1 medium **red onion**, thinly sliced

1 crisp **apple**, peeled, cored, and chopped

1½ teaspoons **caraway seeds**

2 **bay leaves**

Kosher salt and **pepper**

2 tablespoons **light** or **dark brown sugar**

1 cup cloudy **apple cider**

½ cup **cider vinegar**

WURSTS:

8 **bratwursts, knockwursts,** or **bockwursts**

8 (6-inch) **hot dog rolls** of choice, split open like a book

Spicy brown mustard

8 slices deli-sliced **Swiss cheese**

DRESSING:

1 cup **sour cream**

¼ cup good-quality **ketchup**, such as Heinz Organic

2 rounded tablespoons **dill relish**

TIP: Any leftover cabbage is a great sandwich topper for smoked turkey or ham sammies as well as a super side dish for schnitzel or roast beef dinners later in the week.

KIELBASA CHILI DOGS

SERVES 4

Melt the butter in a small skillet over medium heat. Add the sliced onions and cook, stirring frequently, until sweet and caramelized, 25 to 30 minutes.

Meanwhile, bring a few inches of water to a boil in a deep skillet. Place the kielbasa ring in the water and keep at a low boil to heat through, 7 to 8 minutes.

Heat a drizzle of oil in a small saucepan or skillet over medium-high heat. Add the beef or turkey and cook until browned, 5 to 6 minutes, crumbling it as it cooks. Add the grated onion (grate it right into the pan), the garlic, pimiento or roasted pepper, paprika, and chili powder. Cook 5 minutes, then add the tomato paste. Cook half a minute, then stir in the stock and reduce the heat to low. Season with salt and pepper.

Cut the kielbasa ring into 6 pieces. Split the kielbasa pieces lengthwise and open them up like a book. Heat a drizzle of oil in a large nonstick skillet or griddle over medium-high heat. Crisp up the kielbasa pieces on both sides.

Place the crispy kielbasa on the roll bottoms. Top with chili, caramelized onions, a dollop of sour cream, and a sprinkle of dill. Set the roll tops in place.

4 tablespoons (½ stick) **butter**

2 **onions**, 1½ onions thinly sliced, ½ onion grated

1 ring **kielbasa**

EVOO (extra-virgin olive oil) or **vegetable oil**, for drizzling

¾ pound **ground beef chuck** or **ground turkey**

2 cloves **garlic**, grated or finely chopped

3 to 4 tablespoons finely chopped **bottled pimiento** or **roasted red pepper**

1 tablespoon **smoked sweet paprika**

1½ teaspoons **chili powder**

1 generous tablespoon **tomato paste**

1 cup **beef stock** (if using ground beef) or **chicken stock** (if using ground turkey)

Kosher salt and **pepper**

6 **potato hamburger rolls**, or **hamburger roll** of choice, split

Sour cream

Chopped **fresh dill**

CREOLE ANDOUILLE DAWGS

MAKES 8 DAWGS

Preheat a large grill pan or griddle over medium-high heat.

Bring a few inches of water to a boil in a deep skillet. Reduce to a low boil, add the sausages, and cook 6 to 8 minutes to heat through. Drain the sausages and drizzle with a little oil. Add to the hot grill pan and crisp up the casings, 3 to 4 minutes.

Meanwhile, heat 3 tablespoons oil, 3 turns of the pan, in a skillet over medium-high heat. Add the celery, onion, bell pepper, and garlic; season with salt and black pepper. Cook, stirring frequently, until tender, 5 to 6 minutes. Add the flour and stir for a couple of minutes. Add the thyme and beer and stir for 30 seconds to thicken. Stir in the tomato paste. Add the stock, Worcestershire sauce, and hot sauce and bring to a bubble; reduce the heat to low.

Nestle the andouille in the baguette (or other rolls) and top with the sauce and scallions. *Ooh oui, chérie!* That's a dawg!

CREOLE ANDOUILLE DAWGS WITH GUMBO SAUCE

When the sauce is done and the heat is lowered, stir in 24 medium shrimp that have been peeled (including tails), deveined, and chopped. Simmer in the sauce until pink, 2 to 3 minutes.

8 **andouille sausages**

3 tablespoons **canola oil**, plus more for drizzling

2 small ribs **celery**, with leafy tops, finely chopped

1 medium **onion**, finely chopped

1 small **green bell pepper**, seeded and finely chopped

2 large cloves **garlic**, finely chopped

Kosher salt and black **pepper**

2 tablespoons **flour**

3 to 4 sprigs **fresh thyme**, leaves stripped and chopped

½ cup **lager beer**

2 tablespoons **tomato paste**

1 cup **chicken stock**

1 tablespoon **Worcestershire sauce**

Hot sauce, to taste

Baguette bread cut to fit sausages or other **crusty dawg rolls**, split open like a book

Chopped **scallions**

7-LAYER CHILI DOG DIP

SERVES 6 TO 8 AS A SNACK

Preheat the oven to 375°F.

Make the chili: Heat 1 tablespoon oil, 1 turn of the pan, in a large saucepan over medium-high heat. When the oil ripples, add the beef and cook 3 minutes, crumbling the beef with a wooden spoon. Add the onion, garlic, chile powder, grill seasoning, cumin, and coriander. Cook another 5 minutes. Pour in the beer and cook another minute, stirring to loosen any bits from the bottom of the pan. Add the stock and crushed tomatoes and bring to a bubble. Reduce the heat and simmer 10 minutes.

Make the dip: While the chili cooks, arrange the bacon on a slotted broiler pan or a cooling rack set over a baking sheet and bake until crisp, 12 to 15 minutes. Remove from the oven and when cool enough to handle, coarsely chop the bacon.

Heat 1 tablespoon EVOO, 1 turn of the pan, in a medium skillet over medium-high heat. Add the diced hot dogs and stir until lightly browned.

Ladle the chili into an 8-inch square glass baking dish. Top with a layer of dogs, followed by cheese. Bake until the cheese is melted, 12 to 15 minutes. Dollop the sour cream on top and scatter the bacon, diced tomatoes, red onion, and cilantro (if using) over the top.

Serve with tortilla chips.

CHILI CON CARNE:

1 tablespoon **EVOO** (extra-virgin olive oil), **corn oil**, or **vegetable oil**

1 pound **ground beef chuck**

1 small **onion**, chopped

2 cloves **garlic**, chopped

2 tablespoons **ancho chile powder**

1½ teaspoons **grill seasoning**, such as McCormick Montreal Steak Seasoning

1½ teaspoons **ground cumin**

1 teaspoon **ground coriander**

½ bottle (¾ cup) **lager beer**

½ cup **beef stock**

1 (14-ounce) can **chunky-style crushed tomatoes**

7-LAYER DIP:

½ pound **bacon**

1 tablespoon **EVOO** (extra-virgin olive oil)

4 all-natural **beef** or **pork hot dogs**, diced

1½ cups shredded **cheddar cheese**

1 cup **sour cream**

1 cup diced **vine-ripened tomatoes**

¼ cup diced **red onion**

¼ cup chopped **cilantro** (optional)

Good-quality **corn tortilla chips**

SLOPPIES

BEEF, PORK, and LAMB SLOPPIES

216 Philly Cheesesteak Sloppy Joes

218 Sloppy Chili Sliders

219 Sloppy Chipotle Joes

220 Sloppy Joaquins

221 Sloppy Joe DiMaggios

222 Tango Joes

223 Sloppy Sausage, Pepper, and Onion Joes

225 Messy Giuseppe

226 Sloppy Cubanos

227 Sloppy Dawgs

228 Sloppy Porchetta

229 Sloppy Merguez

CHICKEN, TURKEY, and VEGGIE SLOPPIES

230 BBQ Chicken Sloppy Joes with Pickled
Slaw Salad

232 Buffalo Joes

233 Cincinnati Sloppy Sliders

234 Sloppy Suizas

235 Sloppy Maple-BBQ Joes

237 Sloppy Veg-Head Joes with Beans

238 Sloppy Veg-Head Joes

PHILLY CHEESESTEAK SLOPPY JOES

SERVES 4

Heat 1 tablespoon EVOO, 1 turn of the pan, in a large skillet over medium-high heat. Add the beef and cook 5 to 6 minutes, crumbling with a wooden spoon as it browns. Add the onion and season with salt and pepper. Cook until the onions are tender, 7 to 8 minutes. Stir in the steak sauce and beef stock, bring the mixture up to a bubble, and cook for 2 minutes.

While the meat is cooking, melt the butter in a small skillet or saucepan over medium heat. Stir in the flour and cook for 1 minute, then whisk in the milk and let it come up to a bubble. Cook for a minute or two to thicken, then stir in the cheese. Remove from the heat.

Spoon the filling onto the roll bottoms and top with the super thick provolone cheese sauce. Set the roll tops in place.

4 tablespoons **EVOO** (extra-virgin olive oil)

1 pound **ground sirloin**

1 softball-size **onion**, chopped

Kosher salt and **pepper**

¼ cup **steak sauce**, such as A-1

1 cup **beef stock**

2 tablespoons **butter**

2 tablespoons **flour**

1 cup **milk**

1 cup shredded **provolone cheese**

4 **ciabatta rolls, hoagie rolls**, or 6-inch lengths of **Italian bread**, split

SLOPPY CHILI SLIDERS

MAKES 24 SLOPPY SLIDERS

To reconstitute the chiles, bring the anchos and stock to a simmer in a saucepan over low heat. Transfer the chiles and liquid to a food processor or blender and puree until smooth. Set the ancho puree aside.

Heat the EVOO, 1 turn of the pan, in a saucepan over medium-high heat. Add the beef or turkey and cook 5 to 6 minutes, crumbling it into fine bits with a wooden spoon as it browns. Add the onion and garlic, and cook a few minutes to soften. Stir in the coriander, cumin, and paprika; season with salt and pepper.

In a small bowl, stir together the brown sugar, vinegar, Worcestershire sauce, and tomato sauce. Add to the beef and onion along with the ancho puree and stir to combine. Bring to a simmer to thicken and combine the flavors, about 5 minutes.

Spoon the chili over the roll bottoms and set the tops in place. Pass the cheddar, onions, and pickles separately.

3 **dried ancho chiles**, stemmed and seeded

2 cups **beef stock** (if using ground beef) or **chicken stock** (if using ground turkey)

1 tablespoon **EVOO** (extra-virgin olive oil)

2 pounds **ground beef chuck** or **ground turkey**

1 **onion**, finely chopped

3 to 4 large cloves **garlic**, finely chopped

1 tablespoon **ground coriander**

1 tablespoon **ground cumin**

1 tablespoon **sweet paprika** or **smoked sweet paprika**

Kosher salt and **pepper**

2 tablespoons **light brown sugar**

2 tablespoons **cider vinegar**

2 tablespoons **Worcestershire sauce**

1 cup or 1 (8-ounce) can **tomato sauce**

24 **slider rolls** or **small dinner rolls**, split

TOPPINGS:

Shredded **sharp cheddar cheese**

Chopped **onions**

Chopped **pickles**

TIP: When working with hot liquid in a blender, be very careful that the steam doesn't blow the top right off the blender jar. Remove the cap from the blender lid and, using a potholder, keep the lid clamped down tightly and start at low speed.

SLOPPY CHIPOTLE JOES

SERVES 6

Heat the EVOO, 2 turns of the pan, in a large skillet over medium-high heat. Add the beef and cook 4 to 5 minutes, breaking it up with a potato masher or a wooden spoon as it browns. Add the onion, bell pepper, garlic, and chipotle puree and cook, stirring every now and then, until the onion and pepper start to get a little tender, 3 to 4 minutes.

In a small bowl, stir together the brown sugar, Worcestershire sauce, and tomato sauce. Add to the skillet when the veggies are tender; season with a little salt and pepper. Bring up to a bubble and simmer until nice and thick.

Spoon the filling over the roll bottoms. Set the roll tops in place. Serve with toppings of your choice.

2 tablespoons **EVOO** (extra-virgin olive oil)

1½ pounds **ground beef chuck**

1 large **onion**, finely chopped

1 **red bell pepper**, seeded and finely chopped

3 cloves **garlic**, grated or finely chopped

2 tablespoons pureed **chipotle in adobo sauce** (see Tip, page 14)

2 tablespoons **light brown sugar**

2 tablespoons **Worcestershire sauce**

1 cup or 1 (8-ounce) can **tomato sauce**

Kosher salt and **pepper**

6 **soft burger rolls** or 12 **slider rolls**

TOPPINGS:

Diced **avocado**

Crushed **Fritos**

Minced **onion**

Shredded **cheddar cheese**

SLOPPY JOAQUINS

SERVES 6

Sloppy Joaquin is the Spanish cousin to Sloppy Joe—HA, get it?! (Hey, have you met his Italian cousin, Messy Giuseppe, on page 225?) Chimichurri is in and on everything in Argentina, and they have no shortage of meat. Chimichurri is great on chicken, fish, sandwiches, stews, and, of course, sliced steak.

Preheat the broiler.

Make the chimichurri: Pulse together the parsley, thyme, oregano, shallot, garlic, red pepper flakes, and vinegar in a food processor until finely chopped. With the machine on, pour in the EVOO. Season with salt and pepper.

Make the sloppies: Heat the EVOO, 2 turns of the pan, in a deep skillet over medium heat. Add the garlic and onion and cook until softened, about 4 minutes. Add the mushrooms and cook until browned, about 5 minutes. Add the beef and cook 5 to 6 minutes, breaking it up with a wooden spoon as it browns. Season with the paprika and salt and pepper. Stir in the sherry and cook, scraping up any browned bits from the bottom of the pan, until slightly reduced, about 1 minute. Stir in the tomato sauce and Worcestershire sauce and simmer to thicken. Stir in half the chimichurri.

While the filling is cooking, toast the rolls: Spread the butter on the rolls, line them up on a baking sheet, and broil until golden.

Sprinkle the parsley on the roll bottoms and pile on the filling. Using a vegetable peeler, shave the cheese over the meat. Spoon the chimichurri over the sloppies and set the roll tops into place.

CHIMICHURRI SAUCE:

¾ cup chopped **flat-leaf parsley** leaves

3 tablespoons chopped **fresh thyme** leaves

1 tablespoon chopped fresh **oregano** or **marjoram**

1 **shallot**, chopped

1 clove **garlic**, grated or pasted (see Tip, page 138)

1 teaspoon **crushed red pepper flakes**

2 tablespoons **red wine vinegar**

⅓ cup **EVOO** (extra-virgin olive oil)

Kosher salt and **pepper**

SLOPPY JOAQUINS:

2 tablespoons **EVOO** (extra-virgin olive oil)

3 to 4 large cloves **garlic**, finely chopped

1 small **onion**, chopped

24 medium **cremini** or **button mushrooms**, chopped

1½ pounds **ground beef chuck**

1 tablespoon **sweet paprika**

½ cup **dry sherry**

1 cup or 1 (8-ounce) can **tomato sauce**

2 tablespoons **Worcestershire sauce**

6 **crusty rolls** or 12 **slider rolls**, split

2 tablespoons **butter**, softened

A handful of **flat-leaf parsley** leaves, chopped

A wedge of **Manchego cheese**, for shaving

SLOPPY JOE DiMAGGIOS

SERVES 6

Heat the EVOO, 1 turn of the pan, in a deep skillet over medium-high heat. Add the beef and cook, crumbling it with a wooden spoon as it browns. Add the chopped hot dogs after 3 to 4 minutes, then cook 3 to 4 minutes more. Add the onion to the pan and cook to soften, 5 to 6 minutes.

In a bowl, mix the chili powder, brown sugar, Worcestershire sauce, and tomato sauce. Pour the sauce mixture over the meat and simmer a few minutes to combine the flavors.

Spoon the filling onto the roll bottoms and top with relish (or pass the relish separately). Set the roll tops in place.

1 tablespoon **EVOO** (extra-virgin olive oil)

1 pound **lean ground beef chuck**

4 all-natural **beef** or **pork hot dogs**, chopped

½ small **onion**, finely chopped

1 tablespoon **chili powder**

1 tablespoon **dark brown sugar**

2 tablespoons **Worcestershire sauce**

1 cup or 1 (8-ounce) can **tomato sauce**

6 **soft burger rolls** (like at the ballpark)

Dill relish

TANGO JOES

SERVES 4

Preheat the oven to 300°F.

Pulse together the onion, garlic, parsley, oregano, thyme, rosemary, and vinegar in a food processor until finely chopped. With the machine on, pour in ⅓ cup EVOO. Turn off the machine when emulsified.

Heat the remaining 1 tablespoon EVOO, 1 turn of the pan, in a large skillet over high heat. Add the beef and cook, breaking it up with a wooden spoon, until browned, about 7 minutes. Season with the paprika and salt and pepper.

In a small bowl, combine the tomato sauce, Worcestershire sauce, and brown sugar. Stir into the meat and bring to a simmer. Stir in half of the herb sauce and cook for 5 minutes.

Meanwhile, warm the rolls in the oven. Split them and slather the cut sides of the tops with the remaining herb sauce. Pile the filling onto the roll bottoms and set the tops in place.

½ small **onion**, coarsely chopped

2 cloves **garlic**

1 cup **flat-leaf parsley** leaves (3 generous handfuls)

2 tablespoons **fresh oregano** leaves

2 tablespoons **fresh thyme** leaves

1 tablespoon **fresh rosemary**

3 tablespoons **red wine vinegar**

⅓ cup plus 1 tablespoon **EVOO** (extra-virgin olive oil)

2 pounds **ground sirloin**

2 teaspoons **smoked sweet paprika**

Kosher salt and **pepper**

1 cup or 1 (8-ounce) can **tomato sauce**

2 tablespoons **Worcestershire sauce**

2 tablespoons **dark brown sugar**

4 **Portuguese** or **kaiser rolls**

SLOPPY SAUSAGE, PEPPER, and ONION JOES

SERVES 6

Preheat the broiler.

Heat the EVOO, 2 turns of the pan, in a saucepan over medium-high heat. Add the pork and cook 5 to 6 minutes, breaking it up with a potato masher or wooden spoon as it cooks. Add the fennel seeds, paprika, red pepper flakes, garlic, onion, and cubanelle peppers; season with salt and pepper. Cook until the veggies soften, 7 to 8 minutes. Stir in the tomato paste and cook for 1 minute. In a small bowl, stir together the brown sugar, balsamic vinegar, and Worcestershire sauce. Stir in the chicken stock. Stir the sauce mixture into the pork, let come up to a bubble, then reduce the heat and simmer about 10 minutes.

While the filling is simmering, toast the rolls under the broiler. Once they are golden, remove from the broiler and sprinkle each with about a palmful of Parmigiano-Reggiano. Place them back under the broiler to melt the cheese.

Spoon the filling over the roll bottoms and top with some basil. Set the roll tops in place.

2 tablespoons **EVOO** (extra-virgin olive oil)

1½ pounds **ground pork**

1 tablespoon **fennel seeds**

1 tablespoon **sweet paprika**

1 teaspoon **crushed red pepper flakes**

3 to 4 cloves **garlic**, grated

1 small **onion**, finely chopped

2 **cubanelle peppers**, seeded and chopped

Kosher salt and **pepper**

3 tablespoons **tomato paste**

2 tablespoons **light brown sugar**

2 tablespoons good-quality **balsamic vinegar**

1 tablespoon **Worcestershire sauce**

1½ cups **chicken stock**

6 **sandwich-size ciabatta rolls** or 12 **slider-size ciabatta rolls**, split

Grated **Parmigiano-Reggiano cheese**

Shredded **fresh basil** leaves

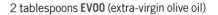

MESSY GIUSEPPE

SERVES 6

Preheat the broiler.

Heat the EVOO, 2 turns of the pan, in a deep skillet or a heavy-bottomed pot over medium-high heat. Add the mushroom and brown 5 minutes. Add the beef and cook, breaking it up with a wooden spoon, until browned, 7 to 8 minutes. Add the bell pepper, onion, garlic, oregano or marjoram, and red pepper flakes; season with salt and pepper and cook 5 minutes. Stir in the tomato paste, then add the wine and cook another minute. Add the beef stock, Worcestershire sauce, and crushed tomatoes or tomato sauce. Stir in the parsley and simmer a few minutes to thicken.

While the filling is simmering, toast the rolls: Brush the cut sides with butter, top with some cheese, and broil to brown.

Spoon the filling onto the roll bottoms and top with a little basil. Set the roll tops in place.

2 tablespoons **EVOO** (extra-virgin olive oil)

1 medium **portobello mushroom cap**, gills scraped off (see Tip), finely chopped

1½ pounds **ground beef chuck**

1 **green bell pepper**, seeded and chopped

1 small **onion**, chopped

3 to 4 cloves **garlic**, finely chopped

1 teaspoon **dried oregano** or **marjoram**

1 teaspoon **crushed red pepper flakes**

Kosher salt and black **pepper**

2 tablespoons **tomato paste**

½ cup (a couple of glugs) **red wine**

1 cup **beef stock** or 1 (10.75-ounce) can **beef consommé**

2 tablespoons **Worcestershire sauce**

1 cup **canned crushed tomatoes** or **tomato sauce**

¼ cup **flat-leaf parsley** leaves, finely chopped

6 **ciabatta rolls** or 12 **slider rolls**, split

4 tablespoons (½ stick) **unsalted butter**, softened

Grated **Parmigiano-Reggiano** or **pecorino Romano cheese**

Shredded **fresh basil** leaves

TIP: The gills on the underside of a portobello mushroom cap can turn sauces and gravies a dark, muddy brown. To keep your sauce nice and clean, just scrape off the gills with a teaspoon. You don't need to worry about the gills if you're cooking the caps whole, like for the Portobello Burgers with Spinach Pesto (page 114).

SLOPPY CUBANOS

SERVES 6

Cubanos are sandwiches offered everywhere in Miami: roast pork and ham with Swiss, pickles, and yellow mustard on a Cuban-style baguette—hot pressed.

Heat the EVOO, 1 turn of the pan, in a large skillet over medium-high heat. Add the chorizo and cook, stirring, until browned, 2 to 3 minutes. Add the pork and cook about 5 minutes, crumbling it with a wooden spoon, until browned. Stir in the onion, garlic, paprika, coriander, and allspice; season with salt and pepper and cook 5 to 6 minutes.

In a small bowl, stir together the brown sugar, Worcestershire sauce, chicken stock, and tomato sauce. Stir the sauce mixture into the pork and simmer to thicken. Just before serving, squeeze in the juice from the lime.

Spoon the filling onto the roll bottoms and top with Swiss cheese, pickles, and lots of yellow mustard. Set the roll tops in place.

1 tablespoon **EVOO** (extra-virgin olive oil)

1 link (4 to 5 ounces) **Spanish chorizo**, casings removed, finely chopped or pulsed in a food processor

1 pound **ground pork**

1 **onion**, finely chopped

2 cloves **garlic**, grated or finely chopped

2 teaspoons **sweet paprika**

2 teaspoons **ground coriander**

1 teaspoon **ground allspice**

Kosher salt and **pepper**

2 tablespoons **light brown sugar**

2 tablespoons **Worcestershire sauce**

½ cup **chicken stock**

1 cup or 1 (8-ounce) can **tomato sauce**

Juice of 1 **lime**

6 **Portuguese rolls** or 12 **slider rolls**, split

TOPPINGS:

Shredded **Swiss cheese**

Chopped **dill pickles**

Yellow mustard

SLOPPY DAWGS

SERVES 6

Heat the EVOO, 1 turn of the pan, in a large skillet over medium-high heat. Add the hot dogs and cook until golden brown, 4 to 5 minutes. Add the onion, garlic, and bell pepper, and cook 3 to 5 minutes to soften. Stir in the baked beans.

In a medium bowl, stir together the brown sugar, vinegar, Worcestershire sauce, and tomato sauce. Stir the sauce mixture into the pan, season with salt and pepper, and simmer over low heat until thickened, about 5 minutes.

Spoon the filling into the hot dog rolls or over the roll bottoms and top with onion, pickles or relish, and mustard. If serving on burger or slider rolls, set the tops in place.

1 tablespoon **EVOO** (extra-virgin olive oil)

$1\frac{1}{2}$ pounds **hot dogs** (**beef, pork, turkey,** or **tofu**), chopped or thinly sliced

1 medium **onion**, finely chopped

2 cloves **garlic**, finely chopped or grated

1 **red bell pepper**, seeded and finely chopped

1 cup **canned baked beans**

2 tablespoons **light brown sugar**

2 tablespoons **red wine vinegar**

2 tablespoons **Worcestershire sauce**

1 cup or 1 (8-ounce) can **tomato sauce**

Kosher **salt** and black **pepper**

6 crusty **split-top hot dog rolls**, 6 **burger rolls**, or 12 **slider rolls**, toasted and lightly buttered

TOPPINGS:

Chopped **onion**

Chopped **pickles** or **relish**

Yellow mustard

SLOPPY PORCHETTA

SERVES 6

Heat the EVOO, 2 turns of the pan, in a large skillet over medium-high heat. Add the pancetta and cook until crisp, 2 to 3 minutes. Add the pork and cook about 5 minutes, breaking it into crumbles with a wooden spoon as it browns. Stir in the fennel seeds, rosemary, garlic, and onion; season with salt and lots of pepper. Cook to soften the vegetables, about 5 minutes. Stir in the Worcestershire sauce, brown sugar, vinegar, and chicken stock. Reduce the heat and simmer to thicken, about 5 minutes.

Spoon the filling onto the roll bottoms and top with giardiniera. Set the roll tops in place.

2 tablespoons **EVOO** (extra-virgin olive oil)

1/4-pound slab **pancetta**, cut into 1/4-inch cubes

1 1/2 pounds **ground pork**

1 teaspoon **fennel seeds**

3 tablespoons finely chopped **rosemary**

3 to 4 cloves **garlic**, grated or finely chopped

1 **onion**, finely chopped

Kosher salt and **pepper**

1 tablespoon **Worcestershire sauce**

1 tablespoon **light brown sugar**

2 tablespoons **white balsamic vinegar** or **white wine vinegar**

1 cup **chicken stock**

6 crusty **ciabatta rolls** or 12 **slider rolls**, split

Finely chopped **giardiniera** (Italian hot pickled vegetables), store-bought or homemade (page 183)

SLOPPY MERGUEZ

SERVES 6

Merguez—spicy lamb sausage—is so delicious but tough to find in many markets. I make my own version often and serve it in patties, crumbled on buns, or as the base for meat sauces.

Puree the roasted pepper in a food processor.

Heat the EVOO, 1 turn of the pan, in a skillet over medium-high heat. Add the lamb and cook 5 to 7 minutes, breaking it up with a wooden spoon as it browns. Add the onion, chile, garlic, fennel seeds, oregano, paprika, and sugar; season with salt and pepper and stir a few minutes more. Add the tomato paste and Worcestershire sauce and stir 1 minute, until fragrant. Add the wine and reduce the heat to low. Stir in the stock and roasted pepper puree and simmer a few minutes to combine the flavors.

Spoon the filling onto the roll or bread bottoms and top with shallot, parsley, mint, and arugula. Slather the roll tops with mustard and set them in place.

1 **roasted red bell pepper**, bottled or homemade (see method for roasting poblano peppers on page 149)

1 tablespoon **EVOO** (extra-virgin olive oil)

1½ pounds **ground lamb**

1 small **onion**, finely chopped

1 small **Fresno chile**, seeded and finely chopped, or 1 teaspoon **crushed red pepper flakes**

4 cloves **garlic**, finely chopped

1 teaspoon **fennel seeds**

1 tablespoon finely chopped **fresh oregano** or 1 teaspoon **dried oregano**

1 tablespoon **sweet paprika** or **smoked sweet paprika**

1 teaspoon **sugar**

Kosher salt and **pepper**

2 rounded tablespoons **tomato paste**

2 tablespoons **Worcestershire sauce**

½ cup **dry red wine**

1 cup **chicken stock**

6 **ciabatta rolls**, or 12 **slider-size ciabatta rolls** or 3-inch lengths of **baguette**, split

TOPPINGS:

1 large **shallot**, finely chopped or sliced very thinly into rings

A handful of **flat-leaf parsley** leaves, finely chopped

A handful of **fresh mint** leaves, finely chopped

Baby arugula leaves

Dijon or **hot mustard**

BBQ CHICKEN SLOPPY JOES with PICKLED SLAW SALAD

SERVES 4

Never know what to do with the liquid left in the pickle jar? Don't toss it—it makes a delish dressing for a slaw that's a natural with these sloppies.

Make the sloppies: Heat the EVOO, 1 turn of the pan, in a large nonstick skillet over medium-high heat. Add the chicken and cook, 5 to 7 minutes, breaking it up with a wooden spoon as it browns. Once the chicken begins to brown, 3 to 4 minutes, stir in the grill seasoning and add the onion and bell pepper. Cook until the vegetables begin to soften, 5 to 6 minutes.

In a bowl, stir together the vinegar, brown sugar, Worcestershire sauce, tomato sauce, and hot sauce. Stir the sauce mixture into the chicken, reduce the heat to a simmer, and let the mixture bubble for 5 minutes.

Meanwhile, make the slaw salad: In a large bowl, combine the pickle juice, honey, and oil. Toss the cabbage with the dressing and season with salt and pepper.

Pile the filling onto the roll bottoms and top with chopped pickles. Set the roll tops in place. Serve with the slaw salad.

SLOPPIES:

1 tablespoon **EVOO** (extra-virgin olive oil)

2 pounds **ground chicken**

1 tablespoon **grill seasoning**, such as McCormick Montreal Steak Seasoning

1 medium **red onion**, chopped

1 small **red bell pepper**, seeded and chopped

3 tablespoons **red wine vinegar**

3 tablespoons **dark brown sugar**

1 tablespoon **Worcestershire sauce**

1 (14-ounce) can **tomato sauce**

1 tablespoon **hot sauce**

SLAW SALAD:

⅓ cup **pickle juice**, from jar

¼ cup **honey**

2 tablespoons **canola** or **vegetable oil**

4 cups packed shredded **cabbage** or ¾ pound **coleslaw mix**

Kosher salt and **pepper**

4 **crusty rolls**, split and toasted

1 cup chopped **dill pickles**

BUFFALO JOES

SERVES 6

A match made in heaven: Buffalo wings meet sloppy joes.

Heat the oil, 1 turn of the pan, in a large skillet over medium-high heat. Melt in the butter. Add the chicken or turkey and cook 5 to 7 minutes, crumbling it with a wooden spoon as it browns. Add the carrot, celery, onion, and garlic; season with salt and pepper and cook 7 to 8 minutes.

In a bowl, stir together the vinegar, brown sugar, Worcestershire sauce, hot sauce, and tomato sauce. Stir the sauce mixture into the pan and simmer a few minutes more.

Pile the filling onto the roll bottoms and top with blue cheese, pickles, and scallions or onions. Set the roll tops in place.

1 tablespoon **vegetable oil**

3 tablespoons **butter**

2 pounds **ground chicken** or **turkey**

1 **carrot**, finely chopped or grated

2 small ribs **celery**, chopped

1 small **onion**, finely chopped

2 to 3 cloves **garlic**, finely chopped or grated

Kosher salt and **pepper**

2 tablespoons **red wine vinegar**

2 tablespoons **light brown sugar**

2 tablespoons **Worcestershire sauce**

¼ cup **hot sauce**, such as Frank's RedHot

1 cup or 1 (8-ounce) can **tomato sauce**

6 **burger rolls** or 12 **slider rolls**, split

TOPPINGS:

Blue cheese crumbles

Chopped **dill pickles**

Chopped **scallions** or **red onions**

CINCINNATI SLOPPY SLIDERS

MAKES 16 SLOPPY SLIDERS

Heat the EVOO, 1 turn of the pan, in a large skillet over medium-high heat. Add the turkey and cook 5 to 7 minutes, crumbling it with a wooden spoon as it browns. Add the chile, onion, and garlic; season with salt and black pepper. Cook until the onion softens, a few minutes, then add the chile powder, cocoa powder, paprika, allspice, cinnamon, cloves, and oregano. Stir to release the flavors of the spices, then add the tomato paste, brown sugar, and Worcestershire, stirring for at least a minute or more.

Add the stock and tomato sauce to the pan and simmer for a few minutes to thicken.

Pile the chili on the rolls and add the toppings of your choice. These are pretty delish straight up as well! Set the roll tops in place.

4- OR 5-WAY SLIDERS

Stir 1 (14-ounce) can red kidney beans, rinsed and drained, and/or 1 cup broken spaghetti pieces, cooked and drained, into the chili after it has thickened.

1 tablespoon **EVOO** (extra-virgin olive oil)

2 pounds **ground turkey**

1 **Fresno** or **jalapeño chile**, seeded and finely chopped

1 **onion**, chopped

4 cloves **garlic**, finely chopped

Kosher salt and **pepper**

1 tablespoon **ancho chile powder**

1 tablespoon **unsweetened cocoa powder**

1½ teaspoons **smoked sweet paprika**

1 teaspoon **ground allspice**

½ teaspoon **ground cinnamon**

A healthy pinch of **ground cloves**

1 teaspoon **dried oregano**, lightly crushed

3 tablespoons **tomato paste**

2 tablespoons **light brown sugar**

1 tablespoon **Worcestershire sauce**

2 cups **chicken stock**

1 cup or 1 (8-ounce) can **tomato sauce**

16 **slider rolls**, split

TOPPINGS:

Finely chopped **red** or **white onions**

Shredded **cheddar** or **pepper jack cheese**

Pickled jalapeño slices

Cilantro or **parsley** leaves

Chopped **giardiniera** (Italian hot pickled vegetables), store-bought or homemade (page 183)

Lightly crushed **tortilla chips**

SLOPPY SUIZAS

SERVES 6

Heat the oil, 2 turns of the pan, in a large skillet over medium-high heat. Add the turkey or chicken, crumbling it with a wooden spoon or spatula as it browns. Add the tomatillos, onion, garlic, chile, coriander, and cumin; season with salt and pepper. Cook to mellow the tomatillos and soften the onion, about 5 minutes.

In a small bowl, stir together the honey, Worcestershire sauce, and stock; squeeze in the lime juice. Stir the sauce mixture into the filling and simmer a few minutes to thicken.

Spoon the filling over the roll bottoms and top with crema or crème fraîche, cheese blend, red onion, and cilantro. Set the roll tops in place.

2 tablespoons **vegetable oil** or **corn oil**

1½ pounds **ground turkey** or **turkey breast**, or **ground chicken**

6 **tomatillos**, husked, rinsed, and chopped

1 **onion**, finely chopped

3 to 4 cloves **garlic**, chopped

1 **jalapeño chile**, seeded and chopped

1 tablespoon **ground coriander**

1 tablespoon **ground cumin**

Kosher salt and **pepper**

1 tablespoon **honey**

2 tablespoons **Worcestershire sauce**

1 cup **chicken stock**

1 **lime**

6 **burger rolls** or 12 **slider rolls**, split

TOPPINGS:

Mexican crema or **crème fraîche**

A blend of shredded **Swiss cheese** and **Monterey Jack cheese**

Chopped **red onion**

Cilantro leaves

SLOPPY MAPLE-BBQ JOES

SERVES 6

Heat the EVOO, 2 turns of the pan, in a large skillet over medium-high heat. Add the turkey and season with the poultry seasoning, salt, and pepper. Cook 6 minutes, crumbling it with a wooden spoon as it browns. Stir in the bell pepper, onion, and garlic and cook until the vegetables are tender, 5 to 6 minutes.

In a bowl, stir together the tomato sauce, maple syrup, soy sauce, vinegar, brown sugar, and mustard. Stir the sauce mixture into the pan and simmer over medium-low heat for a few minutes to combine the flavors.

Spoon the filling onto the roll bottoms and top with shredded cheese, chopped apple, and red onion. Set the roll tops in place.

2 tablespoons **EVOO** (extra-virgin olive oil)

1½ pounds **ground turkey** or **turkey breast**

1 tablespoon **poultry seasoning**

Kosher salt and **pepper**

1 small **red bell pepper**, seeded and finely chopped

1 small **onion**, finely chopped

2 cloves **garlic**, finely chopped

1 cup or 1 (8-ounce) can **tomato sauce**

¼ cup **dark amber maple syrup**

3 tablespoons **soy sauce**

2 tablespoons **cider vinegar**

2 tablespoons **light brown sugar**

1 rounded tablespoon **Dijon mustard**

6 **burger rolls**, split

TOPPINGS:

Shredded **pepper jack cheese** or **extra-sharp cheddar**

Chopped **apple**, such as McIntosh or Granny Smith

Chopped **red onion**

SLOPPY VEG-HEAD JOES with BEANS

SERVES 4

Heat the oil, 1 turn of the pan, in a large skillet over medium-high heat. Add the bell pepper, chiles, onion, and garlic and cook until tender, 6 to 8 minutes. Stir in the black beans, coriander, and cumin; season with salt and pepper.

In a small bowl, stir together the tomatoes, brown sugar, and Worcestershire sauce. Stir the sauce mixture into the pan and simmer for a few minutes to combine the flavors. Squeeze in the lime juice.

Pile the filling onto the roll bottoms and top with cheese, pickles or giardiniera, and cilantro. Set the roll tops in place.

1 tablespoon **vegetable oil**

1 **red**, **green**, or **yellow bell pepper**, seeded and chopped

2 **jalapeño chiles**, seeded and finely chopped

1 **red onion**, chopped

2 large cloves **garlic**, chopped

2 (15-ounce) cans **black beans**, rinsed and drained

1 teaspoon **ground coriander**

1 teaspoon **ground cumin**

Kosher salt and **pepper**

1 (15-ounce) can diced **fire-roasted** or **chunky-style crushed tomatoes**

2 tablespoons **light brown sugar**

2 tablespoons **Worcestershire sauce**

1 **lime**

6 **burger rolls** or 12 **slider rolls**, split

TOPPINGS:

Shredded **pepper jack cheese**

Chopped **pickles** or **giardiniera** (Italian hot pickled vegetables), store-bought or homemade (page 183)

Cilantro leaves

SLOPPY VEG-HEAD JOES

SERVES 6

Heat the EVOO, 4 turns of the pan, in a large skillet over medium-high heat. Add the mushrooms and cook until browned, 10 to 12 minutes. Season with thyme, salt, and pepper. Add the onion, garlic, bell pepper, and chile and cook until the veggies are tender, 5 to 6 minutes. Add the tomato paste and cook 1 minute.

In a small bowl, stir together the brown sugar, vinegar, Worcestershire sauce, and tomato sauce. Stir the sauce mixture into the pan and simmer until thickened.

Pile the filling onto the roll bottoms and top with Gouda and pickles. Set the roll tops in place.

¼ cup **EVOO** (extra-virgin olive oil)

6 medium **portobello mushroom caps**, gills scraped off (see Tip, page 225), diced into small bite-size pieces

2 tablespoons **fresh thyme leaves**, finely chopped

Kosher salt and **pepper**

1 medium **onion**, chopped

3 cloves **garlic**, finely chopped or grated

1 small **red bell pepper**, seeded and chopped

1 **fresh red chile**, such as Fresno, seeded and finely chopped

2 tablespoons **tomato paste**

2 tablespoons **light brown sugar**

2 tablespoons **sherry vinegar**

2 tablespoons **Worcestershire sauce**

1 cup or 1 (8-ounce) can **tomato sauce**

6 **burger rolls** or 12 **slider rolls**, split

TOPPINGS:

Shredded **Gouda cheese**

Sliced or chopped **dill pickles**

BUILDING THE PERFECT BURGER
MICHAEL SYMON

Chef/owner, B Spot Burgers

There are few things I love more in life than a great hamburger. When done right, it gives me even more pleasure and satisfaction than a wonderfully marbled steak. One, you can eat it with your hands, which for me is always a huge plus with food. But what I think really makes it so special is how that first bite of juicy goodness brings me immediately back to my childhood. Hanging out in the backyard with friends and family and admiring my dad work the grill like a deft ninja. Taking temperatures from everyone, adding their favorite cheese and melting it to perfection, and then gently rolling the buns across the hot grill to give them that slight toasting so they would hold up to his perfectly cooked patties.

Although my dad's classic cheeseburger with mayo and a thick slice of red onion may still be my favorite, I have really enjoyed playing with all sorts of different toppings to keep my burgers interesting. The way that I like to come up with toppings is to think about some of my other favorite sandwiches and then use the burger as the vehicle to build the perfect beast. My current fave is the Fat Doug, which is our signature burger at the BSpot and is modeled after a pastrami sandwich: The burger is topped with crispy pastrami, coleslaw, and melted Swiss. It may sound odd to you at first, but just think of the pastrami as you would bacon, and you will soon realize that the options are endless. Here are some of my other favorite combos that can take your burgers to a whole new level: corned beef and sauerkraut for a delicious Reuben; or how about some pulled pork with sweet pickles? I also love fried salami and mozzarella. Really, your only limitation is your own creativity. So go crazy and have some fun! Some of the combos you'll come up with will surprise you and your friends, and will give you a renewed love for this American classic.

Meet Michael Symon.

SIDES AND SAUCES

ALL KINDS OF FRIES

243 Finger Fries with Formaggio

244 Double-Baked Crazy-Crisp Oven Fries

247 Bistro-Style Pommes Frites (French Fries)

248 10-Cut Oven Fries

249 Balsamic Sweet Potato Oven Fries

250 Homemade Tots

252 Garlic, Parmigiano, and Pepper Tots

253 Caesar Tots

254 Crispy Chile Pepper Oven Fries
    with Ranch Dipper

256 Parsnip Oven Fries

257 Eggplant Fries with Yogurt Dipping Sauce

258 Portobello Mushroom Fries

259 Hot Dog Fries

260 Thick-Cut O-Rings and Spicy Dipping
    Sauce

OTHER SIDES

261 Sweet 'n' Spicy Pickles

262 Deviled Eggs

265 Roasted Jalapeño Poppers

266 Honey-Dijon Potato Salad

267 Pickled Potato Salad

268 Pub Hash Browns with Horseradish Sauce

270 Bacon-Wrapped Potato Skins

DIPPERS, FRY GRAVIES, SAUCES, and KETCHUPS

271 Quick Marinara Dipper

271 Horseradish and Sour Cream Fry Dipper

272 Fry Gravy

273 Cheese Fry Topping

273 Chili Cheese Fry Topping

274 Bacon Tomato Jam

275 Basic Mayo and Variations

276 Chipotle Ketchup

276 Israeli Ketchup

277 Moroccan Ketchup

277 Balsamic Ketchup

Bistro-Style Pommes Frites (page 247).

FINGER FRIES with FORMAGGIO

SERVES 6

2 pounds **fingerling potatoes**, halved lengthwise

4 tablespoons (½ stick) **butter**

2 cloves **garlic**, smashed

Kosher salt and **pepper**

½ cup grated **Parmigiano-Reggiano cheese**

Preheat the oven to 425°F.

Put the fingerling potatoes in a large pot and cover with cold salted water. Bring to a boil and cook until just tender, about 8 minutes. Drain.

While the potatoes are cooking, melt the butter in a small saucepan. Add the garlic and cook over medium-low heat 4 to 5 minutes. Pour the garlic butter onto a rimmed baking sheet, add the drained potatoes, and turn to coat them in butter. Arrange cut side down and roast until deeply golden brown, about 20 minutes.

Remove from the oven and flip cut side up with a spatula. Season the potatoes with a little salt and lots of pepper and sprinkle with the Parmigiano-Reggiano. Return the potatoes to the oven for 5 minutes to melt the cheese onto the fries.

DOUBLE-BAKED CRAZY-CRISP OVEN FRIES

SERVES 6

These fries are CRAZY GOOD, hence the name in the title. You'll notice I leave a patch of skin on the end of the potato before I slice them. This is an appearance thing, plus I like some skin on my potato. If you like more skin, you may leave more!

Preheat the oven to 350°F. Set a cooling rack over each of 2 baking sheets.

Peel the potatoes, leaving a patch of the skin at both ends. Cut each potato lengthwise into very thin (⅛- to ¼-inch) slices—the thinner they are, the crispier the end product will be. Cut those slices into strips that are just as thin.

In a large bowl, drizzle the fries very lightly with EVOO—a couple of turns of the bowl should to do the trick. Season with salt and pepper.

Arrange the fries on the racks in a single layer without crowding either rack.

Roast 30 minutes. Remove the fries and increase the oven temperature to 425°F. Toss the fries in a large bowl with one of the optional flavorings (if using). Return the fries to the oven and bake until very crispy and brown, 15 to 20 minutes.

6 medium **starchy potatoes**, such as Idahos

EVOO (extra-virgin olive oil), for drizzling

Kosher salt and **pepper**

OPTIONAL FLAVORINGS (MY FAVE IS GARLIC AND ROSEMARY!):

Minced **garlic** and lots of minced fresh **rosemary**

Old Bay or **Cajun seasoning**

Chipotle chile powder

Minced **garlic**, grated **Parmesan cheese**, and **oregano**

Grated **pecorino Romano cheese** and **pepper**

Melted **butter, parsley,** and **garlic**

Malt vinegar and **salt**

Adobo seasoning

Double-Baked Crazy-Crisp Oven Fries with Cheese Fry Topping (page 273).

BISTRO-STYLE POMMES FRITES (FRENCH FRIES)

SERVES 4

4 russet (baking) potatoes

Peanut oil or vegetable oil, for frying

Fine sea salt

Peel the potatoes, leaving a patch of skin at both ends. Cut lengthwise into ¼-inch-thick slabs, then cut the slabs into ¼-inch-wide sticks. (Or use a mandoline for faster-to-cut fries.) Soak the potatoes in a bowl of icy water 15 minutes. Drain and dry on a thick kitchen towel or layers of paper towels.

Fill a countertop fryer with oil or pour 3 inches of oil into a large Dutch oven. Heat the oil to 275°F. Fry the potato sticks in small batches for about 6 minutes, then remove and drain on cooling racks. Increase the oil temp to 375°F. Refry the fries in small batches until they are as brown as you like, drain on paper towels, and season with sea salt. Serve with Basic Mayo (page 275), ketchup, or Fry Gravy (page 272).

TIP: The potatoes can be fried the first time up to a few hours before serving. Leave them at room temp and fry them for the second time just before serving.

10-CUT OVEN FRIES

SERVES 4 *Nov. 2020*

Preheat the oven to 425°F with a baking sheet on the oven rack.

While the oven is heating, in a large bowl, toss the potatoes with the EVOO, salt, pepper, paprika, granulated onion, granulated garlic, and cayenne until the potatoes are coated with oil and spices.

Pull the hot baking sheet pan out of the oven. Scatter the seasoned potatoes onto the hot baking sheet in one layer. Return the pan to the oven and roast the potatoes, turning occasionally, until golden brown and crispy, 40 to 45 minutes.

3 med. w/ ½ spices

4 large unpeeled **russet (baking) potatoes**, cut lengthwise into 10 wedges each

3 tablespoons **EVOO** (extra-virgin olive oil)

1½ teaspoons **fine sea salt**

½ teaspoon coarsely ground **pepper**

½ teaspoon **sweet paprika**

½ teaspoon **granulated onion**

½ teaspoon **granulated garlic**

¼ teaspoon **cayenne pepper**

*40 min
on parchment
heat pan
cut & soak
potatoes
overnight*

BALSAMIC SWEET POTATO OVEN FRIES

SERVES 4

Preheat the oven to 450°F.

Toss the sweet potato wedges with the EVOO on a baking sheet and season with salt, pepper, and a little nutmeg. Roast until tender and crispy, flipping once, 25 to 30 minutes.

While the potatoes are roasting, bring the vinegar, brown sugar, rosemary, and garlic to a boil in a medium saucepan over high heat. Reduce the heat to medium and cook until thickened and saucy, about 10 minutes. Keep your eye on the sauce; it can go from thick to burnt quickly.

Discard the garlic cloves and rosemary sprig. Transfer the potatoes to a serving dish and drizzle with the balsamic reduction.

2 large unpeeled **sweet potatoes**, scrubbed clean and cut lengthwise into wedges, 10 to 12 wedges per potato

2 to 3 tablespoons **EVOO** (extra-virgin olive oil)

Kosher salt and **pepper**

Freshly grated **nutmeg**

1½ cups **balsamic vinegar**

3 tablespoons **light brown sugar**

1 sprig **fresh rosemary**

2 cloves **garlic**, smashed

HOMEMADE TOTS

MAKES 80 TO 100

Cook the potatoes in a large pot of well-salted boiling water until tender. Drain the potatoes well and pass them through a ricer into a large bowl. Add the grated onion (grate it right over the bowl), flour, egg, and rosemary; season with salt and pepper and mix well.

On a floured surface, roll the potato mix into 1-inch-thick logs and cut into tots.

Fill a countertop fryer with oil or pour a few inches of oil into a large Dutch oven. Heat the oil to 350°F. (The oil is ready when a 1-inch cube of white bread cooks to golden brown in 40 seconds.) Fry the tots in small batches until golden and crisp, about 4 minutes. Remove and drain on paper towels. Season the cooked tots with a little extra salt.

6 medium **starchy potatoes**, such as Idahos, peeled and cubed

Kosher salt

3 tablespoons finely grated **onion**

¼ cup **flour**, plus more for rolling

1 large **egg**

1 tablespoon minced **fresh rosemary**

Pepper

Peanut oil or **vegetable oil**, for frying

Homemade Tots with Chipotle Ketchup (page 276).

GARLIC, PARMIGIANO, and PEPPER TOTS

MAKES 80 TO 100

Cook the potatoes in a large pot of well-salted boiling water until tender. Drain the potatoes well and pass them through a ricer into a large bowl. Add the garlic, flour, egg, and Parmigiano-Reggiano; season with salt and pepper and mix well.

On a floured surface, roll into 1-inch-thick logs and cut into tots.

Fill a countertop fryer with oil or pour a few inches of oil into a large Dutch oven. Heat the oil to 350°F. (The oil is ready when a 1-inch cube of white bread cooks to golden brown in 40 seconds.) Fry the tots in small batches until golden and crisp, about 4 minutes. Remove and drain on paper towels. Season the cooked tots with a little extra salt.

6 medium **starchy potatoes**, such as Idahos, peeled and cubed

Kosher salt

6 cloves **garlic**, finely grated

¼ cup **flour**, plus more for rolling

1 large **egg**

1 cup grated **Parmigiano-Reggiano cheese**

Pepper

Peanut oil or **vegetable oil**, for frying

CAESAR TOTS

MAKES 80 TO 100

Cook the potatoes in a large pot of well-salted boiling water until tender. Drain the potatoes well and pass them through a ricer into a large bowl. Add the garlic, flour, egg, mustard, Worcestershire sauce, anchovy paste, and pecorino; season with salt and pepper and mix well.

On a floured surface, roll into 1-inch-thick logs and cut into tots.

Fill a countertop fryer with oil or pour a few inches of oil into a large Dutch oven. Heat the oil to 350°F. (The oil is ready when a 1-inch cube of white bread cooks to golden brown in 40 seconds.) Fry the tots in small batches until golden and crisp, about 4 minutes. Remove and drain on paper towels. Season the cooked tots with a little extra salt.

6 medium **starchy potatoes**, such as Idaho, peeled and cubed

Kosher salt

6 cloves **garlic**, finely grated

¼ cup **flour**, plus more for rolling

1 large **egg**

1 tablespoon **Dijon mustard**

1 tablespoon **Worcestershire sauce**

1 teaspoon **anchovy paste**

1 cup grated **pecorino Romano cheese**

Pepper

Peanut oil or **vegetable oil**, for frying

CRISPY CHILE PEPPER OVEN FRIES with RANCH DIPPER

SERVES 4

Preheat the oven to 400°F.

Make the fries: Line up 3 shallow bowls on the counter: Spread the flour out in one, beat the eggs with the mustard and 2 tablespoons of flour (from the first bowl) in the second, and mix together the panko, Parmigiano-Reggiano, and some salt and pepper in the third.

Coat the chile strips in the flour, then in egg, and finally in the panko mixture, pressing to make sure the coating sticks.

Arrange the chile strips on a baking sheet in a single layer. Roast the chiles on the baking sheet, turning halfway through baking, until golden brown and crispy, about 18 minutes.

While the fries are roasting, make the ranch dipper: In a medium bowl, mix together the buttermilk, sour cream, vinegar, garlic, hot sauce, chives, dill, and parsley. Season with salt and pepper.

Serve the fries immediately with the ranch dipper.

CHILE PEPPER FRIES:

1 cup **flour**

5 large **eggs**, lightly beaten

2 tablespoons **Dijon** or **yellow mustard**

2 cups **panko breadcrumbs**

¾ cup grated **Parmigiano-Reggiano cheese**

Kosher salt and **pepper**

1½ pounds **chiles** (a combination of **poblano**, **Anaheim**, and **jalapeño**), seeded and cut into 1-inch-wide strips

RANCH DIPPER:

¾ cup **buttermilk**

½ cup **sour cream**

1 tablespoon **white wine vinegar**

1 clove **garlic**, grated or pasted (see Tip, page 138)

1 teaspoon **hot sauce**

3 tablespoons finely chopped **chives**

3 tablespoons finely chopped **fresh dill**

3 tablespoons finely chopped **flat-leaf parsley**

PARSNIP OVEN FRIES

SERVES 4

Preheat the oven to 400°F.

Drizzle the EVOO onto a rimmed baking sheet and place in the oven to get really hot.

Fill a large bowl with ice and water. Bring about 2 inches of water to a boil in a high-sided skillet. Salt the water and cook the parsnips until tender, about 4 minutes. Drain the parsnips and shock them in the ice water. Drain again and pat dry.

While the parsnips are cooking, line up 3 shallow bowls on the counter: Spread the flour out in one and season with salt and pepper. Beat the eggs in the second, and mix together the pecans, breadcrumbs, and Parmigiano-Reggiano in the third. Coat the parsnips in the seasoned flour, then in egg, and finally in the breadcrumb mixture, pressing to make sure the coating sticks.

Arrange the parsnips on the hot oiled baking sheet in a single layer and roast, flipping about halfway through the cooking time, until tender and golden brown, 12 to 15 minutes.

Combine the barbecue sauce and chili sauce and serve alongside the parsnips as a dip.

2 tablespoons **EVOO** (extra-virgin olive oil)

Kosher salt

1 pound **parsnips**, peeled and quartered lengthwise

1 cup **flour**

Pepper

1 large **egg**

1 cup **pecans**, toasted and finely chopped (or pulse-process them in food processor)

¾ cup **fine dry breadcrumbs**

½ cup grated **Parmigiano-Reggiano cheese**

½ cup **barbecue sauce**, homemade or store-bought

½ cup prepared **chili sauce**, such as Heinz

EGGPLANT FRIES with YOGURT DIPPING SAUCE

SERVES 4

I use rice flour to coat the eggplant, which typically gives a crispier crust. If you can't find rice flour, you can add a little cornstarch to regular flour.

Make the eggplant fries: Place the eggplant strips in a large bowl and fill with 3 cups of ice and water, making sure all the eggplant pieces are submerged. Cover with plastic wrap and soak the eggplant in the refrigerator for 2 to 12 hours.

Fill a countertop fryer with oil or pour a few inches of oil into a large Dutch oven. Heat the oil to 325°F.

While the oil is heating, make the sauce: Stir together the yogurt, cumin, garlic, lemon zest and juice, and oregano; season with salt and pepper.

Place the rice flour in a shallow bowl; season with salt and pepper. Drain the eggplant, leaving it a little damp so the rice flour will stick to it. Toss the damp eggplant strips in the seasoned flour to coat. Fry the eggplant strips and chile slices in batches, turning occasionally, until golden brown, 3 to 4 minutes. Drain on paper towels and season with salt while still hot. Serve with the dipping sauce.

EGGPLANT FRIES:

1 (1-pound) unpeeled **eggplant**, cut into ½-inch rounds and then into ½-inch-wide strips

Vegetable oil, for frying

1 cup **rice flour**

1 **fresh red chile**, such as Fresno, thinly sliced

DIPPING SAUCE:

1 cup **Greek yogurt**

1½ teaspoons **ground cumin**

1 small clove **garlic**, grated

Finely grated zest and juice of 1 **lemon**

1 tablespoon **fresh oregano** leaves, chopped

Kosher salt and **pepper**

PORTOBELLO MUSHROOM FRIES

SERVES 4

Preheat the oven to 425°F. Set a cooling rack over a baking sheet.

Brush the mushroom caps with a little oil. Arrange the caps on the cooling rack and roast until tender, 12 to 15 minutes. Cool the mushrooms and cut them into 1-inch-wide strips. Season with salt and pepper.

Line up 3 shallow bowls on the counter: Spread the flour out in one, beat the eggs in the second, and mix together the thyme, panko, Parmesan, and garlic in the third. Coat the mushroom strips in the flour, then in the egg, and finally in the panko mixture, patting gently to make sure the coating sticks.

Heat a thin layer of oil in a nonstick skillet over medium-high heat. Add a batch of fries and cook, flipping once, until browned, 2 or 3 minutes on each side. Serve as is or with Quick Marinara Dipper or Fry Gravy (if you like).

4 large **portobello mushroom caps**, gills scraped off (see Tip, page 225)

EVOO (extra-virgin olive oil) or **vegetable oil**

Kosher salt and **pepper**

1 cup **flour**

2 large **eggs**, beaten

2 tablespoons finely chopped **fresh thyme** leaves

1 cup **panko breadcrumbs**

½ cup shredded or grated **Parmesan cheese**

1 teaspoon **granulated garlic**

Quick Marinara Dipper (page 271) or **Fry Gravy** (page 272), optional

HOT DOG FRIES

SERVES 4

Quarter each hot dog lengthwise.

Set up 3 shallow bowls on the counter: Spread the flour out in one, beat the eggs and mustard in the second, and spread out the panko in the third. Coat the hot dog strips in the flour, then the eggs, and finally in the breadcrumbs, pressing to make sure the coating sticks.

Fill a countertop fryer with oil or pour a few inches of oil into a large Dutch oven. Heat the oil to 350°F. (The oil is ready when a 1-inch cube of white bread cooks to golden brown in 40 seconds.) Add the breaded hot dog strips and cook until golden, 3 to 4 minutes. Drain on a cooling rack or a paper towel–lined plate.

Serve with mustard as a dipper.

1 package (about 8) all-natural **beef** or **pork hot dogs**

1 cup **flour**

6 large **eggs**

1 tablespoon **yellow** or **Dijon mustard**, plus more for dipping

1 cup **panko breadcrumbs**

Vegetable oil, for frying

THICK-CUT O-RINGS and SPICY DIPPING SAUCE

SERVES 4

Fill a countertop fryer with oil or pour a few inches of oil into a large Dutch oven. Heat the oil to 350°F. (The oil is ready when a 1-inch cube of white bread cooks to golden brown in 40 seconds.)

Slice the onions into 1-inch slices and separate the rings, discarding the outer layer of skin. Pour the evaporated milk into a small, deep bowl. Mix together the flour, paprika, cayenne, and mustard in a shallow bowl; season with salt. Dip the individual onion rings in the milk, then coat in seasoned flour.

Fry the onion rings in batches until golden brown. Remove to a flattened-out brown paper bag or paper towel–lined surface to drain. Season with salt while hot.

While the o-rings are frying, make the spicy dipping sauce: In a small bowl, stir together the sour cream and chili sauce.

Serve with the sour cream sauce for dipping.

Vegetable oil or canola oil, for frying

2 large Vidalia onions or other sweet onions

2 (5-ounce) cans evaporated milk

1 cup flour

1 teaspoon sweet paprika

½ teaspoon cayenne pepper

½ teaspoon dry mustard

Coarse salt

1 cup sour cream

¼ cup prepared chili sauce, such as Heinz

SWEET 'N' SPICY PICKLES

MAKES ABOUT 2 CUPS, OR ABOUT 80 SLICES

Bring the vinegar, ⅔ cup water, the sugar, salt, and garlic to a low boil in a saucepan, stirring to dissolve the sugar and salt. Reduce the heat to low.

Layer the onion, cucumbers, chile, bay leaves, dill, coriander seeds, mustard seeds, and peppercorns into a plastic or glass container in which they fit snugly.

Pour the hot brine over the cucumber mixture, cover tightly, and refrigerate 24 hours or several days, turning occasionally. The pickles will keep in the refrigerator for up to 1 month.

2 cups **white balsamic** or **cider vinegar**

½ cup **sugar**

2 teaspoons **sea salt**

1 large clove **garlic**, halved

½ small **red onion**, thinly sliced

4 **Kirby cucumbers**, sliced ⅛ to ¼ inch thick

1 small **fresh red chile**, such as Fresno, sliced

2 **bay leaves**

A few sprigs **fresh dill**

1 teaspoon **coriander seeds**

1 teaspoon **mustard seeds**

1 teaspoon **black peppercorns**

DEVILED EGGS

MAKES 12 WHOLE OR 24 HALVED DEVILED EGGS

Deviled eggs are great for entertaining—I'm the deviled egg queen! All you have to do is make the filling earlier in the day, cover it tightly with plastic wrap, and hold it in the refrigerator. A little before your guests arrive, fill the egg whites and garnish. That way, they'll stay looking fresh and delish!

1 dozen large **eggs**

2 tablespoons grated **onion**

1 clove **garlic**, grated or pasted (see Tip, page 138)

2 tablespoons **sweet pickle relish**

1 tablespoon **yellow** or **Dijon mustard**

2 to 3 teaspoons **hot sauce**

1 teaspoon **Worcestershire sauce**

1 teaspoon **sweet paprika**

3 to 4 tablespoons **mayo**

Kosher salt and **pepper**

1 small **fresh red chile**, such as Fresno, thinly sliced into rings

Place the eggs in a medium pot, cover with water, and bring to a full boil. Turn off the heat, cover the pot, and let stand 10 minutes.

Drain the water and crack the eggshells by shaking the pot. Run cold water into the pot until the eggs are cool enough to handle. Peel the eggs.

Halve them lengthwise to make 24 halves or trim the tops to expose the yolks if you would like to present the eggs whole and upright.

Either way, scoop the yolks into a bowl and add the grated onion (grate it right over the bowl), garlic, relish, mustard, hot sauce, Worcestershire sauce, paprika, and mayo (a few tablespoons to start); season with salt and pepper. Mash to very smooth, adding a bit more mayo if dry. Fill a sturdy plastic food storage bag with the filling and cut off one corner. Pipe the yolk mixture into the egg whites and garnish with a bull's-eye of thinly sliced red chile.

ROASTED JALAPEÑO POPPERS

MAKES 16 POPPERS

Preheat the oven to 425°F.

With the jalapeños on their sides, and cutting lengthwise, slice off one-third of the chiles. Seed the chiles to make "boats" for the filling. Finely chop enough of the trimmings to measure 3 to 4 tablespoons. (Reserve the remainder of the pepper trimmings for another use, such as salsas.) In a bowl, combine the chopped jalapeño and Fresno chiles, the cream cheese, onion, garlic, cumin, and shredded cheeses. Stir until blended and season with salt and pepper. Spoon the filling into the hollowed-out chiles.

Stir the panko and grated Parmigiano-Reggiano together on a plate and roll the stuffed tops of the poppers in the panko-Parm mixture.

Arrange the poppers on a baking sheet and coat with a little cooking spray. Roast until the peppers are tender-crisp and the filling is browned and bubbling, 15 to 18 minutes. Let stand 10 minutes and serve.

16 fat **jalapeño chiles**

1 **Fresno chile**, seeded and finely chopped

8 ounces **cream cheese**, softened

3 tablespoons grated **onion**

2 cloves **garlic**, grated or pasted (see Tip, page 138)

1 teaspoon **ground cumin**

¾ cup shredded **sharp cheddar cheese**

¾ cup shredded **Monterey Jack cheese**

Kosher salt and **pepper**

¾ cup **panko breadcrumbs**

½ cup grated **Parmigiano-Reggiano cheese**

All-natural cooking spray

HONEY-DIJON POTATO SALAD

SERVES 6

Quarter the potatoes and place in a medium pot with water to cover. Bring to a boil and salt the water. Cook the potatoes until just tender, 12 to 15 minutes. Drain the potatoes and spread out on a baking sheet for 5 minutes to cool and dry.

In a serving bowl, whisk together the honey, mustard, and vinegar. Whisk in the EVOO. Season with salt and pepper. Add the radishes, onion, celery, and cress or parsley to the bowl along with the potatoes. Toss the potato salad and adjust the seasoning with salt and pepper.

2 pounds small **red skin potatoes**

Kosher salt

¼ cup **honey**

¼ cup **Dijon mustard**

2 to 3 tablespoons **cider vinegar**

⅓ cup **EVOO** (extra-virgin olive oil)

Pepper

6 **radishes**, quartered

½ medium **red onion**, chopped

3 to 4 ribs **celery**, chopped

1 cup chopped **watercress** or **flat-leaf parsley**

PICKLED POTATO SALAD

SERVES 4

Place the potatoes in a pot with water to cover. Bring to a boil and salt the water. Cook the potatoes until tender, 7 to 8 minutes.

Meanwhile, heat 2 tablespoons EVOO, 2 turns of the pan, in a medium skillet over medium-high heat. Add the bacon and cook until crisp, 2 to 3 minutes. Add the onion, chile, coriander seeds, mustard seeds, and bay leaves. Cook until the onion is tender, about 5 minutes. Sprinkle with sugar, then douse the pan with cider vinegar. Stir in the consommé and boil until reduced to ¾ cup. Pour the dressing into a bowl. Remove the bay leaves.

Drain the potatoes and add to the dressing; season with salt and pepper. Stir in the parsley, drizzle with EVOO, and serve warm or at room temp.

4 medium **starchy potatoes**, such as Idahos, peeled and cut into ¼-inch-thick slices

Kosher salt

2 tablespoons **EVOO** (extra-virgin olive oil), plus more for drizzling

¼ pound **bacon**, finely chopped

1 **red onion**, finely chopped

1 **fresh red chile**, such as Fresno or red finger, seeded and finely chopped

1 teaspoon **coriander seeds**

1 teaspoon **mustard seeds**

2 **bay leaves**

2 teaspoons **superfine sugar**

¼ cup **cider vinegar**

1 (10.75-ounce) can **beef consommé**

Pepper

¼ cup finely chopped **flat-leaf parsley**

PUB HASH BROWNS with HORSERADISH SAUCE

SERVES 4

Heat a drizzle of EVOO in a large skillet over medium-high heat. Scatter the bacon into the pan and cook until browned, 2 to 3 minutes. Transfer the bacon bits to a paper towel–lined plate to drain. Leave the drippings in the pan.

Meanwhile, peel the potatoes and halve them length-wise. Cut each half lengthwise into 4 wedges. Cut the wedges across into thirds so you end up with 24 rustic wedge cuts per potato.

Scatter the potato wedges in the pan of drippings in a single layer; season lightly with salt and more generously with pepper. Cook until crisp and browned, flipping occasionally, 5 to 6 minutes, Cover the skillet with foil and cook 5 to 6 minutes to steam the potatoes. Un-cover and cook, flipping occasionally, until deep, deep golden and very crisp, 3 to 4 minutes. Stir the bacon bits into the potatoes.

While the potatoes are cooking, in a small bowl, thin the sour cream a bit with cream, then stir in the horse-radish and chives; season with salt and pepper. Serve the potatoes with the sauce.

EVOO (extra-virgin olive oil), for drizzling

5 slices **bacon**, cut crosswise into 1-inch pieces

1½ to 2 pounds **starchy potatoes**, such as Idahos (2 large or 3 medium potatoes)

Kosher salt and coarsely ground **pepper**

1 cup **sour cream**

Splash of **heavy cream** or **half-and-half**

2 tablespoons **prepared horseradish**

3 tablespoons finely chopped **chives**

BACON-WRAPPED POTATO SKINS

SERVES 4

Preheat the oven to 400°F.

Rub the potatoes with a little EVOO and season the skins with salt and pepper. Poke with the tines of a fork and roast until just tender, about 40 minutes. Cool.

Halve the potatoes lengthwise. Scoop out the flesh into a bowl. Mash with the sour cream, butter, cheese, horseradish, and chives; season with salt and pepper. Fill the potato skins with the mashed potatoes and wrap the potato and filling entirely in bacon, overlapping the bacon a little as you wrap the slices around the skins. Set a cooling rack over a baking sheet. Arrange the wrapped potatoes on the cooling rack and roast until the bacon is crispy, 15 to 20 minutes.

2 large **russet (baking) potatoes**

EVOO (extra-virgin olive oil), for drizzling

Kosher salt and **pepper**

⅓ cup **sour cream**

2 tablespoons **butter**

½ cup shredded **super-sharp white cheddar cheese**

2 tablespoons **prepared horseradish**

¼ cup chopped **chives**

8 slices **bacon**

QUICK MARINARA DIPPER

MAKES ABOUT 2 CUPS

Heat the EVOO in a small saucepan over medium heat and melt the butter in it. Add the garlic and stir for a couple of minutes. Add the onion, bay leaf, tomato puree, oregano, and basil; season with salt and pepper. Simmer at a low bubble 20 minutes. Discard the onion and bay leaf.

1 tablespoon **EVOO** (extra-virgin olive oil)

2 tablespoons **butter**

2 cloves **garlic**, chopped

½ small **white onion**, peeled and left whole

1 **bay leaf**

2 cups **tomato puree**

½ teaspoon **dried oregano** or **marjoram**

A few **fresh basil** leaves, torn

Kosher salt and **pepper**

HORSERADISH and SOUR CREAM FRY DIPPER

MAKES ABOUT 1½ CUPS

In a small bowl, stir together the applesauce and bread-crumbs and let stand 10 minutes. Stir in the sour cream, horseradish, and chives; season with salt and pepper. Serve with fries of your choice as a dipper. (Our fave is the 10-Cut Oven Fries, page 248.)

¼ cup unsweetened **applesauce**

2 tablespoons **fine dry breadcrumbs**

1 cup **sour cream**

2 rounded tablespoons **prepared horseradish**

¼ cup finely chopped **chives**

Kosher salt and **pepper**

FRY GRAVY

MAKES ABOUT 2 CUPS

Every now and then I like to dunk my fries in a tasty gravy. This one gets its tang from the Dijon mustard. If you're making one of my oven-fry recipes, you can make this while the fries are in the oven.

4 tablespoons (½ stick) **butter**

1 large **shallot**, minced

3 tablespoons **flour**

2 (10.75-ounce) cans **beef consommé** or 2½ cups **beef stock**

2 tablespoons **Worcestershire sauce**

2 rounded tablespoons **Dijon mustard**

Pepper

Melt the butter in a skillet over medium to medium-high heat. Add the shallot, stir 2 minutes, then sprinkle in the flour. Stir 1 to 2 minutes, then whisk in the beef consommé or stock. Bring to a bubble and cook until thickened, 3 to 4 minutes. Add the Worcestershire sauce and Dijon; season liberally with pepper. Keep warm over low heat until the fries are ready.

Pour over fries of your choice or serve as a dipper.

POUTINE

Poutine is a dish that originated in Quebec but is popular across Canada. This is my spin on the original for you!

Pile Double-Baked Crazy-Crisp Oven Fries (page 244) or Bistro-Style Pommes Frites (page 247) into parchment-paper cones. Top with shredded Gruyère or white cheddar and let melt. Top with a ladle of gravy.

CHEESE FRY TOPPING

MAKES ABOUT 2 CUPS

While I do love a good plain and crispy fry, I also appreciate various fry toppings to keep them exciting. This is a basic cheese sauce that I love if I'm in the mood for cheese fries. Note: If you're a chili cheese fry fan . . . see below!

3 tablespoons **butter**

2 tablespoons **flour**

1¼ cups **milk**

Kosher salt and **pepper**

1½ cups **shredded sharp yellow cheddar cheese**

1 rounded tablespoon **yellow mustard**

Melt the butter in a small saucepan over medium heat. Whisk in the flour and cook for 1 minute. Whisk in the milk and cook until thickened, 2 to 3 minutes; season with salt and pepper. Stir in the cheese to melt. Remove the sauce from the heat and stir in the mustard. Pour over fries of your choice or pass as a dipper.

CHILI CHEESE FRY TOPPING

MAKES ABOUT 2½ CUPS

Cheese Fry Topping (above)

1½ teaspoons **vegetable oil** or **corn oil**

⅓ pound **ground beef chuck**

½ cup finely chopped **onion**

1 clove **garlic**, minced

1 small **serrano chile**, seeded and finely chopped

1 tablespoon mild to medium **chile powder**, such as ancho

1 teaspoon **sweet paprika**

½ teaspoon **ground coriander**

½ teaspoon **ground cumin**

Kosher salt and **pepper**

Prepare the cheese fry topping.

Heat the oil in a small skillet over medium-high heat. Add the beef and cook 5 to 6 minutes, crumbling it with a wooden spoon as it browns. Add the onion, garlic, chile pepper, chile powder, paprika, coriander, and cumin; season with salt and pepper. Stir 2 to 3 minutes, then add ½ cup water and let it evaporate, 3 to 5 minutes more.

Stir the beef mixture into the cheese fry topping and pour over fries of your choice.

BACON TOMATO JAM

MAKES ABOUT 1 CUP

Cook the bacon in a medium skillet over medium heat until partially rendered and crisp at the edges, 3 to 5 minutes. Add the onion and garlic and cook for another 5 minutes. Mix in the vinegar, maple syrup, brown sugar, ketchup, and red pepper flakes. Season with pepper. Simmer a few minutes more to marry the flavors. Cool to room temperature.

½ pound **bacon**, chopped into small pieces

1 small **onion**, diced

3 cloves **garlic**, chopped or grated

¼ cup **cider vinegar**

2 tablespoons **dark amber maple syrup**

2 tablespoons **dark brown sugar**

¼ cup good-quality **ketchup**, such as Heinz Organic

¼ teaspoon **crushed red pepper flakes**

Pepper

BASIC MAYO

MAKES ABOUT 1 CUP

1 **organic egg** yolk

A pinch of fine **sea salt**

2 teaspoons **Dijon mustard**

1 cup **grapeseed oil** or other **mild-flavored oil**

Whisk the egg yolk, salt, and mustard in a small bowl. Slowly stream in the oil while you continue to whisk. Once the mayo begins to thicken, you can start to go a bit faster. The whole process will take 4 to 5 minutes. Alternatively, combine the yolk, salt, and mustard in a food processor and process until blended. With the machine running, slowly stream in the oil to emulsify.

DIJON MAYO

Stir ¼ cup Dijon mustard, 1 tablespoon white wine vinegar, 1 tablespoon minced fresh thyme leaves, and 1 teaspoon superfine sugar into the finished mayo.

SAFFRON MAYO

Soak ¼ teaspoon saffron threads (about 2 pinches) in 1 tablespoon warm water for 10 to 15 minutes. Add to the finished mayonnaise.

ROASTED GARLIC MAYO

Roast 1 head of garlic (see page 113). Squeeze the pulp from the cloves and mash to a paste using a knife or fork. Whisk into the finished mayo.

HERB MAYO

Add ½ cup loosely packed mixed fresh herbs, such as chives, thyme, rosemary, parsley, and basil, to the finished mayo in the processor and process until the herbs are finely chopped. If making the mayo by hand, chop the herbs finely and stir into the finished mayo.

DEVILED MAYO

Whisk 2 tablespoons chipotle puree (see Tip, page 14) or minced chipotle chiles into the finished mayo.

KETCHUPS

My fave for all these ketchup recipes: Heinz Organic Ketchup.

CHIPOTLE KETCHUP

MAKES ABOUT 1 CUP

In a small bowl, stir together all the ingredients. Transfer to a dipper bowl and pass with fries of your choice.

1 cup **organic ketchup**

3 tablespoons pureed **chipotle in adobo sauce** (see Tip, page 14)

1½ teaspoons **honey**

ISRAELI KETCHUP

MAKES ABOUT 1 CUP

I use sumac in this recipe, which is used in Israeli cooking. It is a dark red to purplish spice and adds a slight lemony flavor.

In a small bowl, stir together all the ingredients. Transfer to a dipper bowl and pass with fries of your choice.

1 cup **organic ketchup**

1 tablespoon **hot sauce**

1 teaspoon **ground coriander**

1 teaspoon **ground cumin**

1 teaspoon **ground sumac** or **sweet paprika**

½ teaspoon **dried oregano**

½ teaspoon **dried thyme**

MOROCCAN KETCHUP

MAKES ABOUT 1¼ CUPS

In a small bowl, stir together all the ingredients until the preserves are incorporated into the ketchup. Transfer to a dipper bowl and pass with fries of your choice.

1 cup **organic ketchup**

1 teaspoon **ground coriander**

1 teaspoon **turmeric**

½ teaspoon **dried oregano**

½ teaspoon **ground cumin**

A pinch of **ground cinnamon**

1 tablespoon **orange** or **apricot all-fruit preserves**

1½ teaspoons **honey**

Pepper

BALSAMIC KETCHUP

MAKES ABOUT 1 CUP

In a small bowl, combine the ketchup and balsamic drizzle; season with pepper and mix well. Transfer to a dipper bowl and pass with fries of your choice.

1 cup **organic ketchup**

3 tablespoons **balsamic drizzle**, store-bought or homemade (see Tip, page 15)

Pepper

BURGER BASH

SPIKE MENDELSOHN
280 The Smokehouse Burger, Chipotle-Barbecue Sauce, Cliff's Homegrown Vidalia Onion Petals

MASAHARU MORIMOTO
282 Morimoto Kakuni Burger

KATIE LEE
283 Logan County Hamburgers

MICHAEL SYMON
284 Yo Burger, Spicy Ketchup, Pickled Red Onions, Fat Doug Burger

MICHAEL SCHWARTZ
288 Genuine Bacon, Egg, and Cheeseburger with Heirloom Tomato Onion Chutney

BOBBY FLAY
291 Louisiana Burger

MICHAEL SCHLOW
292 The Schlow Burger, Cousin Shari's Coleslaw, Crispy Onions

CRAIG KOKETSU
294 The Fire Eater Burger, Fire Eater Sauce, Pickled Jalapeños

CHRIS SANTOS
296 Short Rib and Lamb Burger, Pickled Red Onions, Harissa Mayo

MARC MURPHY
298 The Big Marc, Homemade Cheddar and Black Pepper Buns, Spiked Ketchup, Jalapeño and Cheddar Tots

FRANKLIN BECKER
302 Wisconsin Cheeseburger

JOSH CAPON
304 The Bash Burger with Caramelized Onion-and-Bacon Jam

Photos courtesy of the Food Network South Beach and New York City Wine & Food Festivals.

Tips from Rachael for hosting your own burger bash!

Experience Rachael Ray's Burger Bash.

Spike Mendelsohn

Chef

THE SMOKEHOUSE BURGER

SERVES 6

Make the barbecue sauce and the onion ring batter. Don't fry the onions until the burgers are cooking.

To make the patties, prepare six 5-ounce balls of ground sirloin and form each ball into a patty. Arrange the patties on a tray, cover, and refrigerate.

Toast the buns.

Heat a large skillet over medium-high heat. Add enough oil to just cover the entire bottom. When the oil begins to smoke, cook the bacon until crispy. Remove with a slotted spoon and drain on the paper towels.

Reduce the heat to medium and place the patties in the skillet. Season with salt and pepper and cook 3 minutes. Flip and repeat on the other side. During the last 2 minutes of cooking, place the bacon and cheddar slices on the patties. Cover with a lid during the last 30 seconds and cook until the cheese melts.

To assemble the burgers, place 1 patty on the bottom of each toasted bun. Top the patty with the Chipotle-Barbecue Sauce and Cliff's Homegrown Vidalia Onion Petals. Cover with the top bun; repeat with each burger. Don't forget to wrap the sandwiches in wax paper. Serve immediately.

Chipotle-Barbecue Sauce (recipe follows)

Cliff's Homegrown Vidalia Onion Petals (recipe follows)

2 pounds **ground sirloin**

6 **potato burger buns**, split

Canola oil

1 (1-pound) package **applewood-smoked bacon**

Salt and freshly ground **black pepper**

6 slices **cheddar cheese**

CHIPOTLE-BARBECUE SAUCE

MAKES 3 CUPS

Spoon half the can of chiles into a blender and puree until smooth. Add the barbecue sauce, ketchup, vinegar, and molasses, and puree until smooth. Strain the mixture through a fine-mesh sieve to remove the seeds.

½ (7-ounce) can **chipotles in adobo** sauce

2 cups sweet, mild **barbecue sauce**

½ cup **ketchup**

¼ cup **cider vinegar**

1 tablespoon **molasses**

CLIFF'S HOMEGROWN VIDALIA ONION PETALS

SERVES 6

Make the onion ring batter: Sift 2 cups flour, the salt, paprika, brown sugar, Old Bay, cumin, black pepper, and cayenne into a large bowl. In a separate bowl, mix together the beer, buttermilk, and egg. Slowly incorporate the dry ingredients into the wet, whisking to prevent lumps. Refrigerate until needed.

While the burgers are cooking, make the onion petals: Heat about 3 inches oil in a large skillet until it reaches 350°F. Line a baking sheet with paper towels.

Toss the onions in a bowl with the remaining 1 cup flour, coating them well, and shake off the excess. Dip the petals into the bowl of batter to coat well. Slowly add the petals one by one into the oil, making sure not to overcrowd the skillet. Cook until golden brown and crispy. Using a slotted spoon, remove the petals and drain them on the paper towels. Season the petals with salt and pepper while still hot. Serve immediately.

3 cups all-purpose **flour**

1 tablespoon **salt**

1 tablespoon **paprika**

1 tablespoon **brown sugar**

1½ teaspoons **Old Bay seasoning**

1 teaspoon **ground cumin**

Pinch of **black pepper**

Pinch of ground **cayenne pepper**

1 cup **beer** (type of beer does not matter)

1 cup **buttermilk**

1 large **egg**, beaten

Canola oil for deep-frying

4 **Vidalia onions**, each cut into 8 wedges

Kosher salt and freshly ground **black pepper** to taste

TIP: The batter for the onion rings can be made up to a day in advance.

Masaharu Morimoto

Chef/owner Morimoto

MORIMOTO KAKUNI BURGER

SERVES 4

Preheat the oven to 250°F.

Make the kakuni: Heat the oil in a large ovenproof skillet over medium heat. Add the pork belly and sear until golden brown. Turn and brown the other side. Pour or spoon off the fat from the pan. Sprinkle the brown rice over the meat and pour in enough cold water to cover the pork by 1 inch. Bring to a simmer over high heat. Cover with the lid and transfer to the oven. Braise gently until the pork is tender when pierced with a knife, about 8 hours.

Remove from the oven, uncover, and let the pork cool in the cooking liquid. Remove the pork from the liquid carefully to keep it in one piece. Discard the rice and cooking liquid.

Cut the pork crosswise into 8 pieces. Bring 4 cups water, the sake, soy sauce, and sugar to a boil in a saucepan. Add the pork belly slices, reduce the heat to low, and simmer until the pork is very tender, about 2 hours.

While the pork is simmering, make the mustard sauce: In a small bowl, whisk together the mustard and mayonnaise. Set aside.

When the pork belly is ready, heat a grill. Form the beef into 4 patties. Season the patties with salt and pepper and grill to the desired doneness.

Place the burgers on the roll bottoms. Top with 2 slices of glazed pork and some glazing liquid, some shaved cabbage, and a drizzle of the mustard sauce. Set the roll tops in place. Serve with pickle slices.

PORK KAKUNI:

1 tablespoon **vegetable oil**

1 pound skinless, boneless **pork belly**

1½ cups **brown rice**

1¾ cups **sake**

¼ cup **soy sauce**

2 tablespoons **sugar**

MUSTARD SAUCE:

½ cup prepared **Japanese mustard**

½ cup **Japanese mayonnaise**, such as **Kewpie**

BURGERS:

1¼ pounds **ground beef (70% lean)**, preferably **Wagyu beef**

Kosher salt and **pepper**

4 **soft burger rolls**, split and toasted

1 cup shaved **green cabbage**

Sweet pickle slices

Katie Lee

Author of The Comfort Table *and* The Comfort Table: Recipes for Everyday Occasions

LOGAN COUNTY HAMBURGERS

SERVES 6

These thin hamburgers are straight out of the Depression era. My grandmother grew up during the Depression in Logan County, in the hills of West Virginia. Since money was scarce, families had to make their meat go a long way. Even though times have changed, she still likes to make good food that's easy on the wallet. I just love the combination of the flavors of the burger, raw onion, cheese, and especially the grilled toast.

Make the burgers: In a medium bowl, combine the beef, egg, grated onion, garlic powder, salt, and pepper. Mix until combined. Form into 6 thin patties.

Spread the butter onto one side of each slice of bread. Heat a large heavy-duty skillet over medium-high heat. Cook the burgers about 3 minutes on each side. Drain on paper towels. Drain the grease from the skillet.

In the same skillet, place 6 slices of bread, butter side down. Top each with a slice of cheese (if using), some sliced onions, and a burger. Top with the remaining cheese (if using) and bread, butter side up. Cook the sandwiches until golden brown, about 2 minutes per side.

Serve with mustard, ketchup, tomatoes, pickles, or any other desired hamburger toppings.

BURGERS:

1 pound **ground beef (85% lean)**

1 large **egg**, lightly beaten

1 medium **yellow onion**, ½ grated, ½ thinly sliced

¼ teaspoon **garlic powder**

1 teaspoon **kosher salt**

1 teaspoon freshly ground **black pepper**

2 tablespoons **unsalted butter**, softened

12 slices **white bread**

12 slices **American cheese** (optional)

TOPPINGS (ANY OR ALL):

Mustard of your choice

Ketchup

Sliced **tomatoes**

Pickles

Michael Symon

Chef/owner, B Spot Burgers (Ohio)

YO BURGER

SERVES 4

We make our own pickled onions and spicy ketchup at B Spot, but if you can find store-bought versions of either that you really like, feel free to use those instead.

Make the spicy ketchup and pickled red onions.

Build a medium-high fire in your grill or preheat a gas grill to medium-high.

Form the beef into four 6-ounce patties, season liberally with kosher salt and cracked black pepper, and place the burgers on the grill. Cook for 3 minutes per side (for medium-rare), adding the cheese after you have flipped the burgers or when they are cooked to your desired doneness.

Place the burgers on the English muffin bottoms and top with cucumber pickle, pickled red onions, salami, and spicy ketchup. Set the muffin tops in place.

4 teaspoons Spicy Ketchup (recipe follows)

4 ounces Pickled Red Onions (page 286)

1½ pounds **ground beef** (equal parts brisket, beef cheek, and sirloin)

Kosher salt and cracked **black pepper**

4 thin slices **Fontina cheese**

4 **English muffins**, toasted

1 **green cucumber pickle**, thinly sliced

8 slices **salami**, cooked until crisp

TIP: The salami can be crisped in a skillet or in the oven on a cooling rack over a baking sheet.

SPICY KETCHUP

MAKES 3 TO 4 CUPS

Heat the oil in a nonreactive 2-quart saucepan over medium heat. Add the onion, garlic, and a three-finger pinch of salt and sweat until the onion is translucent, about 2 minutes. Add the Fresno chiles, ancho chile, and red pepper flakes. Cook for a minute or two. Add the brown sugar, cumin, cinnamon, tomato paste, and vinegar and simmer for 10 minutes. Add 3 cups water, bring to a gentle simmer, and cook over low heat for 2 hours.

Remove from the heat and let cool for 15 minutes. Discard the cinnamon stick. Puree the mixture in a blender and strain through a sieve, pushing any solids through. Let cool, then cover and refrigerate for up to 1 month.

1 tablespoon **olive oil**

1 small **yellow onion**, minced

5 cloves **garlic**, chopped

Kosher salt

5 **Fresno chiles**, seeded and minced

1 **dried ancho chile**, seeded and minced

¼ teaspoon **crushed red pepper flakes**

2 tablespoons **dark brown sugar**

1 tablespoon **cumin seeds**

1 **stick cinnamon**

2 cups **tomato paste**

2 tablespoons **cider vinegar**

PICKLED RED ONIONS

MAKES 6 CUPS

Because you can never know precisely how much of the water-vinegar mixture you will need, fit the onions into the container you are using for pickling, fill it up with water, and then dump the water into a measuring cup. Pour out half the water and replace it with vinegar.

Place the red onions in a jar and cover them with water. Pour off the water into a measuring cup. Note the volume, pour off half the water, and replace it with vinegar. Pour the liquid into a saucepan and add 2 tablespoons sugar and 2 tablespoons salt for every 3 cups of liquid. Add the mustard seeds, chile flakes, coriander seeds, peppercorns, garlic, and bay leaves. Bring to a boil over high heat. Boil for 2 minutes, then remove from the heat.

Layer the onions into a sterilized jar, cover the onions with the hot liquid, and seal the jar. Refrigerate for 2 weeks before using. The pickled onions will keep refrigerated for up to a year.

2 pounds **red onions**, thinly sliced

PICKLING LIQUID:

White wine vinegar

Sugar

Salt

2 teaspoons **mustard seeds**

1 tablespoon **chile flakes**

2 tablespoons **coriander seeds**

2 tablespoons **black peppercorns**

4 cloves **garlic**

2 **bay leaves**

FAT DOUG BURGER

SERVES 4

Make the slaw: in a mixing bowl, toss together all the slaw ingredients. Refrigerate for 1 hour.

Build a medium-high fire in your grill or preheat a gas grill to medium-high.

Make the burgers: Mix the three types of ground beef together really well and form into 4 equal-size patties. Season with salt and pepper. Grill the patties 3 to 5 minutes per side.

Meanwhile, divide the pastrami into 4 piles and put them in a skillet over medium heat. After 2 minutes, top each pile with a slice of Swiss cheese. Remove the pastrami-cheese melts from the pan when the cheese has melted, transfer them to a plate, and set aside.

Pour the butter into the pan you used to make the pastrami-cheese melts. Toast the rolls, cut sides down, for about 2 minutes, or until toasted to your liking.

Place some slaw on the roll bottoms and top with the burgers and pastrami-cheese melts. Set the roll tops in place.

SLAW:

½ head **napa cabbage**, shredded

½ clove **garlic**, minced

½ small **red onion**, thinly sliced

½ **jalapeño pepper**, minced

3 tablespoons **champagne vinegar**

2 tablespoons **mayonnaise**

1 tablespoon **Dijon mustard**

1 tablespoon **spicy mustard**

1 tablespoon **Worcestershire sauce**

1 tablespoon **sugar**

1½ teaspoons **salt**

BURGERS (OR USE 1½ POUNDS OF THE GROUND BEEF OF YOUR CHOICE):

½ pound **ground sirloin**

½ pound **ground brisket**

½ pound **ground boneless short rib**

Salt and **pepper**

½ pound thinly sliced **pastrami**

4 slices **Swiss cheese**

1½ tablespoons **butter**, melted

4 **brioche rolls** or **egg buns**, split

Michael Schwartz

Chef/owner, Michael's Genuine Food & Drink (Miami and Grand Cayman) and Harry's Pizzeria (Miami)

GENUINE BACON, EGG, and CHEESEBURGER with HEIRLOOM TOMATO ONION CHUTNEY

MAKES 12 MINI BURGERS

I'm not generally a fan of "sliders" or mini burgers, but this combo packs such a big punch that I decided to go down that road. Keep in mind that you may eat two or three of these guys! Proportion is really important in making a great burger (or any dish, for that matter), so try not to overload. Less is more here. A small piece of thick-cut bacon, half a slice of cheese, not too much chutney, and that quail egg! And toasting the buns is a must!

Also a quick note on ingredients: Since I always say that the secret to good food is good food, spend some time sourcing the best ingredients. Slab bacon is preferable, grass-fed beef, too. Super-ripe heirloom tomatoes for the chutney. You get it, right?

1 cup Heirloom Tomato Onion Chutney (page 290)

1½ pounds freshly **ground beef chuck**

12 **quail eggs**

6 slices **thickest-cut bacon**

Kosher salt and **pepper**

6 slices **white cheddar cheese**, cut into quarters

12 **potato dinner rolls**, split and toasted

Make the chutney.

Form the beef into twelve 2-ounce balls, being careful not to pack too tight. Press lightly to slightly flatten the balls into patties. Set aside.

Carefully cut off the top of the shell of each quail egg, making the hole big enough for the yolk to fit through when you go to fry them. Set them back into the carton they came in and set aside.

Heat a large griddle over two burners over medium-high heat. Cook the bacon on one side for about 4 minutes; turn and continue cooking until the fat is rendered and the bacon is slightly crisp. We're not going for super-crisp bacon here, as it'll make the burger hard to eat.

Remove the bacon, cut each piece in half, and set on paper towels in a warm place until ready to assemble.

Pour off and reserve the bacon fat, wipe the griddle with a towel, and drizzle some of the bacon fat back onto the griddle. Season the burgers on both sides with salt and pepper and place on the griddle. Using the back of a spatula, flatten the burgers a bit. Brown on one side for about 2 minutes. Flip the burgers and top each with a piece of bacon and 2 quarter-slices of cheddar. Turn the heat down to low. This gives you some time to fry the quail eggs and toast the buns. It'll also slowly melt the cheese.

Place a large nonstick frying pan over medium heat. If the pan is in good shape, you should not need to drizzle with oil. Carefully pour the quail eggs from their shells into the pan, one at a time. Try not to have them touch each other. You may need to do this in two batches, depending on the size of your pan. Season each egg with a pinch of salt and pepper and cook until the white just sets up, about 2 minutes. Use a small spatula to transfer the eggs to a plate.

Place a spoonful of chutney on each of the roll bottoms. Top with a burger and then a quail egg. Set the roll tops in place. Serve with extra tomato chutney on the side.

HEIRLOOM TOMATO ONION CHUTNEY

MAKES 3 CUPS

Bring a large pot of water to a boil. Fill a large bowl with ice and water. Cut a little "X" on the bottom of the tomatoes. Immerse the tomatoes in the boiling water for 15 to 30 seconds, until the skin at the "X" starts to peel away. Using a slotted spoon, transfer the tomatoes to the ice bath to cool quickly and stop the cooking process. Peel the tomato either with your hands or with a paring knife. Halve the tomatoes and squeeze out the seeds. Coarsely chop the tomatoes and set aside. You should have about 3½ cups.

Heat a large skillet over medium heat and add the oil. When the oil gets hazy, add the onions. Cook and stir until the onions soften slightly and get a little bit of color, about 6 minutes.

Add the tomatoes, cloves, salt, and pepper. Cook and stir until the tomatoes start to break down and release their liquid, about 10 minutes. Add the vinegar and agave nectar. Continue to cook, stirring often to prevent burning, until the liquid has evaporated and the chutney is thick, about 5 minutes.

4 **heirloom tomatoes**, cored (about 2 pounds)

¼ cup **extra-virgin olive oil**

24 **cipollini onions** (about 1 pound), halved or quartered lengthwise, depending on size

2 **whole cloves**

1 teaspoon **kosher salt**

½ teaspoon **pepper**

¼ cup **champagne vinegar**

2 tablespoons **agave nectar** or **honey**

Bobby Flay

Executive Chef/owner, Bobby's Burger Palace, Mesa Grill, Bar Americain, and Bobby Flay Steak

LOUISIANA BURGER

SERVES 4

Make the remoulade sauce: In a small bowl, whisk together the mayonnaise, mustards, hot sauce, cornichons, and scallions; season with salt and black pepper. Cover and refrigerate for at least 30 minutes before serving to allow the flavors to meld.

Make the burgers: In a small bowl, combine the paprika, thyme, garlic powder, onion powder, cayenne, 2 teaspoons salt, and 2 teaspoons black pepper. Mold the meat into 4 uniform, fairly flat patties, no thicker than ¾ inch, and then make a deep depression in the center with your thumb. Season one side of each of the patties with the spice mixture, making sure to rub the spices into the meat.

Heat the oil in a cast-iron skillet or on a griddle over high heat until smoking. Place the burgers in the pan, spice-rub side down, and season the top side with salt and pepper. Cook until slightly charred and the spices have formed a crust, about 1½ minutes (be careful not to burn the spices). Turn the burgers over, lower the heat to medium, and continue cooking to the desired doneness. During the last minute of cooking, put 2 slices of cheese on each burger, cover the pan or dome the burgers with aluminum foil if on a griddle, and cook until the cheese has completely melted, about 1 minute.

Spread some of the remoulade sauce on the bun bottoms and tops. Place the onion slices on the bun bottoms and top with the burgers. Top the burgers with the griddled ham and drizzle the ham with some of the hot sauce. Set the bun tops in place.

REMOULADE SAUCE:

½ cup **mayonnaise**

¼ cup **Dijon mustard**

¼ cup **whole-grain mustard**

3 tablespoons **Frank's RedHot sauce**

3 **cornichons**, finely diced

2 **scallions**, white and green parts, finely diced

Kosher salt and freshly ground **black pepper**

BURGERS:

1 tablespoon **sweet paprika**

1 teaspoon **dried thyme**

½ teaspoon **garlic powder**

½ teaspoon **onion powder**

½ teaspoon **cayenne pepper**

1½ pounds **ground beef chuck (80% lean)**

1 tablespoon **canola oil**

8 thin slices **pepper jack cheese**

4 **sesame seed buns**, split and lightly toasted

4 (⅛-inch-thick) slices **red onion**

4 slices **tasso ham**, griddled until golden brown

2 tablespoons **Frank's RedHot sauce**

Michael Schlow

Chef/owner, Radius, Via Matta, Tico, Happy's, and Alta Strada

THE SCHLOW BURGER

MAKES 2 BIG BURGERS

Make the slaw and the onions.

Combine the ground beef with the olive oil, salt, and plenty of black pepper and mix well. Divide the meat into two 10-ounce patties and refrigerate until the grill is ready (don't do this more than an hour in advance).

Meanwhile, in a small bowl, stir together the mayonnaise, horseradish, and lemon juice; season with black pepper.

Heat a grill to high and take the patties out of the refrigerator 5 to 7 minutes before you are ready to grill them.

Grill the burgers for 1½ minutes. Give the burgers a quarter-turn to "mark" them, and cook 1½ more minutes. Flip the burgers over and cook 1½ minutes, then rotate a quarter-turn to "mark," and cook 1½ more minutes. Transfer the burgers to the grill's top shelf or to a cooler section of the grill and cover each one with a slice of cheese. Turn the grill off and shut the lid. After 4 minutes, open the lid. The cheese will be melted and the burgers cooked to rare to medium-rare. (If you like your burgers more well done, cook them 30 seconds longer for each of the 4 turns and leave the grill on low instead of turning it off while the cheese is melting.)

Toast the buns, if desired. Place the burgers on the bun bottoms and top with plenty of the horseradish sauce; it should drip down the sides. Top with the onions and season with pepper. Slather more horseradish sauce on the bun tops and set them in place. Plate the slaw on the side. Grab a cold beer or iced tea and get ready to make a mess. This is not a dainty meal!

Cousin Shari's Coleslaw (recipe follows)

Crispy Onions (recipe follows)

1¼ pounds **ground beef (80% lean)**—ask the butcher for a mixture of ground chuck, ground brisket, and ground sirloin

2 tablespoons **extra-virgin olive oil**

Salt and freshly ground **black pepper**

¼ cup **mayonnaise**

2 teaspoons **prepared horseradish**

Juice of ½ **lemon**

2 thick slices **Vermont** or **English Cheddar cheese**

2 **brioche buns**, split

COUSIN SHARI'S COLESLAW

SERVES 4 TO 6

In a large bowl, toss together the onion and sugar and let sit for 30 minutes.

Add the olive oil, mayonnaise, vinegar, salt, and pepper to the onion and stir well to combine. Fifteen to 30 minutes before serving, add the cabbage, toss well, and refrigerate until serving time.

1 medium **yellow onion**, chopped into small dice

1 cup **sugar**

1 cup **pure** or **extra-virgin olive oil**

⅔ cup **mayonnaise**

½ cup **cider vinegar**

1 teaspoon **salt**

½ teaspoon **pepper**

1 large head **green cabbage**, shredded

CRISPY ONIONS

MAKES ½ CUP, ENOUGH FOR 2 BIG BURGERS

Pour the oil into a countertop fryer or deep, heavy pot. Heat the oil to 375°F.

Dip the onion rings in the seasoned rice flour and shake off any excess. Quickly fry the onions until they're golden brown. Drain the onions in a single layer on paper towels.

2 cups **canola oil**

1 large **yellow onion**, cut into ⅛-inch-thick rings

Rice flour seasoned with **salt** and **pepper**

Craig Koketsu

Chef/partner, The Hurricane Club (New York City)

THE FIRE EATER BURGER

SERVES 4

Make the fire eater sauce and pickled jalapeños.

Form the beef into 4 patties. Season the patties with salt and pepper and grill to the desired doneness (about 2 to 3 minutes per side for a medium-rare to medium burger). When the burgers are almost done, place a heaping spoonful of the sauce on top of each, then place a slice of jack cheese on top of the sauce and allow it to melt.

While the burgers are cooking, butter the cut side of the buns and toast in a pan over medium-high heat until golden brown.

To assemble: Place a generous dollop of yogurt on the bun bottoms. Top with the burgers and pickled jalapeños. Set the bun tops in place. Eat immediately.

Fire Eater Sauce (recipe follows)

Pickled Jalapeños (recipe follows)

2 pounds **ground beef** (I use a blend of 50% chuck, 25% brisket, and 25% short rib)

Kosher salt and **pepper**

4 thick slices **pepper jack cheese**

Butter, softened

4 **burger buns**, preferably sourdough-cheese rolls, split

1 cup **labne yogurt** or **Greek yogurt**

FIRE EATER SAUCE

MAKES ENOUGH FOR ABOUT 12 BURGERS

Heat the oil in a heavy-bottomed pan over medium heat. Add the onion, garlic, bell peppers, paprika, cumin, and cayenne. Cook the vegetables over low heat until the spices are fragrant. Add the chopped chipotles and the sauce from the can. Cook until the liquid is completely evaporated. Add the ketchup and salt and simmer until thickened, about 10 minutes.

¼ cup **canola oil**

1 large **onion**, finely chopped

2 tablespoons finely chopped **garlic**

3 **red bell peppers**, chopped

2 teaspoons **smoked paprika**

2 teaspoons **ground cumin**

1 teaspoon **cayenne pepper**

1 (7-ounce) can **chipotles in adobo**, chopped, adobo sauce reserved

1 cup **ketchup**

½ teaspoon **salt**

PICKLED JALAPEÑOS

Place the jalapeños in a heatproof container. Bring the vinegar, sugar, and salt to a boil and pour over the jalapeños. Cover with plastic wrap and refrigerate until completely cool (about 2 hours). The pickled jalapeños will keep in the fridge for up to 1 week.

6 **jalapeño chiles**, sliced into thin rings with seeds left in

1 cup **rice vinegar**

⅓ cup **sugar**

1 teaspoon **salt**

Chris Santos

Executive Chef and owner, Beauty & Essex and The Stanton Social Club (New York City)

SHORT RIB and LAMB BURGER

SERVES 6

Make the pickled onions and the harissa mayo.

Make the burgers: Preheat the broiler or a toaster oven. In a mixing bowl, combine the different types of ground meat with the cumin, paprika, and salt and pepper and form into 6 (approximately 7-ounce) patties. Grill the burgers to medium-rare over high heat, 4 to 5 minutes per side.

Meanwhile, season the slices of tomato with salt and pepper and top with the crumbled feta. Broil the tomatoes on a small baking sheet under the broiler or in the toaster oven until the cheese is golden brown. Melt the butter in a large sauté pan over medium heat and, working in batches, toast the rolls until golden.

Smear the harissa mayo on both sides of the toasted rolls. Place a romaine leaf on the bottom of the rolls. Place the burger on top of the romaine. Place the broiled tomato with feta cheese on top of the burger. Top the burger with drained pickled onions and the roll top.

Note: The burger blend is made up of 50% lamb, 25% boneless beef short rib, and 25% beef brisket.

Pickled Red Onions (recipe follows)

Harissa Mayo (recipe follows)

2½ pounds **ground burger blend** (see Note; approximately 7 ounces per patty)

1 tablespoon **ground cumin**

1 tablespoon **paprika**

Salt and **pepper**

6 thick slices **tomato**

½ cup crumbled **goat-milk feta cheese**

4 ounces (1 stick) **butter**, very soft

6 **sourdough rolls**, split

6 **heart of romaine** leaves

PICKLED RED ONIONS

MAKES ¾ CUP, ENOUGH FOR 6 BURGERS

Heat the cider vinegar, sugar, 1 cup water, the cinnamon stick, bay leaf, jalapeño, salt, and peppercorns to a simmer in a saucepan. Simmer for 5 minutes and remove from the heat. Pour the pickling liquid over the onions in a mixing bowl and let cool to room temperature. Reserve the onions in the liquid until you are ready to use them.

Note: Onions will hold refrigerated for 7 to 10 days.

⅓ cup **cider vinegar**

2 tablespoons **sugar**

½ **cinnamon stick**

1 **bay leaf**

¼ **red jalapeño chile**

½ tablespoon **kosher salt**

1 teaspoon **black peppercorns**

¼ pound **red onions**, julienned

HARISSA MAYO

MAKES ABOUT 1 CUP

Preheat the oven to 400° F. Peel away the outer layers of the 2 heads of garlic and cut off the top ½ inch from each. Place each bulb over a piece of aluminum foil and drizzle with olive oil. Wrap each bulb in the foil and bake until the cloves feel soft when pressed, 30 to 45 minutes. Squeeze the soft garlic from the cloves and puree. Transfer the garlic to a small mixing bowl and fold in the mayo, harissa, and paprika.

2 heads **garlic**

Olive oil, for drizzling

⅔ cup **Kewpie mayo**

1 tablespoon **harissa**

½ tablespoon **Spanish paprika**

Marc Murphy

Chef/owner, Benchmarc Restaurants by Marc Murphy (Landmarc and Ditch Plains, New York City) and Benchmarc Events by Marc Murphy

THE BIG MARC

SERVES 6

Make the cheddar and black pepper buns, spiked ketchup, and tot mixture. Wait until the burgers are just about to go in the pan before frying the tots.

Form the beef into 6 patties. Heat a skillet over high heat or heat an outdoor grill to high. Season the patties with salt and pepper, coat with the oil, and sear for about 2 minutes per side. Flip and cook for another 1½ minutes. Take the burgers off the heat and set aside.

Split the cheddar buns horizontally and brush with the melted butter. Toast in the skillet or on the grill.

Place 8 pickle slices on each of the bun bottoms and top with a burger. Slather 2 tablespoons spiked ketchup over each burger and set the bun tops in place. Serve immediately with a side of Jalapeño and Cheddar Tots.

6 Homemade Cheddar and Black Pepper Buns (recipe follows)

¾ cup Spiked Ketchup (page 300)

Jalapeño and Cheddar Tots (page 301)

2½ pounds **ground beef (80% lean)**

Salt and **pepper**

2 tablespoons **canola oil**

6 tablespoons **butter**, melted

48 **bread-and-butter pickle** slices

HOMEMADE CHEDDAR AND BLACK PEPPER BUNS

MAKES 6 BUNS

Stir the yeast, sugar, and water together in a small bowl to activate the yeast. (You can tell when the yeast is activated—little bubbles will have formed, which will take about a minute or two.) Add 3 eggs and the melted butter and mix until incorporated.

Add 4 cups of the flour and the salt to the bowl of a stand mixer. Use the dough hook attachment and start the mixer at low speed to mix the flour and salt. Stop the mixer and add the wet ingredients. Continue to mix for 5 minutes, until the dough is very smooth in texture. The dough should be sticky but workable, so you may want to add a little bit more flour as you mix.

Transfer the dough to a bowl. Cover the bowl with a kitchen towel, place in a warm area, and let rise until the dough has doubled in size.

After the dough has proofed (risen), turn it out onto a countertop and knead in the cheddar and black pepper. Try not to overwork the dough; once the cheese is mixed in, you can stop. Cut the dough into 6 equal portions and round them. Place on a buttered baking sheet and flatten them out with your hand.

Cover the pan and let them rise again in a warm area until they have doubled in size. When they are almost doubled in size, preheat the oven to 350°F.

Beat the remaining egg in a small bowl and brush the tops of the buns with the egg. Bake for 10 minutes, or until golden brown, rotating the pan halfway through. Transfer to a cooling rack.

$1\frac{1}{2}$ ounces **fresh yeast**

$\frac{1}{2}$ cup **sugar**

1 cup **warm water**

4 **large eggs**

4 ounces (1 stick) **butter**, melted

4 to 5 cups **flour**

$1\frac{1}{2}$ teaspoons **salt**

2 cups shredded **cheddar cheese**

2 tablespoons cracked **black pepper**

SPIKED KETCHUP

MAKES 3 CUPS

In a small bowl, whisk together the mayonnaise, mustard, and roasted garlic paste. Stir in the ketchup and vodka. This will keep for up to 6 days in the refrigerator.

1 cup **mayonnaise**

2 tablespoons **Dijon mustard**

1 tablespoon **roasted garlic paste** (see Note)

1½ cups **ketchup**

5 ounces (about ⅔ cup) **vodka**

NOTE: To make roasted garlic paste, cut 1 head of garlic in half crosswise and season with salt, pepper, and olive oil. Wrap in foil and place in a 300°F oven for 1 hour, or until the garlic is soft. Remove the garlic from the skin and mix into a paste.

JALAPEÑO AND CHEDDAR TOTS

MAKES 40 TOTS

Place the potatoes in a pot and cover with cold water. Bring to a boil and adjust the heat to simmering; cook until parboiled, about 20 minutes. Drain the potatoes and let cool to room temp. Once the potatoes have cooled, grate on a box grater right into a bowl. Mix in the cheddar and jalapeños and season with salt and pepper.

Make the pâte à choux: Bring the butter, milk, and 1 cup water to a boil in a medium saucepan. Once the butter has melted, add the flour all at once and stir until the dough is very smooth; continue stirring over heat for a minute or two to cook out the flour a little bit. Place the dough in the bowl of a stand mixer fitted with the paddle attachment. Turn on the mixer and add the eggs one by one, waiting to add the next egg until the previous one has been completely mixed in. Season with a pinch of salt.

Fill a countertop fryer with oil or pour a few inches of oil into a heavy pan. Heat the oil to 350°F.

Fold the pâte à choux into the grated potatoes until the potato mixture is sticky and can form a ball. Using a 1-ounce (2-tablespoon) scoop, form the potato mixture into tots.

Fry the tots until golden brown. Remove them with a slotted spoon or spider and drain on paper towels. Season with salt and pepper.

2 pounds **Yukon Gold potatoes**

10 ounces shredded **cheddar cheese** (about 2½ cups)

1½ cups chopped **pickled jalapeños**

Salt and **pepper**

PÂTE À CHOUX:

½ pound (2 sticks) **butter**

1 cup **milk**

2 cups **flour**

8 large **eggs**

Salt

Oil, for frying (preferably soybean)

Franklin Becker

Corporate Executive Chef, EMM Group, Abe and Arthur's, Lexington Brass, Catch (New York City)

WISCONSIN CHEESEBURGER

SERVES 8

Make the condiment sauce: Mix all the sauce ingredients together until smooth.

Make the cheese sauce: In a double boiler, stir together both cheeses until melted and smooth. Add the sour cream and season with salt and pepper. Keep warm.

Make the fried shallots: Fill a countertop fryer with oil or pour about 3 inches of oil into a large, heavy pot. Heat the oil to 360°F. Shave the shallots, i.e., slice them very, very thin. A mandoline works well for this. Dredge the shaved shallots in Wondra flour to coat them and bounce them around to get rid of excess flour. Fry the shallots in batches till golden. Season with salt and pepper while still hot.

Preheat a griddle. You want it to be hot, but there must be areas on the griddle that are cooler.

Make the burgers: Shape the beef into 8 patties, loosely packing the beef to avoid warming it and melting the fat. The key to a good burger is tenderness.

Season the burgers with salt and pepper. Cook the burgers to the desired doneness. Use the "hot spots" on the griddle to sear the burgers and give them a nice crust. Once seared, move them to cooler spots to finish cooking. Generally speaking, a 1-inch-thick burger will be cooked medium rare after 2½ minutes on each side and medium after another minute on each side.

SPECIAL CONDIMENT SAUCE:

½ cup **Heinz ketchup**

¼ cup **Hellmann's mayonnaise**

2 tablespoons **Dijon mustard**

2 tablespoons **sriracha sauce**

2 tablespoons **maple syrup**

2 tablespoons **red wine vinegar**

CHEESE SAUCE:

6 ounces **Joe Widmer's Four-Year-Old Cheddar Cheese** or a good-quality cheddar cheese

8 ounces **Joe Widmer's Aged Brick Spread** (see Note)

2 tablespoons **sour cream**

Salt and **pepper**

FRIED SHALLOTS (OR JUST BUY DURKEE'S FRENCH FRIED ONIONS IF YOU'RE LAZY):

1 pound **shallots**, peeled

About ¾ cup **Wondra flour**

Oil, for frying

NOTE: To order Joe Widmer's cheeses, visit www.widmerscheese.com.

Place the burgers on the bun bottoms and top with the cheese sauce, condiment sauce, pickle strip, and fried shallots. Add tomato and lettuce or a slice of bacon if you like, and enjoy. For best results, allow the burger to rest for 4 minutes before downing it. Otherwise you will end up with a stained shirt!

BURGERS:

4 pounds **ground beef** (We use a proprietary blend specially designed by Pat LaFrieda consisting of brisket, skirt steak, and chuck, but a good-quality ground beef chuck will work fine.)

Salt and **pepper**

8 **brioche buns**, split (We make our own at the restaurant, but any store-bought version will do at home.)

TOPPINGS:

Bread-and-butter pickle slices (At the restaurant, we make our own, but Vlasic is an excellent store-bought alternative.)

Sliced **tomato** (optional)

Lettuce leaves (optional)

Cooked **bacon** strips (optional)

Josh Capon

Chef/partner, Burger & Barrel (New York City)

THE BASH BURGER with CARAMELIZED ONION-AND-BACON JAM

SERVES 4

¼ cup **ketchup**

¼ cup **mayonnaise**

1 teaspoon **red wine vinegar**

1 teaspoon **Worcestershire sauce**

Kosher salt and **black pepper**

6 slices **bacon**

¼ cup **vegetable oil**

1 large **white onion**, chopped (2 cups)

1½ pounds **ground beef chuck**

4 teaspoons **Dijon mustard**

4 slices **American cheese**

4 **soft rolls**, such as Parker House or potato rolls, split and toasted

4 **dill pickles**, shaved into slices

In a small bowl, stir together the ketchup, mayonnaise, vinegar, and Worcestershire sauce; season with salt and pepper.

Preheat the oven to 375°F. Line a rimmed baking sheet with parchment paper.

Arrange the bacon on the baking sheet and bake until crisp, 30 to 35 minutes; drain. Finely chop the bacon and transfer it to a medium bowl.

Meanwhile, in a large skillet, heat the oil over medium heat. Add the onion and cook, stirring occasionally, until softened and golden brown, 15 to 20 minutes; season with salt and pepper. Add to the bacon.

Heat a grill pan over high heat.

Make four 6-ounce patties from the ground beef and season them with salt and pepper on both sides. Brush 1 teaspoon Dijon mustard on the top of each patty. Grill, turning once, for about 10 minutes for medium (adjust the cooking time for rarer or more well-done burgers). During the last 2 minutes of cooking, top each patty with an American cheese slice.

Spread 1 tablespoon of the sauce on the roll bottoms and tops. Place the burgers on the roll bottoms and top with some of the onion-and-bacon jam and shaved pickles. Set the roll tops in place, slice in half, and enjoy!

INDEX

(Page references in *italic* refer to illustrations.)

A

Adirondacker, 35
Adirondack Red Wing Burgers, 78
Albondigas Subs: Spicy Spanish Meatball Subs, 186–87
American cheese:
  Bash Burger with Caramelized Onion-and-Bacon Jam, 304
  Logan County Hamburgers, 283
anchovy fillets:
  Holsteiner-Style Schnitzel-wich, 184
  Pissaladière Topping, 83
andouille:
  Cajun Pork Burgers, 69
  Dawgs, Creole, 212
  Dawgs with Gumbo Sauce, Creole, 212
apple:
  Green, Slaw, 192–93, *193*
  and Onion Chutney, Chunky, *190*, 191
Argentinean (flavors):
  Bife de Chorizo Sliders, 131
  Chimichurri, 131, 220
  Sloppy Joaquins, 220
Artichoke-Spinach Burgers, 103
arugula, in Blue-Rugula Burgers, 58, *59*
Asian (flavors):
  Banh Mi Burgers, 71
  BBQ "Bun"-Mi Sliders, 157
  Black Sesame and Panko–Crusted Tuna Sliders, *170*, 171
  5-Spice Burgers with Warm Mu Shu Slaw, *66*, *67*
  5-Spice Tuna Sliders with Hoisin, 173
  Garlic-Ginger Salmon Burgers with Wasabi Mayo, 122
  Morimoto Kakuni Burger, 282
  Satay Sliders, 162
  see also Indian (flavors)
Audacious, Herbacious Beef Burgers, 7
avocado(s):
  California Turkey Club Burgers, 90
  Green Ranch Dressing, 91
  Guacamole, 8, 150
  Guaca-Salsa, 154, *155*
  Ranch Dressing, 168, *169*
  Sauce, 149, 156, 196

B

Baba Ghanoush, *108*, 109
bacon:
  Adirondacker, 35
  Beer-Braised, Bacon Cheeseburgers, 40
  Biscuits, Beer and Beef Chili Sliders on, with Tomatillo Ketchup, 132–33
  Bits, Burgers with Blue and, 9
  BL(FG)T Sliders, 136–38, *137*, *138*
  California Turkey Club Burgers, 90
  and Caramelized Onion Jam, 304
  Chipotle Burgers with Nacho Top, 14
  Club Burger Sliders with Avocado-Ranch Dressing, 168, *169*
  Cobb-Style Turkey Burger Club with Green Ranch Dressing, 91
  Egg, and Cheeseburger, Genuine, with Heirloom Tomato Onion Chutney, 288–90
  Grilled Cheese Burgers with Tomato and, 20
  Patty Melts with Eggs, 27
  7-Layer Chili Dog Dip, 213
  Smokehouse Burger, 280–81
  Tomato Jam, 274
  Turkey Club Sliders, Deluxe, 167
  Welsh Rarebit Burgers, 38
  -Wrapped Chipotle Burgers, "Smoke and Fireworks," 45
  -Wrapped Potato Skins, 270
Bagel, Everything, Salmon Burgers, *118*, 119
baked beans, in Sloppy Dawgs, 227
balsamic:
  drizzle, making, 15
  Ketchup, 277
  Sweet Potato Oven Fries, 249
Banh Mi Burgers, 71
barbecue, *see* BBQ; BBQ Sauce
Bash Burger with Caramelized Onion-and-Bacon Jam, 304
BBQ:
  Bourbon Pulled Chicken Sandwiches and Green Apple Slaw, 192–93, *193*
  "Bun"-Mi Sliders, 157
  Chicken Burgers, Italian, 80, *81*
  Chicken Sloppy Joes with Pickled Slaw Salad, 230, *231*
  Chipotle, 281
  Maple Joes, Sloppy, 235

BBQ Sauce, 80, *81*, 157, 192
  Bourbon, 139
  Chipotle Barbecue, 281
  My Almost Famous, 45
  Smoky, 141–42, 180
bean(s):
  baked, in Sloppy Dawgs, 227
  Beef 'n,' Burrito Burgers, 8
  chickpeas, in Falafel Burgers,
    116
  refried, in Green and Red Chile
    Nacho Sliders, 144–45
  refried, in Pigs in Ponchos:
    Quesadilla-Wrapped Franks
    and Beans, *202*, 203
  refried, in South by Southwest
    7-Layer Sliders, 150–51, *151*
  Sloppy Veg-Head Joes with,
    236, 237
Becker, Franklin, 302–3
beef, ground, x
  Cheeseburger Egg Rolls with
    Russian Dressing Dipper, 152
  Chili con Carne, 213
  Coney Chili Dogs, 206
  Kielbasa Chili Dogs, *210*, 211
  Michigan Sauce, 201
beef, ground mix of pork, veal
  and:
  Florentine Burgers, 44
  Lasagna Burgers, 21
  "The Wurst" Reuben Burgers,
    74, *75*
beef and pork burgers:
  Italian Meat Loaf Long Boy, 64
  Long Boy Sausage, with Pickled
    Fennel and Pepperonata,
    76–77
  Meatball Hero, 50–51
  Salami, Ultimate, 52–53
beef burger blends:
  cuts for, x
  forming into patties, 60, x
  grinding your own meat for,
    24–25

mixing your own, xi
RR, xi
beef burgers, 4–64
  Adirondacker, 35
  all'Amatriciana, 10
  Audacious, Herbacious, 7
  Bacon, Egg, and Cheeseburger,
    Genuine, with Heirloom
    Tomato Onion Chutney,
    288–90
  with Bacon Bits and Blue, 9
  Bacon-Wrapped Chipotle,
    "Smoke and Fireworks," 45
  Bash, with Caramelized Onion-
    and-Bacon Jam, 304
  Beef 'n' Bean Burrito Burgers, 8
  Beer-Braised Bacon Bacon
    Cheeseburgers, 40
  Big, with Crunchy Sour Cream
    Onion Rings, 4–6, *5*
  Big Marc, 298–301
  "Big Spicy Mac," Rach's, 42, *43*
  Bloody Mary Cheeseburgers, 31
  Blue-Rugula, 58, *59*
  Bœuf Bourguignon, 30
  Buttered-Toast Swiss Patty, 11
  Chili, with Charred Pico de
    Gallo, 36
  Chili Mac 'n' Cheese, 12, *13*
  Chipotle, with Nacho Top, 14
  Coarse-Ground Chuck,
    with Garlic–Black Pepper
    Parmesan Sauce and Roasted
    Tomatoes with Basil and
    Balsamic Drizzle, 15
  Cuban Patty Melts with Yellow
    Mustard Slaw, 26
  Double-Decker Animal Style, 41
  Drunken, with Stilton, 18
  Fat Doug, 287
  Fire Eater, 294–95
  French Onion, *62*, 63
  French Onion Dip, 16, *17*
  Goat Cheese, with Beets, 19
  Goulash, 39

Grilled Cheese, with Bacon and
    Tomato, 20
  Logan County Hamburgers, 283
  Louisiana, 291
  Meat and Mashed Potatoes, 22
  Meat Lover's, 23
  Morimoto Kakuni, 282
  Patty Melts with Eggs, 27
  Pimiento Mac 'n' Cheese
    Cheeseburgers, 28
  au Poivre with Brandy Cream
    Sauce, Uptown, 56
  with Porcini Steak Sauce,
    Uptown, 57
  Sage-Scented, with Fontina and
    Roasted Squash, *46*, 47
  Sauerbraten, 29
  Schlow, 292–93
  Shepherd's Pie Knife-and-Fork,
    54–55
  Shish Ka, 112
  Short Rib and Lamb, 296–97
  Smokehouse, 280–81
  Spaghetti and Meatball, 48–49
  Stroganoff-Style Knife-and-
    Fork, *32*, 33–34
  Wellington, 37
  Welsh Rarebit, 38
  Wisconsin Cheeseburger, 302–3
  Yo, 284–86
beef sandwiches, 177–83
  Best Sandwich I Ever Made (and
    My Husband Ever Tasted) aka
    The 7-Hour Smoked Brisket
    Sandwich with Smoky BBQ
    Sauce, Sharp Cheddar, Red
    Cabbage Slaw, and Horseradish
    Sauce, *178*, 179–80
  Chicagoan-Italian Roast Beef
    Heroes, 182–83
  Red Wine and Garlic Marinated
    Sliced Steak, 181
  Sliced Steak Reubens with
    Horseradish Russian
    Dressing, 177

beef slider(s), 131–55
  Beer and Beef Chili, on Bacon
    Biscuits with Tomatillo
    Ketchup, 132–33
  Bife de Chorizo, 131
  Bistro, à la Rachael, *134*, 135
  BL(FG)T, 136–38, *137*, *138*
  Bourbon Barbecue Sliced Steak,
    139
  Brooklyn Beer Chili, with
    Smoky BBQ Sauce, Oil-and-
    Vinegar Slaw, and Sweet 'n'
    Spicy Pickles, *140*, 141–42
  Green and Red Chile Nacho,
    144–45
  Jalapeño Popper, 143
  Mac 'n' Cheese-Burger, 146
  Pimiento Cheese, 148
  Poblano Popper Super-Sliders,
    149
  St. Paddy's-Style Reuben,
    153
  Salad with Yellow Mustard
    Vinaigrette, 147
  Sliced Steak Soft Taco, with
    Guaca-Salsa, 154, *155*
  Sloppy Chili, 218
  South by Southwest 7-Layer,
    150–51, *151*
beef sloppies, 216–22
  Chili Sliders, 218
  Chipotle Joes, 219
  Dawgs, 227
  Joaquins, 220
  Joe DiMaggios, 221
  Messy Giuseppe, *224*, 225
  Philly Cheesesteak Sloppy Joes,
    216, *217*
  Tango Joes, 222
beer:
  -Battered Tex-Mex Fishwiches
    with Avocado Sauce, 196
  and Beef Chili Sliders on Bacon
    Biscuits with Tomatillo
    Ketchup, 132–33

  -Braised Bacon Bacon
    Cheeseburgers, 40
  Brooklyn, Chili Sliders with
    Smoky BBQ Sauce, Oil-and-
    Vinegar Slaw, and Sweet 'n'
    Spicy Pickles, *140*, 141–42
  Chili Burgers with Charred Pico
    de Gallo, 36
  Mexican Pulled Pork Sliders,
    158–59
  South by Southwest 7-Layer
    Sliders, 150–51, *151*
  stout, in Welsh Rarebit Burgers,
    38
Beets, Goat Cheese Burgers with,
  19
Berber Burgers, 113
Big, Beefy Mushroom Cheddar
  Melts, 198
Big Beef Burgers with Crunchy
  Sour Cream Onion Rings, 4–6,
  5
Big Marc, 298–301
"Big Spicy Mac," Rach's, 42, *43*
biscuit:
  Chicken and, Sliders with Spicy
    Orange-Maple Drizzle and
    Crunchy Oil-and-Vinegar
    Slaw, 163
  Fried Chicken and, Sliders with
    Smoky Chard, *164*, 165
bistro-style:
  Pommes Frites (French Fries),
    246, 247
  Sliders à la Rachael, *134*, 135
black beans:
  Beef 'n' Bean Burrito Burgers, 8
  Sloppy Veg-Head Joes with
    Beans, *236*, 237
Blackberry-Pinot Gravy, 185
black pepper, *see* pepper(corn)
Black Sesame and Panko–Crusted
  Tuna Sliders, *170*, 171
blenders, working with hot liq-
  uids in, 218

Bloody Mary Cheeseburgers, 31
BL(FG)T Sliders, 136–38, *137*, *138*
blue (cheese):
  Adirondack Red Wing Burgers,
    78
  Buffalo Turkey Sliders, 166
  Burgers with Bacon Bits and, 9
  Cobb-Style Turkey Burger Club
    with Green Ranch Dressing, 91
  Dressing, Buffalo Turkey
    Burgers with, 88, *89*
  Rugula Burgers, 58, *59*
  Sauce, 166
  Stilton, Drunken Burgers with,
    18
bockwursts, in Reuben Dogs, 209
Bœuf Bourguignon Burgers, 30
bourbon:
  Barbecue Sliced Steak Sliders,
    139
  BBQ Pulled Chicken
    Sandwiches and Green Apple
    Slaw, 192–93, *193*
Brandy Cream Sauce, 56
Brat Burgers with Sauerkraut or
  Sweet Onions, 68
bratwursts, in Reuben Dogs, 209
breads:
  freezing trimmings for
    breadcrumbs or stuffing, 160
  see also rolls, buns, or breads
Brisket, 7-Hour Smoked, Sand-
  wich with Smoky BBQ Sauce,
  Sharp Cheddar, Red Cabbage
  Slaw, and Horseradish Sauce,
  178, 179–80
broccoli rabe:
  Hot Sausage Burgers with, *72*,
    73
  Pulled Pork with, Subs, 188
Brooklyn Beer Chili Sliders with
  Smoky BBQ Sauce, Oil-and-
  Vinegar Slaw, and Sweet 'n'
  Spicy Pickles, *140*, 141–42
brown rice, in Pork Kakuni, 304

buffalo:
   Joes, 232
   Turkey Burgers with Blue
      Cheese Dressing, 88, *89*
   Turkey Sliders, 166
"Bun"-Mi Sliders, BBQ, 157
buns, *see* rolls, buns, or breads
burger blends:
   forming into patties, 60, x
   grinding your own meat for,
      24–25
   ingredients for, x–xi
   mixing your own, xi
   RR, xi
Burrito Burgers, Beef 'n' Bean, 8
Buttered-Toast Swiss Patty Burger,
   11

C

cabbage:
   leftover, uses for, 209
   Red, 29, 209
   see also sauerkraut; Slaw(s)
caesar:
   Pesto, 102
   Tots, 253
Cajun Pork Burgers, 69
California Turkey Club Burgers,
   90
Cambozola blue cheese, in Blue-
   Rugula Burgers, 58, *59*
Capon, Josh, 304
Caribbean (flavors):
   Burgers with Mango Salsa, 96,
      97
   Jerk Burgers, 99
carrots:
   Giardiniera, 183
   Lemon Slaw, 194, *195*
cast-iron skillets, cooking burgers
   in, x
cauliflower, in Giardiniera, 183
celery, in Giardiniera, 183

Chard, Smoky, *164*, 165
cheddar cheese:
   Adirondacker, 35
   Bacon, Egg, and Cheeseburger,
      Genuine, with Heirloom
      Tomato Onion Chutney,
      288–90
   Bacon Biscuits, Beer and
      Beef Chili Sliders on, with
      Tomatillo Ketchup, 132–33
   Beer-Braised Bacon Bacon
      Cheeseburgers, 40
   Big, Beefy Mushroom Melts,
      198
   "Big Spicy Mac," Rach's, 42, *43*
   and Black Pepper Buns,
      Homemade, 299
   Bloody Mary Cheeseburgers, 31
   Brat Burgers with Sauerkraut or
      Sweet Onions, 68
   Cheeseburger Egg Rolls with
      Russian Dressing Dipper, 152
   Chili Fry Topping, 273
   Chili Mac 'n' Cheese Burgers,
      12, *13*
   Chorizo Sliders, 156
   Fry Topping, *245*, 273
   Green and Red Chile Nacho
      Sliders, 144–45
   Jalapeño Popper Sliders, 143
   and Jalapeño Tots, 301
   Mac 'n' Cheese-Burger Sliders,
      146
   Michigan Dogs with Cheese
      Sauce, 201
   Patty Melts with Eggs, 27
   Pimiento Cheese Sliders, 148
   Pimiento Mac 'n' Cheese
      Cheeseburgers, 28
   Poblano Popper Super-Sliders,
      149
   Pork Schnitzel Sandwiches with
      Chunky Apple and Onion
      Chutney, *190*, 191
   Poutine, 272

   Roasted Jalapeño Poppers, 265,
      266
   Schlow Burger, 292–93
   7-Layer Chili Dog Dip, 213
   Slider Salad with Yellow
      Mustard Vinaigrette, 147
   "Smoke and Fireworks" Bacon-
      Wrapped Chipotle Burgers,
      45
   Smokehouse Burger, 280–81
   Welsh Rarebit Burgers, 38
   Wisconsin Cheeseburger, 302–3
cheese:
   American, in Bash Burger with
      Caramelized Onion-and-
      Bacon Jam, 304
   American, in Logan County
      Hamburgers, 283
   Chili Fry Topping, 273
   Comté, in Double-Decker
      Animal Style, 41
   Fry Topping, *245*, 273
   Goat, Burgers with Beets, 19
   Gouda, Smoked, Hungarian
      Turkey Burgers with, 98
   Grilled, Burgers with Bacon and
      Tomato, 20
   herb, in Audacious, Herbacious
      Beef Burgers, 7
   Manchego, in Chorizo Sliders,
      156
   Manchego, in 3-Cheese *Queso*
      Sauce, 14
   Pimiento, Sliders, 148
   ricotta, in Florentine Burgers,
      44
   ricotta, in Lasagna Burgers, 21
   Sauce, Michigan Dogs with, 201
   3-, *Queso* Sauce, 14
   see also blue (cheese); cheddar
      cheese; cream cheese;
      Emmentaler Swiss cheese;
      feta cheese; Fontina cheese;
      Gruyère cheese; Monterey
      Jack cheese; mozzarella

cheese; Parmigiano-Reggiano cheese; pepperjack cheese; provolone cheese; Swiss cheese

cheeseburger(s):
Adirondacker, 35
Adirondack Red Wing Burgers, 78
Audacious, Herbacious Beef Burgers, 7
Bacon, Egg and, Genuine, with Heirloom Tomato Onion Chutney, 288–90
Bash Burger with Caramelized Onion-and-Bacon Jam, 304
Beer-Braised Bacon Bacon, 40
Berber Burgers, 113
"Big Spicy Mac," Rach's, 42, 43
Bloody Mary, 31
Blue-Rugula Burgers, 58, 59
Brat Burgers with Sauerkraut or Sweet Onions, 68
Burgers with Bacon Bits and Blue, 9
Chili Burgers with Charred Pico de Gallo, 36
Cubano Burgers, 100, 101
Cuban Patty Melts with Yellow Mustard Slaw, 26
Double-Decker Animal Style, 41
Drunken Burgers with Stilton, 18
Egg Rolls with Russian Dressing Dipper, 152
Fat Doug Burger, 287
Fire Eater Burger, 294–95
Fresh Tuna French-Style, 126
Hot Sausage, with Broccoli Rabe, 72, 73
Hungarian Turkey Burgers with Smoked Gouda, 98
Italian Meat Loaf Long Boy Burgers, 64
Logan County Hamburgers, 283
Louisiana Burger, 291

Marsala Burgers, 86
Meat Lover's Burger, 23
Mediterranean Veggie Burgers with Provolone and Italian Ketchup, 117
Onion-and-Mushroom-Smothered Turkey Burgers with Swiss, 104
Patty Melts with Eggs, 27
Pimiento Mac 'n' Cheese, 28
Provençal Burgers with Pissaladière Topping, 83
Rachel Patty Melts, 87
Sage-Scented Burgers with Fontina and Roasted Squash, 46, 47
Schlow Burger, 292–93
"Smoke and Fireworks" Bacon-Wrapped Chipotle Burgers, 45
Smokehouse Burger, 280–81
Spaghetti and Meatball Burgers, 48–49
Spinach-Artichoke Burgers, 103
Wisconsin, 302–3
"The Wurst" Reuben Burgers, 74, 75
Yo Burger, 284–86
Cheesesteak Sloppy Joes, Philly, 216, 217
Chicagoan-Italian Roast Beef Heroes, 182–83
chicken burgers, 78–86
Adirondack Red Wing, 78
with Caesar Pesto, 102
Caribbean, with Mango Salsa, 96, 97
5-Spice, with Warm Mu Shu Slaw, 66, 67
Goulash, 39
Gyro, 111
Indian-Spiced Patties with Yogurt Sauce, 84, 85
Italian BBQ, 80, 81
Jerk, 99
Kiev, with Russian Slaw, 79

Marsala, 86
Provençal, with Pissaladière Topping, 83
Saltimbocca, 65
Spanikopita, 82
Spinach-Artichoke, 103
testing doneness of, 80
chicken sandwiches:
Bourbon BBQ Pulled, and Green Apple Slaw, 192–93, 193
Sliced Pork and, Hoagies, Italian, 189
chicken sliders, 162–65
and Biscuit, with Spicy Orange-Maple Drizzle and Crunchy Oil-and-Vinegar Slaw, 163
Fried, and Biscuit, with Smoky Chard, 164, 165
Satay, 162
chicken sloppies:
BBQ Sloppy Joes with Pickled Slaw Salad, 230, 231
Buffalo Joes, 232
Suizas, 234
chickpeas, in Falafel Burgers, 116
chile(s):
Giardiniera, 183
green, in Rach's "Big Spicy Mac," 42, 43
Green, Sauce, 144
Green and Red, Nacho Sliders, 144–45
Oven Fries, Crispy, with Ranch Dipper, 254, 255
poblano, in Patty Melts with Eggs, 27
Poblano Popper Super-Sliders, 149
Red, Paste, 144
see also chipotle(s); jalapeño(s)
chili:
Beer and Beef, Sliders on Bacon Biscuits with Tomatillo Ketchup, 132–33

chili (continued)
  Brooklyn Beer, Sliders with
    Smoky BBQ Sauce, Oil-and-
    Vinegar Slaw, and Sweet 'n'
    Spicy Pickles, *140*, 141–42
  Burgers with Charred Pico de
    Gallo, 36
  con Carne, 213
  Cheese Fry Topping, 273
  Dog Dip, 7-Layer, 213
  Dogs, Coney, 206
  Dogs, Kielbasa, *210*, 211
  Mac 'n' Cheese Burgers, 12,
    13
  Sliders, Sloppy, 218
Chimichurri Sauce, 131, 220
Chinese (flavors):
  5-Spice Burgers with Warm Mu
    Shu Slaw, 66, *67*
  5-Spice Tuna Sliders with
    Hoisin, 173
chipotle(s):
  in adobo sauce, tip for, 14
  Barbecue Sauce, 281
  Burgers, "Smoke and
    Fireworks" Bacon-Wrapped,
    45
  Burgers with Nacho Top, 14
  Deviled Mayo, 275
  Fire Eater Sauce, 295
  Joes, Sloppy, 219
  Ketchup, 276
chorizo:
  Albondigas Subs: Spicy Spanish
    Meatball Subs, 186–87
  Bife de Chorizo Sliders, 131
  Sliders, 156
  Sloppy Cubanos, 226
chutneys:
  Apple and Onion, Chunky, *190*,
    191
  Heirloom Tomato Onion, 290
Cincinnati Sloppy Sliders, 233
Cliff's Homegrown Vidalia Onion
  Petals, 281

club:
  Burger Sliders with Avocado-
    Ranch Dressing, 168, *169*
  Cobb-Style Turkey Burger, with
    Green Ranch Dressing, 91
  Turkey, Burgers, California, 90
  Turkey, Sliders, Deluxe, 167
Coarse-Ground Chuck Burgers
  with Garlic–Black Pepper Par-
  mesan Sauce and Roasted To-
  matoes with Basil and Balsamic
  Drizzle, 15
Cobb-Style Turkey Burger Club
  with Green Ranch Dressing, 91
cod, in Fishwiches, 194–95, *195*
Coleslaw, Cousin Shari's, 293
Comté cheese, in Double-Decker
  Animal Style, 41
condiments and garnishes:
  Apple and Onion Chutney,
    Chunky, *190*, 191
  Baba Ghanoush, *108*, 109
  Bacon Tomato Jam, 274
  Chard, Smoky, *164*, 165
  Cucumber Relish, 162
  Giardiniera, 183
  Guacamole, 8, 150
  Guaca-Salsa, 154, *155*
  Heirloom Tomato Onion
    Chutney, 290
  Honey Mustard, 121
  Marinated Vegetables, 52–53
  Onion Ring Garnish, *32*, 33
  Onion Rings, Sour Cream, 4, *5*
  Onions, Caramelized, 41, 58
  Onion Topping, French, *134*, 135
  Pepperonata, 76–77
  Pissaladière Topping, 83
  Potato-Kraut, 153
  Red Cabbage, 29, 209
  saucy, as bun's worst enemy, 61
  Spicy Sour Cream, 150
  see also ketchups; mayo; pickle(d)
    (s); Salsa; Slaw(s)
Coney Chili Dogs, 206

Coney Island Sauce, 206
cooking burgers, x
Corn, Indian, Turkey Tikka Burgers
  with, 106
corn dogs:
  Firecracker Deviled, 204, *205*
  L'il Devils (Corn Dog Sliders),
    204
corned beef, in St. Paddy's-Style
  Reuben Sliders, 153
Country Pork and Peppercorn
  Burgers, 70
couscous, in Mediterranean Veg-
  gie Burgers with Provolone and
  Italian Ketchup, 117
Cousin Shari's Coleslaw, 293
Cranberry Bog Turkey Burgers,
  92, *93*
cream cheese:
  Jalapeño Popper Sliders, 143
  Roasted Jalapeño Poppers, 265,
    266
  Sauce, 119
cremini mushrooms, in Mediter-
  ranean Veggie Burgers with
  Provolone and Italian Ketchup,
  117
Creole Andouille Dawgs, 212
  with Gumbo Sauce, 212
crescent roll dough, in Pigs in a
  Blanket with the Works, 208
Crouton Rolls, 102
Cuban (flavors):
  Cubano Burgers, *100*, 101
  Cubano Dogs, 199
  Patty Melts with Yellow
    Mustard Slaw, 26
  Sloppy Cubanos, 226
cucumber(s):
  Relish, 162
  Sweet 'n' Spicy Pickles, 141, 261
  Tzatziki, 111
Curried Turkey Burgers, 94
curry powder, making your own,
  94

D

deviled:
  Corn Dogs, Firecracker, 204, *205*
  Eggs, 262, *263*
  Mayo, 275
Dijon (mustard):
  Double-Decker Animal Style, 41
  Honey Potato Salad, 266
  Mayo, 275
  Remoulade Sauce, 291
dips and dipping sauces:
  Horseradish and Sour Cream Fry Dipper, 271
  Marinara Dipper, Quick, 271
  Ranch Dipper, 254
  Russian Dressing Dipper, 152
  7-Layer Chili Dog Dip, 213
  Spicy Dipping Sauce, 260
  Yogurt Dipping Sauce, 257
Double-Baked Crazy-Crisp Oven Fries, 244, *245*
Double-Decker Animal Style, 41
dressing(s):
  Avocado-Ranch, 168, *169*
  Blue Cheese, 88, *89*
  Hoagie, 189
  Horseradish Russian, 177
  Italian, 53
  Ranch, 167
  Ranch, Dipper, 254
  Ranch, Green, 91
  Ranch, Red, 6
  Russian, Dipper, 152
  Russian-Style, 87
  Yellow Mustard Vinaigrette, 147
Drunken Burgers with Stilton, 18

E

E. coli, 25
egg(s):
  Bacon, and Cheeseburger,
    Genuine, with Heirloom Tomato Onion Chutney, 288–90
  Deviled, 262, *263*
  fried, in Holsteiner-Style Schnitzel-wich, 184
  hard-boiled, in Niçoise-Style Pan Bagnats, 197
  Patty Melts with, 27
eggplant:
  Berber Burgers, 113
  Fries with Yogurt Dipping Sauce, 257
  Middle Eastern Lamb Burgers with Baba Ghanoush, *108*, 109
Egg Rolls, Cheeseburger, with Russian Dressing Dipper, 152
Emmentaler Swiss cheese:
  Berber Burgers, 113
  Onion-and-Mushroom-Smothered Turkey Burgers with Swiss, 104
  Rachel Patty Melts, 87
  Sliced Steak Reubens with Horseradish Russian Dressing, 177
  "The Wurst" Reuben Burgers, 74, *75*
Everything Bagel Salmon Burgers, *118*, 119

F

Falafel Burgers, 116
Fat Doug Burger, 287
fennel:
  Lemon Slaw, 194, *195*
  Pickled, 76
  seeds, crushing, 77
feta cheese:
  Short Rib and Lamb Burger, 296–97
  Spanikopita Burgers, 82
  Walnut Sauce, 110
Finger Fries with Formaggio, 243
Firecracker Deviled Corn Dogs, 204, *205*
Fire Eater Burger, 294–95
Fire Eater Sauce, 295
Fishwiches, 194–95, *195*
  Tex-Mex Beer-Battered, with Avocado Sauce, 196
5-spice:
  Burgers with Warm Mu Shu Slaw, 66, *67*
  Tuna Sliders with Hoisin, 173
Flay, Bobby, 291
Florentine Burgers, 44
Fontina cheese:
  Marsala Burgers, 86
  Sage-Scented Burgers with Roasted Squash and, *46*, 47
  Saltimbocca Burgers, 65
  Yo Burger, 284–86
forming patties, 60, x
French (flavors):
  Bistro Sliders à la Rachael, *134*, 135
  Bistro-Style Pommes Frites (French Fries), *246*, 247
  Bœuf Bourguignon Burgers, 30
  Fresh Tuna Cheeseburgers, 126
  Niçoise-Style Pan Bagnats, 197
  Onion Burgers, *62*, 63
  Onion Dip Burgers, 16, *17*
  Provençal Burgers with Pissaladière Topping, 83
  Tuna Burgers, 123
French Fries (Bistro-Style Pommes Frites), *246*, 247
Fried Chicken and Biscuit Sliders with Smoky Chard, *164*, 165
fries, 241–60
  Balsamic Sweet Potato Oven, 249
  Bistro-Style Pommes Frites (French Fries), *246*, 247

fries (continued)
  Caesar Tots, 253
  Cheese Topping for, *245*, 273
  Chili Cheese Topping for, 273
  Crispy Chile Oven, with Ranch
    Dipper, 254, *255*
  Double-Baked Crazy-Crisp
    Oven, 244, *245*
  Eggplant, with Yogurt Dipping
    Sauce, 257
  Finger, with Formaggio, 243
  frying ahead of time, 247
  Garlic, Parmigiano, and Pepper
    Tots, 252
  Gravy for, 272
  Horseradish and Sour Cream
    Dipper for, 271
  Hot Dog, 259
  Jalapeño and Cheddar Tots,
    301
  Onions, Crispy, 293
  Parsnip Oven, *164*, 256
  Portobello Mushroom Fries,
    258
  Poutine, 272
  Shallots, 302
  10-Cut Oven, 248
  Thick-Cut-O-Rings and Spicy
    Dipping Sauce, 260
  Tots, Homemade, 250, *251*
  Vidalia Onion Petals, Cliff's
    Homegrown, 281

G

garlic:
  Black Pepper Parmesan Sauce,
    15
  Bread Rolls, 49
  Ginger Salmon Burgers with
    Wasabi Mayo, 122
  Parmigiano, and Pepper Tots,
    252
  "pasted," making, 138

and Red Wine Marinated Sliced
    Steak Sandwiches, 181
  Roasted, Mayo, 275
Giardiniera, 183
  Marinated Vegetables, 52–53
Ginger-Garlic Salmon Burgers
    with Wasabi Mayo, 122
Giuseppe, Messy, *224*, 225
Goat Cheese Burgers with Beets,
    19
Gouda, Smoked, Hungarian Tur-
    key Burgers with, 98
Goulash Burgers, 39
Gravy, 54–55
  Fry, 272
  Pinot-Blackberry, 185
  Potpie, 105
  Sauerbraten, 29
Greek (flavors):
  Gyro Burger, 111
  Spanikopita Burgers, 82
  Tzatziki, 111
Green Raita Sauce, 161
Green Ranch Dressing, 91
griddles, cooking burgers on, x
Grilled Cheese Burgers with
    Bacon and Tomato, 20
grilling burgers outdoors, x
grinding your own meat, 24–25
Gruyère cheese:
  Bistro Sliders à la Rachael, *134*,
    135
  French Onion Burgers, *62*, 63
  Fresh Tuna French-Style
    Cheeseburgers, 126
  Mac 'n' Cheese-Burger Sliders,
    146
  Poutine, 272
  Provençal Burgers with
    Pissaladière Topping, 83
Guacamole, 8, 150
Guaca-Salsa, 154, *155*
Gumbo Sauce, Creole Andouille
    Dawgs with, 212
Gyro Burger, 111

H

ham:
  Cubano Burgers, *100*, 101
  Cubano Dogs, 199
  Meat Lover's Burger, 23
Harissa Mayo, 297
Hash Browns, Pub, with Horse-
    radish Sauce, 268, *269*
Hawaii Burgers, 95
hazelnuts, in Portland Pork
    Schnitzel-wiches with Pinot-
    Blackberry Gravy, 185
herb:
  cheese, in Audacious,
    Herbacious Beef Burgers, 7
  Mayo, 275
hoagies (heroes):
  Chicagoan-Italian Roast Beef,
    182–83
  Italian Sliced Chicken and Pork,
    189
Hoisin, 5-Spice Tuna Sliders with,
    173
Holsteiner-Style Schnitzel-wich, 184
honey:
  Dijon Potato Salad, 266
  Mustard, 121
horseradish:
  Bloody Mary Cheeseburgers, 31
  Russian Dressing, 177
  Sauce, 180, 268, *269*
  and Sour Cream Fry Dipper, 271
Hot and Sweet Pepper Dogs, 200
Hot Dog Salsa, 207
hot dogs and sausages, 199–213
  Coney Chili Dogs, 206
  Creole Andouille Dawgs, 212
  Cubano Dogs, 199
  Firecracker Deviled Corn Dogs,
    204, *205*
  Hot and Sweet Pepper Dogs, 200
  Hot Dog Fries, 259
  Jalapeño Popper Dogs, 207
  Kielbasa Chili Dogs, *210*, 211

L'il Devils (Corn Dog Sliders), 204

Michigan Dogs with Cheese Sauce, 201

Pigs in a Blanket with the Works, 208

Pigs in Ponchos: Quesadilla-Wrapped Franks and Beans, *202*, 203

Reuben Dogs, 209

7-Layer Chili Dog Dip, 213

Sloppy Dawgs, 227

Sloppy Joe DiMaggios, 221

Hot Sausage Burgers with Broccoli Rabe, *72*, 73

Hungarian (flavors):
    Goulash Burgers, 39
    Turkey Burgers with Smoked Gouda, 98

I

I'll Have What Charlie's Having Sliders, 160

Indian (flavors):
    Corn, Turkey Tikka Burgers with, 106
    Lamb Sliders with Green Raita Sauce and Red Onions, 161
    -Spiced Patties with Yogurt Sauce, *84*, 85

Israeli Ketchup, 276

Italian (flavors):
    BBQ Chicken Burgers, 80, *81*
    Burgers all'Amatriciana, 10
    Chicagoan-, Roast Beef Heroes, 182–83
    Giardiniera, 183
    Hot Sausage Burgers with Broccoli Rabe, *72*, 73
    Lasagna Burgers, 21
    Meat Loaf Long Boy Burgers, 64
    Meat Lover's Burger, 23
    Messy Giuseppe, *224*, 225

Salami Burgers, Ultimate, 52–53

Sicilian-Style Tuna or Swordfish Burgers, 124, *125*

Sliced Chicken and Pork Hoagies, 189

Sloppy Porchetta, 228

Italian Dressing, 53

J

jalapeño(s):
    and Cheddar Tots, 301
    Pickled, 295
    Popper Dogs, 207
    Poppers, Roasted, 265, *266*
    Popper Sliders, 143

jams:
    Bacon Tomato, 274
    Caramelized Onion-and-Bacon, 304

Japanese flavors, in Morimoto Kakuni Burger, 282

Jerk Burgers, 99

Joaquins, Sloppy, 220

Joe DiMaggios, Sloppy, 221

Joes:
    BBQ Chicken Sloppy, with Pickled Slaw Salad, 230, *231*
    Buffalo, 232
    Sloppy Chipotle, 219
    Sloppy Maple-BBQ, 235
    Sloppy Sausage, Pepper, and Onion, 223
    Sloppy Veg-Head, 238
    Sloppy Veg-Head, with Beans, *236*, 237
    Tango, 222

K

Kakuni Burger, Morimoto, 282

ketchup(s), 276–77
    Balsamic, 277

Bloody Mary Sauce, 31

Chipotle, 276

Israeli, 276

Italian, 117

Moroccan, 277

Spicy, 285

Spiked, 300

Tomatillo, 132

Kielbasa Chili Dogs, *210*, 211

Kiev, Chicken, Burgers with Russian Slaw, 79

knife-and-fork burgers:
    Shepherd's Pie, 54–55
    Stroganoff-Style, *32*, 33–34

knockwursts:
    Cubano Dogs, 199
    Reuben Dogs, 209

Koketsu, Craig, 294–95

L

LaFrieda, Pat, 24–25

lamb:
    Sliders, Indian, with Green Raita Sauce and Red Onions, 161
    Sloppy Merguez, 229

lamb burgers, 109–13
    Berber, 113
    Gyro, 111
    Indian-Spiced Patties with Yogurt Sauce, *84*, 85
    Middle Eastern, with Baba Ghanoush, *108*, 109
    Shish Ka, 112
    Short Rib and, 296–97
    with Walnut and Feta Cheese Sauce, 110

Lang, Adam Perry, 60–61

Lasagna Burgers, 21

Lee, Katie, 283

Lemon Slaw, 194, *195*

lentils, in Mediterranean Veggie Burgers with Provolone and Italian Ketchup, 117

L'il Devils (Corn Dog Sliders), 204
Logan County Hamburgers, 283
long boy burgers:
    Italian Meat Loaf, 64
    Sausage, with Pickled Fennel
        and Pepperonata, 76–77
Louisiana Burger, 291

M

mac 'n' cheese:
    Burger Sliders, 146
    Chili, Burgers, 12, *13*
    Pimiento, Cheeseburgers, 28
Manchego cheese:
    Chorizo Sliders, 156
    3-Cheese *Queso* Sauce, 14
Mango Salsa, 96, *97*
maple:
    BBQ Joes, Sloppy, 235
    Orange Drizzle, 163
Marinara Dipper, Quick, 271
Marinated Vegetables, 52–53
Marsala Burgers, 86
mayo:
    Basic, 275
    Cranberry, 92, *93*
    Deviled, 275
    Dijon, 275
    Garlic, Roasted, 275
    Harissa, 297
    Herb, 275
    Remoulade Sauce, 291
    Saffron, 275
    Wasabi, 122
Meat and Mashed Potatoes Burger, 22
meatball(s):
    Albondigas Subs: Spicy Spanish
        Meatball Subs, 186–87
    Hero Burgers, 50–51
    Spaghetti and, Burgers, 48–49
Meat Lover's Burger, 23

Mediterranean Veggie Burgers
    with Provolone and Italian
    Ketchup, 117
melts:
    Big, Beefy Mushroom Cheddar,
        198
    see also patty melts
Mendelsohn, Spike, 280–81
Merguez, Sloppy, 229
Messy Giuseppe, *224*, 225
Mexican (flavors):
    Beef 'n' Bean Burrito Burgers, 8
    Chipotle Burgers with Nacho
        Top, 14
    Chorizo Sliders, 156
    Green and Red Chile Nacho
        Sliders, 144–45
    Pigs in Ponchos: Quesadilla-
        Wrapped Franks and Beans,
        202, 203
    Pulled Pork Sliders, 158–59
    Sliced Steak Soft Taco Sliders
        with Guaca-Salsa, 154, *155*
    Sloppy Suizas, 234
    Tex-Mex Beer-Battered
        Fishwiches with Avocado
        Sauce, 196
    3-Cheese *Queso* Sauce, 14
Michigan Dogs with Cheese
    Sauce, 201
Middle Eastern (flavors):
    Falafel Burgers, 116
    Lamb Burgers with Baba
        Ghanoush, *108*, 109
    Shish Ka Burgers, 112
Monterey Jack cheese:
    Green and Red Chile Nacho
        Sliders, 144–45
    Patty Melts with Eggs, 27
    Pigs in Ponchos: Quesadilla-
        Wrapped Franks and Beans,
        202, 203
    Roasted Jalapeño Poppers, 265,
        266
    3-Cheese *Queso* Sauce, 14

Morimoto Kakuni Burger, 282
Moroccan Ketchup, 277
mortadella, in Italian Meat Loaf
    Long Boy Burgers, 64
mousse pâté:
    Bœuf Bourguignon Burgers, 30
    Wellington Burgers, 37
mozzarella cheese:
    Italian Meat Loaf Long Boy
        Burgers, 64
    Lasagna Burgers, 21
    Meatball Hero Burgers, 50–51
    Portobello Burgers with
        Spinach Pesto, 114, *115*
    Spaghetti and Meatball Burgers,
        48–49
    Spinach-Artichoke Burgers, 103
Murphy, Marc, 298–301
mushroom(s):
    Cheddar Melts, Big, Beefy, 198
    cremini, in Mediterranean
        Veggie Burgers with
        Provolone and Italian
        Ketchup, 117
    -and-Onion-Smothered Turkey
        Burgers with Swiss, 104
    Porcini Steak Sauce, 57
    shiitake, in Mu Shu Slaw, 66,
        67
    Sloppy Joaquins, 220
    Stroganoff-Style Knife-and-Fork
        Burgers, *32*, 33–34
    see also portobello (mushroom
        caps)
Mu Shu Slaw, 66, *67*
mustard:
    Dijon, Double-Decker Animal
        Style, 41
    Dijon-Honey Potato Salad, 266
    Dijon Mayo, 275
    Honey, 121
    Remoulade Sauce, 291
    Sauce, Japanese, 304
    Yellow, Slaw, 26
    Yellow, Vinaigrette, 147

N

naan breads, in Indian-Spiced
  Patties with Yogurt Sauce, *84*, 85
nacho:
  Sliders, Green and Red Chile,
    144–45
  Top, Chipotle Burgers with,
    14
napa cabbage, in Slaw, 287
Niçoise-Style Pan Bagnats, 197
North African (flavors):
  Berber Burgers, 113
  Harissa Mayo, 297
  Moroccan Ketchup, 277
  Sloppy Merguez, 229

O

Oil-and-Vinegar Slaw, 141, 163
olives, black, in Pissaladière Top-
  ping, 83
onion(s):
  and Apple Chutney, Chunky,
    190, 191
  Burgers, French, *62*, 63
  Caramelized, 41, 58, 74
  Caramelized, -and-Bacon Jam,
    304
  Crispy, 293
  Dip, French, 16, *17*
  Heirloom Tomato Chutney, 290
  -and-Mushroom-Smothered
    Turkey Burgers with Swiss, 104
  Pickled, 149, 158, 161
  Red, Pickled, 286, 297
  Ring Garnish, *32*, 33
  Rings, Sour Cream, 4, *5*
  Sausage, and Pepper Joes,
    Sloppy, 223
  Sweet, Brat Burgers with, 68
  Thick-Cut-O-Rings and Spicy
    Dipping Sauce, 260
  Topping, French, *134*, 135

Vidalia, Petals, Cliff's
  Homegrown, 281
open-face burgers:
  Salmon, with Honey Mustard,
    121
  Turkey, with Potpie Gravy, 105
  Welsh Rarebit, 38
Orange-Maple Drizzle, 163
Oscar's (Warrensburg, N.Y.), 35,
  40, 91
Ozersky, Josh, 172

P

Pan Bagnats, Niçoise-Style, 197
pancetta:
  Burgers all'Amatriciana, 10
  Meat Lover's Burger, 23
Panko and Black Sesame–Crusted
  Tuna Sliders, *170*, 171
Parmigiano-Reggiano cheese:
  Finger Fries with Formaggio,
    243
  Florentine Burgers, 44
  Garlic, and Pepper Tots, 252
  Garlic–Black Pepper Sauce, 15
  Italian BBQ Chicken Burgers,
    80, *81*
  Spinach-Artichoke Burgers,
    103
  3-Cheese *Queso* Sauce, 14
parsley, in Chimichurri Sauce,
  131, 220
Parsnip Oven Fries, *164*, 256
pasta:
  Spaghetti and Meatball Burgers,
    48–49
  see also mac 'n' cheese
pastrami:
  Fat Doug Burger, 287
  I'll Have What Charlie's Having
    Sliders, 160
pâté, mousse-style:
  Bœuf Bourguignon Burgers, 30

Wellington Burgers, 37
patties, forming, 60, x
patty melts:
  Cuban, with Yellow Mustard
    Slaw, 26
  with Eggs, 27
  Rachel, 87
  see also cheeseburgers
pecorino Romano cheese:
  Chicken or Turkey Burgers with
    Caesar Pesto, 102
  Italian BBQ Chicken Burgers,
    80, *81*
  Italian Meat Loaf Long Boy
    Burgers, 64
pepper(corn):
  Black, and Cheddar Cheese
    Buns, Homemade, 299
  Black, Garlic Parmesan Sauce,
    15
  Garlic, and Parmigiano Tots,
    252
  Pork and, Burgers, Country,
    70
  Uptown Burger au Poivre with
    Brandy Cream Sauce, 56
pepper(s):
  Giardiniera, 183
  Hot and Sweet, Dogs, 200
  Pepperonata, 76
  red, in Fire Eater Sauce, 295
  Sausage, and Onion Joes,
    Sloppy, 223
  Sloppy Veg-Head Joes with
    Beans, *236*, 237
pepper jack cheese:
  Chili Burgers with Charred Pico
    de Gallo, 36
  Fire Eater Burger, 294–95
  Louisiana Burger, 291
  Poblano Popper Super-Sliders,
    149
  South by Southwest 7-Layer
    Sliders, 150–51, *151*
Pepperonata, 76–77

pesto:
  Caesar, 102
  Spinach, 114
Philly Cheesesteak Sloppy Joes,
  216, *217*
pickle(d)(s):
  Fennel, 76
  Jalapeños, 295
  Onions, 149, 158, 161
  Potato Salad, 267
  Red Onions, 286, 297
  Slaw Salad, 230, *231*
  spears, in Cubano Dogs, 199
  Spears, Sweet 'n' Spicy, 199
  Sweet 'n' Spicy, 141, 261
Pico de Gallo, Charred, 36
Pigs in a Blanket with the Works,
  208
Pigs in Ponchos: Quesadilla-
  Wrapped Franks and Beans,
  202, 203
pimiento:
  Cheese Sliders, 148
  Mac 'n' Cheese Cheeseburgers, 28
pineapple, in Hawaii Burgers, 95
Pinot-Blackberry Gravy, 185
Pissaladière Topping, 83
poblano chiles:
  Green Chile Sauce, 144
  Patty Melts with Eggs, 27
Pommes Frites, Bistro-Style
  (French Fries), *246*, 247
popper(s):
  Jalapeño, Dogs, 207
  Jalapeño, Roasted, 265, *266*
  Jalapeño, Sliders, 143
  Poblano, Super-Sliders, 149
Porchetta, Sloppy, 228
Porcini Steak Sauce, 57
pork, ground mix of beef, veal
  and:
  Florentine Burgers, 44
  Lasagna Burgers, 21
  "The Wurst" Reuben Burgers,
    74, 75

pork and beef burgers:
  Italian Meat Loaf Long Boy, 64
  Long Boy Sausage, with Pickled
    Fennel and Pepperonata, 76–77
  Meatball Hero, 50–51
  Salami, Ultimate, 52–53
pork burgers, 66–77
  Banh Mi, 71
  Brat, with Sauerkraut or Sweet
    Onions, 68
  Cajun, 69
  Caribbean, with Mango Salsa,
    96, *97*
  5-Spice, with Warm Mu Shu
    Slaw, 66, *67*
  Goulash, 39
  Hot Sausage, with Broccoli
    Rabe, *72, 73*
  Jerk, 99
  Peppercorn, Country, 70
Pork Kakuni, 304
pork sandwiches, 185–91
  Albondigas Subs: Spicy Spanish
    Meatball Subs, 186–87
  Italian Sliced Chicken and Pork
    Hoagies, 189
  Portland Schnitzel-wiches with
    Pinot-Blackberry Gravy, 185
  Pulled Pork with Broccoli Rabe
    Subs, 188
  Schnitzel, with Chunky Apple
    and Onion Chutney, *190*, 191
pork sliders, 156–60
  BBQ "Bun"-Mi, 157
  Chorizo, 156
  Green and Red Chile Nacho,
    144–45
  I'll Have What Charlie's Having,
    160
  Poblano Popper Super-Sliders,
    149
  Pulled, Mexican, 158–59
  Satay, 162
pork sloppies:
  Cubanos, 226

Porchetta, 228
Sausage, Pepper, and Onion
  Joes, 223
port, in Drunken Burgers with
  Stilton, 18
Portland Pork Schnitzel-wiches
  with Pinot-Blackberry Gravy,
  185
portobello (mushroom caps):
  Big, Beefy Mushroom Cheddar
    Melts, 198
  Burgers with Spinach Pesto,
    114, *115*
  Fries, 258
  Marsala Burgers, 86
  Messy Giuseppe, *224*, 225
  removing gills on underside
    of, 225
  Shish Ka Burgers, 112
  Sloppy Veg-Head Joes, 238
potato(es):
  Bistro-Style Pommes Frites
    (French Fries), *246*, 247
  Caesar Tots, 253
  Double-Baked Crazy-Crisp
    Oven Fries, 244, *245*
  Finger Fries with Formaggio,
    243
  Garlic, Parmigiano, and Pepper
    Tots, 252
  Jalapeño and Cheddar Tots, 301
  Kraut, 153
  mashed, in Shepherd's Pie
    Knife-and-Fork Burgers,
    54–55
  Mashed, Meat and, Burger, 22
  Poutine, 272
  Pub Hash Browns with
    Horseradish Sauce, 268, *269*
  Salad, Honey-Dijon, 266
  Salad, Pickled, 267
  Skins, Bacon-Wrapped, 270
  10-Cut Oven Fries, 248
  Tots, Homemade, 250,
    251

Potpie Gravy, Open-Face Turkey
    Burgers with, 105
Poutine, 272
prosciutto:
    Italian Meat Loaf Long Boy
        Burgers, 64
    Meat Lover's Burger, 23
    Saltimbocca Burgers, 65
Provençal Burgers with Pissala-
    dière Topping, 83
provolone cheese:
    Chicagoan-Italian Roast Beef
        Heroes, 182–83
    Hot Sausage Burgers with
        Broccoli Rabe, 72, 73
    Lasagna Burgers, 21
    Meatball Hero Burgers, 50–51
    Meat Lover's Burger, 23
    Mediterranean Veggie Burgers
        with Italian Ketchup and, 117
    Philly Cheesesteak Sloppy Joes,
        216, 217
    Pulled Pork with Broccoli Rabe
        Subs, 188
    Salami Burgers, Ultimate,
        52–53
    Spaghetti and Meatball Burgers,
        48–49
    Spinach-Artichoke Burgers,
        103
Pub Hash Browns with Horserad-
    ish Sauce, 268, 269
Pulled Chicken, Bourbon BBQ,
    Sandwiches and Green Apple
    Slaw, 192–93, 193
pulled pork:
    with Broccoli Rabe Subs, 188
    Sliders, Mexican, 158–59

Q

Quesadilla-Wrapped Franks and
    Beans (Pigs in Ponchos), 202,
    203

Queso Sauce, 3-Cheese, 14
quinoa, in Mediterranean Veggie
    Burgers with Provolone and
    Italian Ketchup, 117

R

Rachel Patty Melts, 87
Raita Sauce, Green, 161
Ranch Dressing, 167
    Avocado, 168, 169
    Dipper, 254
    Green, 91
    Red, 6
Red Cabbage, 29, 209
    Oil-and-Vinegar Slaw, 141
    Slaw, 180
Red Ranch Dressing, 6
red wine:
    Bœuf Bourguignon Burgers,
        30
    and Garlic Marinated Sliced
        Steak Sandwiches, 181
    Pinot-Blackberry Gravy, 185
    port or sherry, in Drunken
        Burgers with Stilton, 18
    sherry, in Wellington Burgers,
        37
refried beans:
    Green and Red Chile Nacho
        Sliders, 144–45
    Pigs in Ponchos: Quesadilla-
        Wrapped Franks and Beans,
        202, 203
    South by Southwest 7-Layer
        Sliders, 150–51, 151
relishes:
    Cucumber, 162
    Giardiniera, 183
    Pepperonata, 76
Remoulade Sauce, 291
Reuben(s):
    Burgers, "The Wurst," 74, 75
    Dogs, 209

Sliced Steak, with Horseradish
    Russian Dressing, 177
Sliders, St. Paddy's-Style, 153
ricotta cheese:
    Florentine Burgers, 44
    Lasagna Burgers, 21
Roast Beef Heroes, Chicagoan-
    Italian, 182–83
rolls, buns, or breads, 60–61, xi
    assembling burgers on, 61
    Cheddar Cheese and Black
        Pepper Buns, Homemade,
        299
    cold-toasting, 61
    Crouton Rolls, 102
    Garlic Bread Rolls, 49
    toasting, 9
romaine lettuce:
    Caesar Pesto, 102
    Slider Salad with Yellow
        Mustard Vinaigrette, 147
Russian Dressing, 87
    Dipper, 152
    Horseradish, 177
Russian Slaw, 79

S

Saffron Mayo, 275
Sage-Scented Burgers with Fontina
    and Roasted Squash, 46, 47
St. Paddy's-Style Reuben Sliders,
    153
salads:
    Pickled Slaw, 230, 231
    Potato, Honey-Dijon, 266
    Potato, Pickled, 267
    Slider, with Yellow Mustard
        Vinaigrette, 147
salami:
    Burgers, Ultimate, 52–53
    Meat Lover's Burger, 23
salmon burgers:
    Everything Bagel, 118, 119

salmon burgers (continued)
   Garlic-Ginger, with Wasabi
      Mayo, 122
   Open-Face, with Honey
      Mustard, 121
   with Tartar Sauce, 120
Salsa, 150
   Charred Pico de Gallo, 36
   Hot Dog, 207
   Mango, 96, *97*
   Warm Fire-Roasted, 186
salt, kosher, x
Saltimbocca Burgers, 65
sandwiches, 174–98
   Big, Beefy Mushroom Cheddar
      Melts, 198
   Bourbon BBQ Pulled Chicken,
      and Green Apple Slaw, 192–
      93, *193*
   Fishwiches, 194–95, *195*
   Holsteiner-Style Schnitzel-wich,
      184
   Niçoise-Style Pan Bagnats, 197
   Schnitzel-wich with Garlic
      Butter and Hot Relish, 184
   Tex-Mex Beer-Battered
      Fishwiches with Avocado
      Sauce, 196
   see also beef sandwiches; pork
      sandwiches
Santos, Chris, 296–97
Satay Sliders, 162
sauces:
   Avocado, 149, 156, 196
   BBQ, *see* BBQ Sauce
   Bloody Mary, 31
   Blue Cheese, 166
   Brandy Cream, 56
   Chimichurri, 131, 220
   Coney Island, 206
   Cream Cheese, 119
   Fire Eater, 295
   Garlic–Black Pepper Parmesan, 15
   Green Chile, 144
   Green Raita, 161

Horseradish, 180, 268, *269*
Michigan, 201
Mustard, Japanese, 304
Orange-Maple Drizzle, 163
Pimiento Cheese, 148
Porcini Steak, 57
Remoulade, 291
Sour Cream, 74, 138, *138*
Spicy Dipping, 260
Spinach Pesto, 114
Stroganoff, 33–34
Tahini, 116
Tartar, 120, 194
3-Cheese *Queso*, 14
Tzatziki, 111
Walnut-Feta, 110
Yogurt, *84*, 85
Yogurt Dipping, 257
see also Gravy; ketchups; mayo;
   Salsa
Sauerbraten Burgers, 29
sauerkraut:
   Brat Burgers with, 68
   Potato-Kraut, 153
   Rachel Patty Melts, 87
   Sliced Steak Reubens with
      Horseradish Russian
      Dressing, 177
   "The Wurst" Reuben Burgers,
      74, *75*
sausage(s):
   andouille, in Cajun Pork
      Burgers, 69
   Burgers, Hot, with Broccoli
      Rabe, *72*, 73
   chorizo, in Albondigas Subs:
      Spicy Spanish Meatball Subs,
      186–87
   chorizo, in *Bife de Chorizo* Sliders,
      131
   chorizo, in Sloppy Cubanos, 226
   Chorizo Sliders, 156
   Long Boy Burgers with Pickled
      Fennel and Pepperonata,
      76–77

   Merguez, Sloppy, 229
   Pepper, and Onion Joes, Sloppy,
      223
   see also hot dogs and sausages
scallions, in Mu Shu Slaw, 66, *67*
Schlow, Michael, 292–93
Schlow Burger, 292–93
schnitzel-wiches:
   with Garlic Butter and Hot
      Relish, 184
   Holsteiner-Style, 184
   Pork, with Chunky Apple and
      Onion Chutney, *190*, 191
   Pork, with Pinot-Blackberry
      Gravy, Portland, 185
Schwartz, Michael, 288–90
seafood burgers, 119–27
   Salmon, Everything Bagel, *118*,
      119
   Salmon, Garlic-Ginger, with
      Wasabi Mayo, 122
   Salmon, Open-Face, with
      Honey Mustard, 121
   Salmon, with Tartar Sauce, 120
   Shrimp, 127
   Tuna, French, 123
   Tuna, Fresh, French-Style
      Cheeseburgers, 126
   Tuna or Swordfish, Sicilian-
      Style, 124, *125*
seafood sandwiches:
   Fishwiches, 194–95, *195*
   Niçoise-Style Pan Bagnats, 197
   Tex-Mex Beer-Battered
      Fishwiches with Avocado
      Sauce, 196
seafood sliders, 171–73
   Tuna, Black Sesame and Panko–
      Crusted, *170*, 171
   Tuna, 5-Spice, with Hoisin, 173
seasoning burgers, x
Sesame, Black, and Panko–Crusted
   Tuna Sliders, *170*, 171
7-Hour Smoked Brisket Sandwich
   with Smoky BBQ Sauce, Sharp

Cheddar, Red Cabbage Slaw, and Horseradish Sauce aka The Best Sandwich I Ever Made (and My Husband Ever Tasted), *178*, 179–80

7-layer:
Chili Dog Dip, 213
Sliders, South by Southwest, 150–51, *151*

Shallots, Fried, 302

Shepherd's Pie Knife-and-Fork Burgers, 54–55

sherry:
Drunken Burgers with Stilton, 18
Wellington Burgers, 37

shiitake mushrooms, in Mu Shu Slaw, 66, *67*

Shish Ka Burgers, 112

Short Rib and Lamb Burger, 296–97

shrimp:
Burgers, 127
Creole Andouille Dawgs with Gumbo Sauce, 212

Sicilian-Style Tuna or Swordfish Burgers, 124, *125*

sides, 240–70
Eggs, Deviled, 262, *263*
Hash Browns, Pub, with Horseradish Sauce, 268, *269*
Jalapeño Poppers, Roasted, 265, *266*
Pickles, Sweet 'n' Spicy, 141, 261
Potato Salad, Honey-Dijon, 266
Potato Salad, Pickled, 267
Potato Skins, Bacon-Wrapped, 270
see also condiments and garnishes; fries; Slaw(s)

skillets, cast-iron, cooking burgers in, x

Slaw(s), 287
Coleslaw, Cousin Shari's, 293
Green Apple, 192–93, *193*
Lemon, 194, *195*
Oil-and-Vinegar, 141, 163
Pickled, Salad, 230, *231*
Red Cabbage, 180
Russian, 79
Yellow Mustard, 26

sliders, 128–73, xi
Corn Dog (L'il Devils), 204
Lamb, Indian, with Green Raita Sauce and Red Onions, 161
Tuna, Black Sesame and Panko–Crusted, *170*, 171
Tuna, 5-Spice, with Hoisin, 173
see also beef slider(s); chicken sliders; pork sliders; turkey sliders

sloppies, 214–38
Merguez, 229
Philly Cheesesteak Sloppy Joes, 216, *217*
Veg-Head Joes, 238
Veg-Head Joes with Beans, *236*, 237
see also beef sloppies; chicken sloppies; pork sloppies; turkey sloppies

"Smoke and Fireworks" Bacon-Wrapped Chipotle Burgers, 45

Smokehouse Burger, 280–81

Smoky BBQ Sauce, 141–42, 180

sour cream:
and Horseradish Fry Dipper, 271
Onion Rings, 4, *5*
Russian Dressing Dipper, 152
Sauce, 74, 138, *138*
Spicy, 150

South by Southwest 7-Layer Sliders, 150–51, *151*

Spaghetti and Meatball Burgers, 48–49

Spanikopita Burgers, 82

Spanish Meatball Subs, Spicy (Albondigas Subs), 186–87

Spicy Dipping Sauce, 260

Spicy Ketchup, 285

Spicy Sour Cream, 150

Spicy Spanish Meatball Subs (Albondigas Subs), 186–87

Spiked Ketchup, 300

spinach:
Artichoke Burgers, 103
Florentine Burgers, 44
Pesto, Portobello Burgers with, 114, *115*
Spanikopita Burgers, 82

Squash, Roasted, Sage-Scented Burgers with Fontina and, 46, 47

steak, sliced:
Red Wine and Garlic Marinated, Sandwiches, 181
Reubens with Horseradish Russian Dressing, 177
Sliders, Bourbon Barbecue, 139
Soft Taco Sliders with Guaca-Salsa, 154, *155*

Steak Sauce, Porcini, 57

Stilton:
Burgers with Bacon Bits and Blue, 9
Drunken Burgers with, 18

stout, in Welsh Rarebit Burgers, 38

Stroganoff-Style Knife-and-Fork Burgers, *32*, 33–34

subs:
Albondigas: Spicy Spanish Meatball Subs, 186–87
Pulled Pork with Broccoli Rabe 4, 188

Suizas, Sloppy, 234

Sweet 'n' Spicy Pickles, 141, 261

Sweet 'n' Spicy Pickle Spears, 199

Sweet Potato Oven Fries, Balsamic, 249

Swiss cheese:
Berber Burgers, 113
Bistro Sliders à la Rachael, *134*, 135

Swiss cheese (continued)
Buttered-Toast Swiss Patty Burger, 11
Cubano Burgers, *100*, 101
Cubano Dogs, 199
Cuban Patty Melts with Yellow Mustard Slaw, 26
Double-Decker Animal Style, 41
Fat Doug Burger, 287
Grilled Cheese Burgers with Bacon and Tomato, 20
Mac 'n' Cheese-Burger Sliders, 146
Onion-and-Mushroom-Smothered Turkey Burgers with, 104
Provençal Burgers with Pissaladière Topping, 83
Rachel Patty Melts, 87
Reuben Dogs, 209
St. Paddy's-Style Reuben Sliders, 153
Sliced Steak Reubens with Horseradish Russian Dressing, 177
"The Wurst" Reuben Burgers, 74, *75*
Swordfish Burgers, Sicilian-Style, 124, *125*
Symon, Michael, 239, 284–86

T

Taco Sliders, Sliced Steak Soft, with Guaca-Salsa, 154, *155*
Tahini Sauce, 116
Tango Joes, 222
Tartar Sauce, 120, 194
10-Cut Oven Fries, 248
Tex-Mex Beer-Battered Fishwiches with Avocado Sauce, 196
Thai flavors, in Satay Sliders, 162
Thick-Cut-O-Rings and Spicy Dipping Sauce, 260

3-Cheese *Queso* Sauce, 14
Tikka Burgers, Turkey, with Indian Corn, 106
tomatillo(s):
Green Chile Sauce, 144
Ketchup, 132
Pigs in Ponchos: Quesadilla-Wrapped Franks and Beans, *202*, 203
Sloppy Suizas, 234
tomato(es):
Bacon Jam, 274
Charred Pico de Gallo, 36
fried green, in BL(FG)T Sliders, 136–38, *137*, *138*
Heirloom, Onion Chutney, 290
Hot Dog Salsa, 207
Italian Ketchup, 117
Marinara Dipper, Quick, 271
Salsa, 150
Sloppy Veg-Head Joes with, *236*, 237
Warm Fire-Roasted Salsa, 186
see also ketchups
tortillas:
Pigs in Ponchos: Quesadilla-Wrapped Franks and Beans, *202*, 203
Sliced Steak Soft Taco Sliders with Guaca-Salsa, 154, *155*
tots:
Caesar, 253
Garlic, Parmigiano, and Pepper, 252
Homemade, 250, *251*
Jalapeño and Cheddar, 301
tuna:
Burgers, French, 123
Burgers, Sicilian-Style, 124, *125*
Fresh, French-Style Cheeseburgers, 126
Niçoise-Style Pan Bagnats, 197
Sliders, Black Sesame and Panko–Crusted, *170*, 171

Sliders, 5-Spice, with Hoisin, 173
turkey, ground, x–xi
turkey burgers, 87–106
Adirondack Red Wing, 78
Buffalo, with Blue Cheese Dressing, 88, *89*
with Caesar Pesto, 102
California Club, 90
Caribbean, with Mango Salsa, 96, *97*
Cobb-Style Club with Green Ranch Dressing, 91
Cranberry Bog, 92, *93*
Cubano, *100*, 101
Curried, 94
Hawaii, 95
Hungarian, with Smoked Gouda, 98
Onion-and-Mushroom-Smothered, with Swiss, 104
Open-Face, with Potpie Gravy, 105
Provençal, with Pissaladière Topping, 83
Rachel Patty Melts, 87
Spanikopita, 82
Spinach-Artichoke Burgers, 103
testing doneness of, 80
Tikka, with Indian Corn, 106
turkey sliders, 166–68
Buffalo, 166
Cincinnati Sloppy, 233
Club, Deluxe, 167
Club Burger, with Avocado-Ranch Dressing, 168, *169*
Sloppy Chili, 218
turkey sloppies:
Buffalo Joes, 232
Chili Sliders, 218
Cincinnati Sliders, 233
Maple-BBQ Joes, 235
Suizas, 234
Tzatziki, 111

U

uptown burgers:
  au Poivre with Brandy Cream
    Sauce, 56
  with Porcini Steak Sauce, 57

V

veal:
  Brat Burgers with Sauerkraut or
    Sweet Onions, 68
  Holsteiner-Style Schnitzel-wich,
    184
  Marsala Burgers, 86
  Provençal Burgers with
    Pissaladière Topping, 83
  Sage-Scented Burgers with
    Fontina and Roasted Squash,
    46, 47
  Saltimbocca Burgers, 65

Schnitzel-wich
    with Garlic Butter and Hot
      Relish, 184
veal, ground mix of beef, pork
    and:
  Florentine Burgers, 44
  Lasagna Burgers, 21
  "The Wurst" Reuben Burgers,
    74, 75
Vegetables, Marinated, 52–53
veggie burgers, 114–17
  Falafel, 116
  Mediterranean, with Provolone
    and Italian Ketchup, 117
  Portobello Burgers with
    Spinach Pesto, 114, 115
Veg-Head Joes, Sloppy, 238
  with Beans, 236, 237
Vidalia Onion Petals, Cliff's
    Homegrown, 281
Vietnamese (flavors):
  Banh Mi Burgers, 71

BBQ "Bun"-Mi Sliders, 157
Vinaigrette, Yellow Mustard, 147

W

Walnut-Feta Sauce, 110
Wasabi Mayo, 122
Wellington Burgers, 37
Welsh Rarebit Burgers, 38
Wisconsin Cheeseburger, 302–3
"The Wurst" Reuben Burgers, 74, 75

Y

Yo Burger, 284–86
yogurt:
  Dipping Sauce, 257
  Green Raita Sauce, 161
  Sauce, 84, 85
  Tzatziki, 111

ABOUT THE AUTHOR

RACHAEL RAY is best known as the host of the hit syndicated Emmy Award–winning daytime television show *Rachael Ray,* produced by CBS Television Distribution in association with Harpo Productions, Scripps Networks, and Watch Entertainment. Rachael's warmth, energy, and boundless curiosity also reach thousands of fans through her popular Food Network shows and lifestyle magazine, *Every Day with Rachael Ray.* She has her own line of cookware created by Meyer, knives by Füritechnics, and signature food ingredients by Colavita. In 2011, Rachael won the People's Choice Award for "Favorite TV Chef." In 2007, Rachael launched Yum-o!, a nonprofit organization dedicated to empowering kids and their families to develop healthy relationships with food and cooking, and in 2008 she partnered with Ainsworth Pet Nutrition to create a line of pet food, from which all her proceeds are donated to organizations that help animals in need. Most recently, it was announced that Rachael was given her own publishing imprint called Rachael Ray Presents under Atria Books, which will allow the bestselling author of more than eighteen books to publish a line of titles by up-and-coming cooks, food writers, and experts. For more information, visit www .rachaelray.com.

View the latest bonus content.